2,—

To Dr. Kud
Best W...
[signature]
18 September '02

The Corporate Executive Survival Guide International Operations

A framework of contingency planning tools for the International Professional

by

James R. Doyle

James R. Doyle

Published by
World Security Press
Berkeley, California USA
ISBN 1-930916-66-3
© Copyright 2002 by James R. Doyle

The Author

About James R. Doyle

Mr. Doyle was the president of Emergency Data Systems, Inc. Emergency Data Systems, Inc. provided *Risk Management* consulting solutions for countries, companies and individuals. Topics included: *Crisis Management, Foreign Office and Residential Site Security, Aircraft Operations, Espionage, Communications, International Travel and Terrorist Threats, Personal Protection.* In addition to this book, Mr. Doyle has produced a series of Personal Protection video tape training films. Over the past 20 years, Mr. Doyle's extensive international experience has included the Middle East, Europe, Far East, Latin America and the Pacific.

During his 20 years as an international consultant, Mr. Doyle has provided consulting services for a wide variety of domestic and international clients including government agencies and the military. During Operation Desert Storm, Mr. Doyle provided support services for U.S. and Royal Saudi Air Forces.

Emergency Data Systems, Inc. was a registered constituent with the U.S. Department of State, Overseas Security Advisory Council (OSAC) and the F.B.I. Awareness of National Security Issues and Response (ANSIR) program. Mr. Doyle was board certified and licensed by the Texas Board of Private Investigators and Private Security Agencies.

James R. Doyle

<u>Dedication</u>

To my lovely wife Corazon

She has shown that retirement is not the end
of great adventures but the beginning

Acknowledgements

Any acknowledgement has to start with my daughter Jaimi and my son Curt. Their support and encouragement throughout my career and through the development of this book has been a source of strength and inspiration.

My greatest honor has been to serve in the United States Marine Corps. The friends I had there are truly the kind of people you can trust your life with as I did. It was an honor to serve with them and for those who are gone, they are not forgotten. *Semper Fidelis!*

In conclusion, I would like to thank the many dedicated individuals I have had the pleasure of working with in the U.S. Department of State, Secret Service, F.B.I., C.I.A., U.S. Air Force and of course, the U.S. Marine Corps. They quietly go about the business of protecting us all.

Contents

INTRODUCTION xvii
   Mission Statement xvii
DISCLAIMER xviii
MOBILIZATION 1
   Recruiting 1
   Documentation 2
   Orientations 2
   Culture Shock 3
   Driving Abroad 3
   Arrest 4
   Children 4
   American Attitudes 5
   Personal Conduct 5
INTERNATIONAL TRAVEL 6
   Planning 6
   Airline Travel 9
   Airports 11
   Public Transportation 11
   Hotels 12
   Trains 15
FOREIGN OFFICE SECURITY 16
SITE SELECTION GUIDELINES 16
   PHYSICAL OFFICE SITE SECURITY 17
   Establish a Fire Plan 21
   Employees Surveillance Reporting 21
   Procedural Security Techniques 23
   Trash Disposal Security Techniques 24
   Monitor Local Terrorism Indicators 25
   Establish a Terrorism Read File 25
   The Potential Effect of the Word "American" 26
   Suspicious Activity Reporting Checklist 26
   Security Guard Selection Criteria 27
   Protective Window Film 29
   OFFICE SURVEY CHECKLIST 30

PERIMETER SECURITY 32
Lighting Evaluation 32
Security Force 32
Perimeter Protection 33
INTERNAL SECURITY 34
Lock / Key Control 34
Alarms and Electronics 35
Theft Control Procedures 35
Security of Proprietary Information 37
Personnel Security 38
Emergency Procedures 38
Office Computer Security 39
Threat Information 39
FACILITY THREAT QUESTIONNAIRE 40
New Office Building Considerations 41
Topography 41
Siting 42
Environmental Considerations 42
Existing Office Building Considerations 43
Common Office Site Requirements 44
Design Standards for Site and Building Security 45
Security Design Objectives 45
EXTERIOR PROTECTION 46
Perimeter Barrier 46
Vehicle Entrances 47
Vehicle Control 48
Vehicle Checks 48
Primary Entrance Security Booth 50
Capabilities: 50
Gate Requirements 51
Parking 52
Lighting 52
Non-walled Facilities 52
Facade 53
External Doors 53
Windows 54
Roof 55
Parking 55
Garages 56
Physical Barriers 56
Construction Activities 56
Exterior Lighting 57
Building Access 57
Building Entrances 57
Doors 57

The Corporate Executive Survival Guide

Windows 58
Lobby 58
Other Building Access Points 59
INTERIOR PROTECTION 59
Walls and Partitions 59
Doors 60
Other Public Areas 60
Storage Requirements 61
Elevators 61
Cable Runs 61
Security Control Center 62
Access Systems 62
Alarm Systems 62
Closed-Circuit TV (CCTV) 63
Stairwell Door Reentry System 63
Special Functional Requirements 64
PUBLIC ACCESS CONTROLS 64
Security Officers and Watchmen 64
Security Hard-line 65
Walls 65
Security Doors 66
Security Windows 66
Public Access Entry Requirements 66
Alarms and Intercoms 67
Designated Secure Area 67
Emergency Exits 67
Executive Offices 68
General Office Security 69
Develop and Improve Employee Security Procedures 70
Office Security Countermeasures 70
Advice for Secretaries 71

BOMB THREAT PLAN 72

Introduction 72
TELEPHONE THREAT GUIDE 73
LETTER AND PARCEL BOMB GUIDE 76

VEHICLE TRAVEL SECURITY 78

Introduction 78
Vehicle Equipment Checklist 79
Travel Procedures Checklist 80
Defense Strategy Checklist 81
Local Travel Guidelines 82
Family and Company Cars 83
Safety and Security Precautions 83

Auto Travel Countermeasures 84
Parking of vehicles: 87

VISITING VIP PROTECTION 88

General Principles 88
Security Coordination 88
Air Travel 89
Aircraft Security 89
Local Transportation 90
Accommodations 90
Official Functions and Activities 91
Liaison With Local Authorities 91
Information Packets 91
Unarmed Security Escort 92
Armed Protective Security Detail 93
High Risk Professional Body Guards 94
VIP Group Activities Guidelines 95

RESIDENTIAL & DEPENDENT SECURITY 96

Introduction 96
RESIDENTIAL PERIMETER SECURITY 98
RESIDENCE PHYSICAL SECURITY 99
DEPENDENT CHILDREN SECURITY 101
SERVANT SECURITY 101
SOCIAL AND RECREATIONAL ACTIVITIES 102
PERSONAL PROTECTION DURING LOCAL TRAVEL 104
RESIDENCE PROTECTION WHILE TRAVELING 109
SECURITY GUDELINES FOR FAMILIES 110
Introduction 110
Residential Security Planning 110
Assessing the Level of Risk at Foreign Sites 111
Location of the Residence 112
Selection of Residence Type 113
After Moving In The Residence 114
Perimeter Security 117
Outer Perimeter 118
Inner Perimeter 119
Intrusion Alarms and Security Lighting 121
Minimum Desired Alarm System Features 122
Lighting 122
Extended Absences From the Residence 124
Domestic Hires - Screening and Responsibilities 124
SERVANT CAUTIONS 125
Residential Telephone Security 128
Residential Mail 131

The Corporate Executive Survival Guide

    SUSPICIOUS PACKAGES 132
    Banking and Charge Accounts 133
    Residential Trash Security 133
    Quality of Law Enforcement Protection 133
    Firearms in Foreign Countries 134
    Children's School 135
    Coups d'etat 135
    Social Activities 137
    Watchdogs 138
    Recreation and Exercise 138
    Illicit Drugs 139
    RESIDENCE SECURITY EVALUATION WORKSHEET 140
    RESIDENTIAL EXTERIOR 143
    BUILDING DOORS 144
    MISCELLANEOUS DEPENDENT CONCERNS 144
    SAFEHAVEN 145
    ALARMS 146
    WINDOWS 146
    EXTERIOR OF APARTMENT 147
    DOORS 147
    EXTERIOR OF SINGLE-FAMILY OR DUPLEX DWELLING 148
    SAFE NEIGHBORHOODS 148
    EXTERIOR OF SINGLE-FAMILY OR DUPLEX DWELLING 149

COMMUNICATION SYSTEMS 149

    Communication Facilities 149
    Systems 149
    Integration 149
    Telecommunications 150
    Electronic Media Path 152
    Electronic Transmission Threats and Vulnerabilities 152
    Threats 153
    Vulnerabilities 153
    Suggested Counter-Measures 154
    Effects of Telecommunications on Computer Security 155
    Video Conferencing 156
    Couriers 157
    Computer Technology 157
    Travel with Computers 158
    Computer Theft 158
    Unauthorized Access 159
    Portable Computers & Foreign Customs 159
    Working With Computers From Hotels 160
    Special Risks When Using Cellular PCs 160
    Virus Contamination And Detection 161

The Computer Systems Manager 161
Physical Access To Computing Facility 162
Telecommunications Lines 162
Magnetic Media Control 162
Use of Encryption 163
Distributed Printer Control 163
International Travel & Computers 163
Environment 164
Physical Security 164
System Security 165
Virus Protection 165

THE ESPIONAGE THREAT 166

INTRODUCTION 166
COUNTERING THE ESPIONAGE THREAT 169
Foreign Travel Precautions 169

THE TERRORIST THREAT 173

Introduction 173
COUNTERING THE TERRORIST THREAT 174
U.S. Terrorist Policy 176
Specific U.S. Policy Guidance 177
Use of Force 177
Humanitarian Appeals 178
Kidnapping Survival Guidelines 179
Hostage Survival 182
Hijacking Survival 182
Armed Assault on the Ground 185
Terrorist Demands 185
Terrorist Surveillance 185
Captivity 187
Behavior During Captivity 187
Avoidance of Capture or Escape 189
Rescue 190
COUNTER-TERRORIST TECHNIQUES 190

CRISIS MANAGEMENT 191

Introduction 191
CRISIS MANAGEMENT GENERAL 193
CRISIS MANAGEMENT ORGANIZATION 193
Crisis Management Team 193
Crisis Management Planning Guide 194
Crisis Management Team FUNCTIONS 195
Responsibilities of the Corporate Crisis Management Team 196
Responsibilities of the Local Crisis Management Team 197

The Corporate Executive Survival Guide

SECURITY INCIDENT COORDINATOR 198
ACTIONS DURING A CRISIS 199
Crisis Management Team RESPONSE TO ACTS OF TERRORISM 200
Crisis Reports 202
Crisis Management Team ASSESSMENT OF A HOSTAGE SITUATION 203
Terrorists 204
Host Government 204
Hostages and Other Victims 204
Action Options 205
Hostage Negotiations 206
Crisis Management Team AND CATASTROPHES AND NATURAL
DISASTERS 206
COMMUNICATIONS IN A CRISIS SITUATION 208
Crisis Management Team AND PUBLIC AFFAIRS INFORMATION 208
Responsibilities of the Spokesperson 208
Handling Media Interests 209
CRISIS MANAGEMENT EVALUATION 210
BUSINESS RECOVERY 211
EMERGENCY MANAGEMENT EXERCISES GENERAL 211
EXERCISE GUIDELINES 212
DEVELOPING AN EXERCISE SCENARIO 213
EMERGENCE EXERCISE SUMMARY 215
Top Management 215
Exercise Control Team 215
CIVIL UNREST 217
CRIMINAL ACTS 219
Residential Safety 219
Personal Safety 220
CIVIL UNREST 221
WAR OR ACTS OF WAR 223
SABOTAGE 224
NATURAL DISASTERS 225
CYCLONES/HURRICANES/TYPHOONS 225
Recommended Action to Lessen the Effect of Cyclones 226
Safety Rules—Before the Storm 227
When the Cyclone Has Passed 229
TORNADOES 231
If You Are in a House or Apartment 232
If You Are in a Mobile Home 232
If You Are in a Motor Vehicle 233
If You Are Outdoors 233
If You Are in a Long-Span Building 233
In a School, Hospital, Nursing Home, or Office Building 234
EARTHQUAKES 235
Home Checklist 236

Emergency Supplies	237
Organizing Your Neighborhood	238
Community Preparedness	238
During an Earthquake	239
After an Earthquake	240
How to Shut Off a Gas Supply	242
How to Shut Off Electricity	242
Disinfecting of Water	242
THUNDERSTORMS AND LIGHTNING	244
First Aid for Victims of Lightning Strikes	244
Precautions To Take During Thunderstorms	245
OTHER NATURAL DISASTERS	247
Winter Storms	247
Winter Storms Checklist	248
Flash Floods	251
General Floods	252
Flood Safety Rules	252
Before the flood:	252
After a flood warning:	253
During the flood:	253
After the flood:	254
Heat Wave	254
Problems for Special Populations	255
Heat Wave Safety Tips	255
EPIDEMICS AND EMERGENCY CARE	256
INTRODUCTION	256
EPIDEMICS	256
EMERGENCY CARE	258
Types of Disasters Common to an Area	260
INDUSTRIAL ACCIDENTS	263
Planning	263
EVACUATION PLANNING	264
GENERAL	264
ORGANIZATION	265
EVACUATION PREPLANNING	266
EVACUATION PROCEDURE STAGES	268
EVACUATION GUIDELINES	269
EVACUATION DEPARTURE KIT	271
Supplies & Equipment	272
Evacuation Documents & Checklist	273
Warden Systems - General Considerations	273
EVACUATION ACTION RESPONSIBILITIES	274
Warden Coordinator	274
Wardens	275
EVACUATION TRANSPORTATION	276

The Corporate Executive Survival Guide

Introduction 276
Assessing Travel Options 277
METHODS OF TRANSPORTATION 279
Scheduled Airlines 279
Nonscheduled (Chartered) Airlines 279
Sea Transportation 280
Land Transportation 280
INDUSTRIAL CHEMICAL ACCIDENTS 282
INDUSTRIAL FIRES 289
NUCLEAR AND RADIOLOGICAL INCIDENTS 295
Control of Human Resources 296
Area Shelter 299
CRISIS MANAGEMENT CONCLUSION 300
U.S. DEPARTMENT OF STATE SERVICES 301
Legal Limitations 301
Practical Limitations 301
Privacy Act Limitations 302
Arrest 302
Financial Assistance 303
Medical Assistance 304
Death of American Citizens 304
Citizen Welfare/Whereabouts 305
Travel Advisories 305
Search and Rescue 306

AIRCRAFT OPERATIONS 306
INTRODUCTION 306
GENERAL CONSIDERATIONS 307
BASIC AIRCRAFT PROTECTION MEASURES 308
HANGAR SECURITY 310
Remain-Over-Night (RON) AIRPORT CONSIDERATIONS 313
IN-FLIGHT SECURITY CONSIDERATIONS 314
LAW ENFORCEMENT CONSIDERATIONS 316
GUIDELINES FOR INTERNATIONAL FLIGHT OPERATIONS 318

CONCLUSION 319

APPENDIX 321
References and Reviews 321
Document A: Letter from John Ashcroft 324
Document B: Invitation for the Evening Parade (Louis J. Freeh) 325

The Corporate Executives Survival Guide
International Operations

Introduction

Mission Statement

The objective of this book is to provide the international professional with a framework of contingency planning tools associated with business operations in a foreign setting. The material covered in this book includes:

Mobilization, Orientation, International Travel, Foreign Office Security, Vehicle Travel Security, Visiting VIP Protection, Communication Systems, Espionage Threats, Terrorist Threats, Residential Security, Crisis Management and Aircraft Operations.

The material offered in this book is applicable in any international setting. This material will provide the international professional with a valuable set of contingency planning tools.

We have been international project managers for over 20 years with emphasis in high security military projects in the Middle East. In addition to our personal experiences, we have relied on a variety of government sources for our information and training material, including but not limited to the U.S. Military, National Counterintelligence Center, Secret Service, F.B.I., C.I.A. and the U.S. Department of State. In an attempt to protect classified sources and methods, we have intentionally avoided identifying some sections of this book with some government agencies.

While the U.S. Department of State does an excellent job of supporting Americans in an international setting, it is incumbent on each individual and company to assume a high level of personal responsibility for their actions.

James R. Doyle

Disclaimer

The Corporate Executive Survival Guide is intended to be a *guide*. It is intended to provide the international professional with a framework of contingency planning tools associated with international operations. It is incumbent on each individual reading this book to assume a high level of personal responsibility for their actions. Information in this book is subject to change and may be updated in future editions.

Although this book contains many suggestions for traveling, working and living in a foreign country, it is by no means intended to be all inclusive. Each foreign assignment requires unique planning and the enclosed material is intended to provide a framework for that planning process.

We recognize that the level of risk varies from country to country and from time to time. That is why we have developed this book in an electronic version which will facilitate an update of information as times and events change.

Advance planning and preparation from a variety of sources will significantly reduce your risk.

MOBILIZATION

Recruiting

Recruiting key personnel for any assignment is always a challenge. However, recruiting personnel for an international assignment is especially challenging.

Typically, international projects do not have an excess in staffing. Each person fulfills a key role. Replacing an individual from a foreign assignment means, among other things, recruiting another person with international experience, obtaining new documentation including passports, visas, security clearances, employment physicals and other mobilization cost. Therefore, is preferable to recruit personnel with international experience and if your plans are to mobilize the individual's family, it is preferable that the family understand all aspects of the foreign assignment.

No one recruiting source should be relied on. The best leads come from current employees with a proven track record to accurately assess how a candidate will perform in a foreign environment. Newspapers will result in volumes of résumés however; selecting the right candidates for an interview will require significant staff time. A professional recruiter could be a helpful tool in doing the initial screening however, remember that the recruiter is selling a product i.e. his candidate.

Employees in a foreign country are prime candidates to be approached by foreign intelligence personnel and competing companies in an attempt to gain an economic or military advantage. Because of this, background checks should include credit history to determine any financial problems that may compromise the employee.

Documentation

Documentation may require more than just a passport. Depending on the nature of the project, some level of security screening may be required as in the case of military projects we have been associated with. In some cases, visas can be obtained immediately. In others, the process could take weeks depending on the country and nature of the project. In addition, some countries may require extensive physicals including drug and aids test. Some countries may require independent certification of academic credentials through an Academic Attaché at their embassy.

Orientations

Country Orientations are critical to reducing the risk of personnel returning from a foreign assignment prior to completion of the assignment. Contracts with penalty clauses such as the employee loosing *Annual Completion Bonuses*, *Foreign Assignment Premiums* can provide a financial incentive for the employee to stay on the assignment however; a lot of problems can be significantly reduced or eliminated with a candid and realistic orientation. The orientation is not only critical for the employee but also so his or her family will have a clear understanding of their responsibilities.

The orientation process can have ***legal consequences!*** Recently, a large international company lost a $6 million dollar lawsuit. They had mobilized an employee who was later arrested at the foreign work site. The employee returned to the United States and sued his former employer on the grounds that his employer did not provide sufficient orientation on the hazards of living and working in a foreign environment. The case is on appeal by the company however, after paying legal fees and the negative publicity, a reversal still means they lost.

While there is any number of valuable topics to be covered in an employee orientation, particular attention should be paid to the following:

Culture Shock

Culture Shock is the physiological and psychological stress experienced when a traveler is suddenly deprived of old familiar cues including language, customs etc. This will affect not only the employee but also the employee's wife and children. The condition may be mild or could be severe lasting for months. These factors could affect work and morale. Culture Shock is most prevalent in the second or third month after arrival when the novelty of the new country fades. Traveler disorientation is a form of culture shock. You may encounter so many strange sounds, sights, and smells upon arrival in a country new to you that you may be more vulnerable to accidents or crime. You may experience this disorientation on a fast-paced business trip to several different countries. You can combat traveler disorientation by gathering advance information of a practical nature about the country, customs, airport, public transportation, knowing the exchange rates, etc. Pay particular attention to any host nation cultural customs which may affect your security or safety. As with any type of stress, culture shock may manifest itself both physically and emotionally. If you should experience it at a time when you need to be alert to security concerns, your awareness could be impaired. But if you understand it, you can successfully deal with it. Symptoms in adults and children may be: Sleepiness, apathy, depression, compulsive eating or drinking, exaggerated homesickness, decline in efficiency, negative stereotyping of nationals, recurrent minor illnesses. The orientation should be equally balanced with the reality of culture shock and the advantages of a foreign assignment including learning about a new culture, learning new languages and of course the financial benefits usually associated with a foreign assignment.

Driving Abroad

Employees and dependents should be aware of the restrictions other countries may impose on drivers. Some cultures prohibit male and female in the same vehicle. Employees should be aware of significant penalties imposed by some countries. Driving laws, rules and customs may vary considerably. Employees with dependents should be advised if family members will not be allowed to drive due to customs or insurance restrictions. There are a number of criminal activities aimed at the American visitor driving in a foreign country. Fake personal injuries are common as are minor auto accidents in an attempt to extort some sort of settlement on the spot. While it sounds like common sense, everyone should be aware of the dangers in picking up strangers in a foreign country. Some cultures may condone personal conduct in such a situation that is not acceptable in the United States.

Arrest

One of the most frightening experiences an American citizen can face is arrest and being detained in a foreign country. Depending on the country, you may not be able to contact anyone for hours. Police, Military and Intelligence agencies detain people for a number of reasons and in some instances, for no reason at all other then curiosity. The best advice is to be polite and professional. The employee should ask to contact the embassy or consulate. This may be your right but it does not mean that you will be able to exercise the right. You should maintain your dignity and not be provocative; however, you should be firm with your request to contact an American official. You should not admit or sign anything! Some countries ask the person to sign a "simple statement" in their language. Americans have signed such statements in an attempt to appease the official thinking it would result in immediate release. This is a common trick used by some police and does not result in your release.

Children

In addition to the considerations of culture shock I mentioned earlier, children are particularly vulnerable to accidents in a foreign country. Children should be briefed and included in the decision process as much as possible. Discussions should be around cultural restrictions, health precautions and medical services, stress and being separated from friends and family in the U.S. Teenagers are particularly vulnerable to the relocation process. All of the rules you would normally apply to your child in the U.S. should be emphasized in a foreign country. Particular attention should be paid to child care providers since background checks may be more difficult. Children should not accept packages from strangers or get into a car with a stranger. Children should be thoroughly briefed on country customs and know how to contact authorities in an emergency. Often times, employees unfamiliar with a foreign environment fail to realize the impact of traveling and living in a foreign country. It is for this reason that candidates with families should have international experience with their family members. Children should be aware of the fact that they are guest in the foreign country and should be sensitive to the cultural differences. If children are aware of the cultural differences in advance, they are less likely to laugh or be embarrassed in the foreign setting.

American Attitudes

Americans are sometimes insulated from the fact that not all countries share the American Dream and do not appreciate some of our customs and traditions. Americans typically are very sociable and want to be liked. This may make us more vulnerable to a variety of incidents. Foreign intelligence agencies and criminals often count on this trait to gain our trust in an attempt to obtain information. Industrial espionage is on the increase and often times an individual may divulge sensitive corporate information thinking he's just having a casual conversation with a person interested in Americans. Americans are rightfully proud of accomplishments in business, sports, world leadership, and war. Sometimes we may be viewed as feeling superior and materialistic in achieving status symbols. Expensive clothing and jewelry lead to this perception and invite crime in addition to negative feelings by some nationals.

Personal Conduct

Employees should be aware that while in a foreign country, their personal conduct is always under scrutiny. They should do nothing which might be misconstrued or reflect poorly on their personal judgment, professional demeanor, or embarrassing to the company. Do not enter into discussions of character flaws, financial problems, emotional relationships, marital difficulties of anyone working in the company. This type of information is eagerly sought by people who would compromise you or someone else in the company. In addition to illegal drugs like marijuana or narcotics, some countries have restrictions against some types of medication and food products, including those that contain alcohol. Prescriptions should be carried with any medication in a foreign country. Alcohol, more than any other substance has caused serious problems for employees and companies in foreign countries. Anyone with a drinking problem would not be a good candidate for a foreign assignment and could be easily compromised. Black Market activities in some countries carry serious consequences. Some of these activities include illegal exchange of currency or the purchase of religious icons and other local antiquities. No one should deliver letters or packages from strangers. You have no way of knowing what is in the package. Exporting prohibited items could result in arrest. Americans should not engage in any type of political or religious activity likely to be offensive in the host country. Weapons of any type should not be touched or handled in any manner. No photographs should be taken of any military or internal security facilities including airports, ports, and military installations. This could result in arrest and confiscation of your equipment. As an example, Saudia Airlines is technically a part of the Ministry of Defense and Aviation in Saudi Arabia and as a result, no photographs on the aircraft are permitted. Particular attention should be paid to dress and clothing in a foreign country. Hand gestures should be avoided unless you are familiar with the gesture for the country you are in. Tapping your nose in Britain means secrecy or confidentiality while in Italy it is a friendly warning. In Taiwan, blinking your eyes at someone is considered impolite. I could go on but I think you get the picture.

INTERNATIONAL TRAVEL

Planning

Most people don't consider the possibility of death, serious accident, illness, emergency evacuation or even being held hostage. Travelers should discuss with family members actions to be taken in case of an emergency. The traveler should provide family and or close friends with emergency plans including multiple points of contact telephone numbers. The U.S. Department of State does have an Overseas Citizen Services office that may be able to assist with emergency communications however; due to the "Privacy Act" there may be situations in which they can not tell family members about your location without specific authority so you should not rely on this service as your sole means of communication.

All important papers should be left behind with a family member or in a safe deposit box. You may also want to consider a trusted friend or an attorney, so they know how to retrieve them on your behalf in the event of an emergency. You may want to take copies of some records and in some cases you may want the copies notarized.

The following items should be collected for safe keeping in the U.S. prior to departure:

- Power of Attorney
- Birth Certificates
- Academic Records
- Marriage Certificates
- Veterans Records
- Guardian or Adoption Papers
- Personal Will
- Naturalization Papers
- Deeds
- Mortgages
- Employment Contracts
- Stocks & Bonds
- Car Titles
- Insurance Records
- Valuables
- Tax Records
- Termination of Previous Marriage
- Child Support and Alimony Agreements
- Banking Records
- Medical Records
- Fingerprint card
- Audio/Video recording
- Personal financial statement

- Inventory of household and personal effects including photos of some items

In addition to *copies* of some documents, a *list* should be developed that can be left with a family member, attorney etc. The following suggestions should be considered in developing the list:

- Passport details
- Drivers license numbers
- Bank account numbers
- Stock broker account numbers
- Credit/Debit card numbers
- Vehicle identification numbers
- Personal property serial numbers
- Passwords for safe and computer
- Social Security numbers
- Prescription details
- Safe deposit details
- Personal property
- Household effects
- Property storage locations
- Veterans Affairs details
- Medical/Dental information
- Employment History

The following suggestions should be considered in advance of your departure:

- Prepare instructions for family members, attorney's, accountants, bankers etc. on what should be done on your behalf in the event of an emergency. This may be in the form of a notarized letter of authorization or a "Power of Attorney". Your attorney can best advise you on the structure of your "Power of Attorney".

- Arrange for direct deposit of all funds to your U.S. bank account. This could include payroll, tax refunds, Veterans Administration compensation, Social Security, property rental income etc. ATM machines should provide you and your spouse with easy access to your funds.

- Assure that widely acceptable credit cards are current in the event of an emergency.

- Obtain travelers checks in addition to sufficient amounts of cash prior to departure.

The international traveler should also consider the following:

- Obtain an International Driving Permit from AAA.
- Prepare a Wallet Card with blood type, known allergies, medications, etc.
- Remove all credit cards and other items not necessary for the trip.
- Remove non-essential papers including military, law enforcement.
- Obtain a Passport Cover (U.S. Passport is distinctive and identifies you.
- Use hard, lockable luggage.
- Luggage tags should contain name, address and telephone numbers.
- Luggage tags should be concealed from casual view with a covering flap.
- Family members should have your travel itinerary.
- At least two (2) valid photo identifications i.e. passport & state drivers license.

Airline Travel

Double check all travel documents including Passport, Visas, Currency, Airline Tickets, Credit Cards, Medications, Prescriptions, Eyeglasses and any personal records required for the trip. Always obtain a small amount of foreign currency in advance for the country you are traveling to and any stops on the way. Double check on import restrictions for the country you are traveling to. Some magazines, religious articles may be confiscated depending on the country being visited. Do not pack items such as medications, airline tickets, cash, checks, credit cards, jewelry, or your passport. In the event of accident or theft, you may be separated from your luggage. Avoid any logos or identifying emblems on your luggage. Do not use a laminated "business card" for your luggage. Never leave your bags unattended. Never accept anything from anyone to carry with you. It is also recommended that a small travel hand bag be carried as opposed to use of a wallet that could fall out or easily be picked from your pocket. These bags are readily available in most airports and are most visible in other countries. Advise anyone of any delays in your trip. When traveling by air in a foreign country, avoid use of your company name when possible. Travelers should consult with corporate travel officials, travel agents and airlines, relative to the safest hotels. Always anticipate that your luggage is at risk when out of your possession and take extra precautions to secure the locks and also assure that the bags do not accidentally open. Check Safety and On-Time records of airlines, make stopovers at airports with good security standards, try to fly wide body planes because hijackers tend to avoid these because they have too many passengers to control. Pick a window seat because this will keep you away from hijackers' actions in the aisle. Keep in mind that eavesdropping on airplanes could cover a radius of 8 seats and is one way you can be targeted. Bars and Restaurants are also often used to target Americans. Dress inconspicuously to blend into the international environment. Remove or loosen shoes after you are seated on the aircraft to avoid swelling and improve circulation. Eat moderately, avoid alcohol, and drink plenty of water. The re-circulated air in the cabin increases the chance of dehydration. Sleep as much as possible on the aircraft. Consider not wearing expensive jewelry. Avoid speaking English as much as possible on foreign carriers. Avoid over-display of your passport when completing landing cards. Scientific conferences and trade association meetings have been targeted by some foreign intelligence agents seeking defense related information. Today, these meetings are still targeted but now the goal is to learn economic information. Individuals engaged in collecting information are not necessarily intelligence officers of a foreign government. Many times they are business persons, managers, corporate officers, sales people, scientist, engineers and other technical personnel. There is a growing trend for foreign corporations to employ former intelligence officers for industrial espionage.

Airports

Maintain a low profile and avoid public areas as much as possible. In the event of any disturbance, move in the opposite direction. Always plan to check in early to avoid being too conspicuous in a long line. Go directly to the gate or secure area after checking your bag. The longer you linger in an unsecured area, the longer you remain a target. Stay away from glass wall areas and airport coffee shops which are open to the concourse or public waiting areas. When arriving or departing an airport, you should not exchange items from one bag to another. Never leave your luggage unattended. Security personnel assume an unattended bag contains a bomb. Never accept luggage or packages <u>for any reason</u> from strangers and stay away from unattended luggage. Do not discuss travel plans with anyone. Always know where you are in relation to exits. If an incident occurs, your survival may depend on remaining calm and exiting to a safe area. Try to use hotel transportation from the airport to the hotel. If you rent a car, consider choosing a conservative model with locking trunk, hood, and gas cap. The car should also have power brakes and steering, seat belts, quick accelerating engine, heavy duty bumpers, smooth interior locks and air conditioning. The gas tank should be kept at least half full. Before getting into the car, examine it for strange objects or wires inside or underneath it. If a strange object is found, do not touch it but call for security personnel. When driving, keep doors locked and windows rolled up. Avoid being boxed in by other cars. Check for suspicious individuals before getting out of the car. Lock the car when unattended. Never let anyone place a package inside or enter the car.

Public Transportation

Pickpockets and petty thieves use public transportation as a prime vehicle for targeting travelers. Avoid carrying a wallet in your hip or easily accessible coat pocket. Carry a purse or handbag that you can firmly grip or secure to your body. Beware of people bumping into you. Use only licensed taxis. Get a map or ask someone for directions from the airport to the hotel so you will be able to track the route used by the taxi driver. Try not to travel alone in a taxi and never get out at an area other than your destination because the driver could leave with your property in the taxi. If the taxi door does not lock, sit in the middle to avoid easy access by thieves who may open your door to grab your bag. On subways, use a middle car but never an empty car. On buses, sit in an aisle seat near the driver.

Hotels

You can usually expect the same standard of security in hotels owned by American hotel chains when traveling in a foreign country. However, you may be a more visible and inviting target in a foreign hotel. Those who notice you as an American may try to lure you to some point outside the hotel. Your travel and lodging should be kept on a "need to know" basis. Ideally, you could make your own hotel reservations. You may consider using your employer's street address without identifying the company and using your personal credit card. The less others' know about your travel itinerary and who you represent, the better. If you are arriving late, you may want to guarantee your reservation to assure you have a room when you arrive.

You should obtain parking information if you plan to rent a car so as to assure a secure parking spot. Guard your credit card information carefully and always audit your credit card receipts. If you are a member of a premium travel club always ask for an upgrade to an executive or concierge floor. The hotel is one of the points in your travel itinerary where you are the most vulnerable. Do not linger in a parking area or any other unsecured area. Be alert for suspicious persons and behavior. Watch for distractions that are intentionally staged to setup a pickpocket, luggage thief or purse snatch. Remember the cautions presented earlier in "Airports". If a disturbance starts, move in the opposite direction. Stay with your luggage until it is brought into the lobby, or placed into the taxi. Consider using the bellman. Luggage in the "care, custody and control" of the hotel causes the hotel to be liable for your property. Protect claim checks; they are your evidence. There are limits of liability for hotels. Use hotel safe boxes when available. Items like computers, jewelry and sensitive documents should be protected at all times. If you arrive by rental car, park as close as possible to the hotel entrance or a secure area. Remove all personal items and anything of value from the vehicle. Always be aware of your surroundings or strangers around your vehicle. If using a valet service, only leave your ignition key. Often time's valets are not employees of the hotel and work for private contractors. Parking garages are difficult to secure. Avoid dimly lit garages that are not patrolled and do not have security telephones or intercoms. If in doubt about the security of an area, do not be embarrassed to ask for an escort to your vehicle in the parking garage.

In some countries, your passport may be temporarily held by the hotel for review by the police or other authorities. It should be returned as soon as possible. Be aware of anyone in the hotel with undue interest in your arrival. While in the hotel, keep it within your view or touch. You may want to position the luggage next to your leg so you can feel if someone tries to move it. You may want to position other articles in front of you during registration. You need to remember that ground floor rooms that open to a pool or beach area are vulnerable. If provided with a ground floor room, exercise extra care. It is best to have a room away from elevator landings or stairwells. Always accept bellman assistance upon check-in. Allow the bellman to open the room, turn lights on, and check the room to ensure that it is vacant and ready for you. Always inspect the door lock and locks on sliding glass doors. Also inspect the optical viewer, privacy latch or chain, guest room safes and dead bolt locks on interconnecting suite doors. Make a mental note of where the nearest fire escape is. In the case of fire dense smoke may make obscure the exit and you will have to remember where it is. Also make a note of where the nearest hotel house telephone is located. Most security conscious hotels require a caller to identify who they are attempting to telephone rather than providing a room number. Note how hotel staffs are uniformed and identified. Many crimes occur by persons misrepresenting themselves as hotel employees on house telephones to gain access to guest rooms. Avoid permitting a person into the guest room unless you have confirmed that the person is authorized to enter. This can be verified by using the optical viewer and by calling the front desk. Put the "do not disturb" sign on your door to give the impression that the room is occupied. Carry the room key with you rather than leaving it at the front desk. Do not use your name when answering the telephone. Do not accept packages or open doors to workmen without verification from the front desk. If a guide is needed, let the hotel recommend a known guide.

Hotel fires are of particular concern overseas. Many hotels overseas are not as fire resistant as hotels in the United States. Interior materials are often extremely flammable and toxic. Fire exits may be difficult to locate or non-existent. Firefighting equipment and water supplies may be limited. There may be no fast method for alerting a fire department. Sprinkler systems and smoke detectors may be non-existent. You must take responsibility for your safety. You must be thinking contingency in the event of a fire so you will know how to get out alive. Stay in a modern hotel, preferably an American hotel with fire safety standards. Try to use a lower floor that provides an exit. Most fire departments have equipment that will reach the fourth floor. A second floor room will allow you to jump in the event fire equipment is not available. Portable smoke alarms are available as are portable burglar alarms for your hotel room. Test the smoke detector in your room by pushing the button and if it does not work, alert the front desk. If you wake and a fire has started, crawl to your door. Feel the door with your hand before opening. If the door is hot, fire may be at the door. If your exit is clear from your hotel room, crawl into the hallway. Be sure to close the door behind you to keep smoke out in case you have to return to your room. Take your key in case your door locks behind you. Stay close to the wall to avoid others in the hall. Do not use elevators during a fire. If you encounter heavy smoke in the stairwell, do not try to run through it. You may want to consider turning and walking up to the roof fire exit. Once you reach the roof, find the windward side and wait for rescuers. If all exits are blocked, return to your room. If there is smoke in your room, open a window for ventilation. Don't break the window unless it can't be opened. If your phone works, call the desk to let someone know where you are and call the fire department to let them know where you are. Hang a bed sheet out the window as a signal. Fill the bathtub with water to use for Firefighting. Use a waste basket or ice bucket to splash water onto your door or any hot walls. Stuff wet towels into cracks under and around doors where smoke can enter. Tie a wet towel over your mouth and nose to help filter out smoke. If there is fire outside your window, take down the drapes and move everything combustible away from the window. If you are above the second floor, you probably will be better off fighting the fire in your room than jumping. A jump from above the third floor may result in severe injury or death. Remember that a fire's by-products such as super-heated gases and smoke present greater danger than the fire itself.

Trains

As in the case of any form of travel, planning is essential to reducing the risk of becoming a victim. The following guidelines offer some ideas for reducing the risk of train travel.

Many cities have more than one railroad station. Check in advance to confirm the station and train departure information is correct. Make reservations in advance so you do not have to stand in line and become a visible and possibly vulnerable target. Standing in line creates an opportunity for pickpockets, baggage thieves and purse snatchers. A hotel concierge can assist with reservations in advance. Travel light and always keep your luggage under your control. Keep your tickets close at hand and in an inside pocket to avoid providing an opportunity to pickpockets. Retain all travel documentation including canceled tickets. Retain your ticket even if a conductor does not check it or take it from you. Prior to departure of the train, assure you are on the correct train. Know in advance if the train will be switching or making any other changes that you should be aware of. You can learn how to tell if you are in the correct car by referring to name boards. Make sure you know how to spell and pronounce the name of your destination so you will recognize it when announced. Be aware of "train splitting". This is when part of the train is split off and attached to another train while the remainder of the original train continues on its way. Check with the ticket agent or onboard conductor to determine if this will occur. Avoid late night or early morning arrivals so as to prevent being stranded at the station with no transportation. If at all possible, you should arrange to have someone meet you at the terminal.

Although railroads offer safe and reliable forms of transportation they are subject to security risk. Railroads are vulnerable because they are easily accessible and operate over open ground. In some countries, safety is a consideration due to poor equipment and tracks. Railroads offer an easy target for criminals and terrorists. Railroad terminals offer opportunities for pickpockets, purse snatchers, baggage thieves, bombers and other criminals. Railroad terminals and trains are targets for the following type of attacks: *Bombing and other forms of sabotage to railroad tracks, terminals and trains; Robberies and burglaries; Theft of unattended baggage on board trains and in rail terminals; and Thefts from sleeping compartments.*

Always check unneeded luggage into the baggage car. The more bags you carry, the more vulnerable you are to thieves. Keep your luggage with you at all times. If you have to leave your seat, either take the luggage with you or secure it to your seat or the baggage rack with a strong cable-lock. Try to get a window seat. This provides a quick means of escape in the event of an accident. Have necessary international documents including your passport handy and ready for inspection by immigration officials at each border crossing. Always keep your camera and other valuables with you at all times. If you are in a private compartment, keep the door locked and confirm the identity of anyone asking for admittance to your compartment. Some train thieves spray chemicals into compartments to subdue the occupants therefore extreme caution should be used in unlocking your compartment. If you become suspicious of anyone, immediately notify the conductor. If you decide to temporarily get off the train before your destination, assure that you are not far from the train and know when it will leave. Familiarize yourself with military time (24 Hour Clock) i.e. 1 P.M. is 1300 Hours in military time. As in traveling by air, make sure you have some currency from each of the countries you will be traveling through in case of emergency. In some countries, you may want to carry your own food and bottled water.

Make certain that you depart from the train at the correct location. Be careful of local transportation and use only authorized taxis for transportation. Be alert to criminals such as pick-pockets, baggage thieves and unauthorized taxi drivers/guides. If you do not have a hotel reservation, go to the in-station hotel services and reservations desk for help in obtaining a hotel room.

FOREIGN OFFICE SECURITY

SITE SELECTION GUIDELINES

From a security point of view, proper site selection is the most important initial step in providing adequate protection. One objective of this book is to bring to your attention the wide range of security matters that should be addressed and integrated into the site selection process for new or existing office buildings.

Because of the renewed threat of individual suicide bombings in addition to the more traditional car bombing, there is a new awareness given to site selection on a worldwide basis regardless of the geographic location. Therefore, more preparation is needed for what might happen during the life of the building or its occupancy. We have all seen how quickly a benign security situation can evolve into a significant threat to facilities. It is only prudent to incorporate adequate security measures based on an evaluation of the existing threat to protect your employees and visitors for the long term. It will be evident from the factors highlighted that security considerations will impact on operational matters. The implications of this fact may be greater in some geographic regions than in others and will certainly affect some more seriously than others. Where this is the case, it is incumbent on all interested parties to evaluate potential damage while engaged in the site selection process and balance it against security requirements. If, in high threat areas, many of the suggested key criteria cannot be met, the firm should consider choosing another, more secure location.

Everyone involved in the site selection process should be aware of the following criteria.

PHYSICAL OFFICE SITE SECURITY

Conduct a basic security survey of compound, building(s) and office space. Photograph the overall area and all access points. Sketch all facility or office spaces noting access points, elevators, entrance areas, stairwells, fire exits, and all points of pedestrian or vehicle entrance, and control. Note the location of guards, the receptionist, and the general manager's office. Detailed attention should be given to the following:

- Perimeter fences, walls, and lighting.

- Lighting for rear areas and entrances.

- Controlled gates, vehicle access, and parking areas.

- Public Access Control. Entry doors electronically controlled by a guard or receptionist.

The "Sally Port" concept: an airlock entry system where the visitor is held between two locked doors until a guard or receptionist electronically releases one of the doors. Ideally, the guard or receptionist is behind bulletproof or shatter-resistant glass.

Install closed circuit television in all entry areas with VCR recorder capability to tape persons passing through any public access area.

If possible, place a walk-through metal detector and explosive detector at the entrance.

If possible, install a silent alarm system for the guard or receptionist to alert other security staff and the general manager's office in case of an emergency. It could be hooked up to trigger a flashing light at designnated points.

The manager's office door should be constructed of reinforced material with a drop bar or strong bolt to "harden" the office and to enable the office to be used as a safe haven in case of an emergency. This can (and should) be done unobtrusively. Install a peephole in the door. Almost all terrorist attacks directed against individuals in an office environment have been against those perceived to be important. Office workers are generally not considered to be a special target.

Consider shatter-resistant protective window film or "Mylar" for increased protection against flying glass in the event of a bombing or violent demonstration.

Maintain the telephone numbers of the local or district police station. Call them to verify unexpected police.

Install iron grillwork for ground floor windows.

In some cases, large ground floor windows should be made smaller and the walls reinforced to reduce potential bomb damage effects and risk to employees.

If the security survey indicates a number of weak points, or the office is located in a multiple occupancy building with few, if any, access controls, then serious consideration should be given to relocating the office. Controlling access is one of the most important elements of a good security program.

The U.S. Embassy or Consulate General is always interested in comments and suggestions regarding ways to improve the security of the American business community. If you have any suggestions or "lessons learned," please contact the U.S. Embassy. Additionally, the names of any reputable local firms that have done particularly good security related work (i.e., iron grilles, security doors, lighting, CCTV, and alarm installations) would be appreciated so that the information can be shared with other concerned managers.

The Security Survey should also include:

The Security Survey should contain the names and contact information for key managers. Included in this list might include the General Manager, Logistics Manager and Security Manager etc. The following elements should be considered in developing the Security Survey:

- Names, Work Numbers, Home Numbers, Fax Numbers, E-Mail.

- Brief description of firm's operation in city or country including office locations etc.

- Overview of professional and support staff and their respective nationalities.

- Exact location of all offices, plants, and other facilities.

- Brief description of office floor plan and configuration, including all floors.

- Schedule of company office and shift work hours.

- Mark locations of all facilities on an area map.

- Identify guard locations and capabilities.

- Identify and describe public access areas.

- Identify previous security problems and incidents of any type.

- List security procedures and equipment now in place including alarms, CCTV, special lighting, bulletproof glass, shatter-resistant window film, metal and explosive detectors.

- Describe all controlled parking, garage, and vehicle access areas.

- Develop a list of all security concerns and questions.

- Confirm the company is registered with the U.S. Embassy or closest Consulate.

- Identify any security material or guidance received from the U.S. Embassy or Consulate.

- Identify key personnel and other points of contact at the U.S. Embassy or Consulate.

- Confirm if responsible company personnel have attended U.S. Embassy security briefings.

Note: If this Company Security Profile transmitted, assure it is only done through a secure line and follow-up with a secure hard copy.

Operations Security is a term generally associated with the military. It is also a functional concept that can be utilized to enhance the security of American corporations and institutions in an overseas environment. Operations Security can best be defined as "A process to deny potential adversaries information about corporate executives, procedures, capabilities and intentions by identifying, controlling, and protecting corporate vulnerabilities that are susceptible to hostile exploitation".

Establish a Fire Plan

This is extremely important in countries that may not have the same safety standards in construction and fire fighting capabilities as required in the United States.

Employees Surveillance Reporting

All employees should be alert to all unusual inquiries such as, non-bona fide inquiries, callers who refuse to give their number, unidentified callers, under-identified callers, and information seeking calls with no apparent justification. Visitors or callers who show more interest in the nationality of the general manager than in conducting business are cause for concern. An attempt to determine the presence of an American executive or confirm their name by an individual who cannot be identified should be reported to the corporate security manager.

At the onset of the Gulf War, two young women visited an international shipping business in Istanbul. They looked curiously about the office and asked if there was a "foreign" manager. They did this in the course of trying to "ship" a package. The company, however, dealt in ocean-going ships, not parcels. The next day an armed terrorist "bomb team" arrived, forced the workers to a back room and set an explosive charge that detonated after their escape. The two teenage girls had been the "site advance team".

Surveillance detection in its most basic form is simply watching for persons who are observing corporate personnel and facilities, presumeably for hostile reasons. One of the primary reasons that terrorists do surveillance is to determine target suitability. Suspects should never be challenged, confronted, or acknowledged except by security personnel. When surveillance is observed or suspected, the corporate security personnel must be notified immediately. The report should be made in strict confidence and in accordance with an established reporting procedure. This incident should not be discussed in any manner with other company employees.

Employees should pay attention to observers loitering in the area especially when arriving at and departing from the office. Particular caution is also important when going to and from lunch at nearby restaurants known to be frequented by corporate employees.

What does a suspect look like? A suspect can be anyone, including teenage boys and girls. They may be used as advance reconnaissance teams for a follow-on attack or as in recent events; they may be the actual suicide bombers targeting innocent civilians in public places.

In a number of cases, groups have used young men and women of student age and appearance. The groups attempt to use individuals without police records or known affiliations to leftist organizations for some collection assignments. These individuals can stand light scrutiny if stopped and questioned by the police. They will usually have a "cover story" ready to explain their presence. Often their assignments are compartmentalized and they may actually be unaware of the specific nature of the mission that they are supporting as in the case of the 11 September 2001 attacks.

For example, in one case young suspects were told to acquire the license plate numbers and departure times of all foreigners on a particular street. (At one time it was possible to identify any vehicle registered to a foreigner by the distinctive color of their special license plates.) They were never told which individuals were targets, or in fact, if any were targets. If interrogated by the police the collectors had almost no operational knowledge certainly none that could lead back up the group's chain of command because cutouts had been used.

The profile of an armed "operator" who takes part in robberies and assassinations is somewhat different. They are most likely to be men in their mid-20s to early 30s. Many have police records and known connections to leftist groups. They are hard-core members of the group. Between assignments these individuals are likely to be in hiding and living under assumed identities. Typically, they will only surface when given an operational order to carry out an action and then return to the underground.

Employees can be briefed to spot things that are not normal, thereby expanding the company's "early warning network." They can be trained to, in effect, perform a type of counter-surveillance. The scope and level of this training should be tailored to an individual's willingness and capability to assist in this effort. The instruction should be presented in a matter-of-fact, non-threatening manner.

Drivers of executives should be given more detailed instructions because of their direct responsibility for the safety of a principal. They should also be told the importance of paying attention for possible suspects when their principal is with them and when the executive is not in their vehicle. They must be observant whenever approaching or departing the company area and the area of the general manager's residence. Any sightings of people taking notes or using hand signals, cameras, binoculars, telephoto lenses, camcorders, car telephones, or short-wave radios near the office or executive residence should be reported, particularly if any of these actions coincide with the movements of the general manager. Also take note of any "art students" making sketches of the office building or general manager's residence.

Suspicious vehicle repairs of extended duration, and utility crew work near the principal's residence or at various choke-point locations en route, should be noted. Privacy fence screening should be considered for the executive parking area at the office in order to obscure the view of vehicles, passengers, and license plates.

Observant employees, when noticed by suspects, signal a firm with a strong security posture that is a potential hard-target. Early detection or the perceived threat of detection, by suspects can and has deterred attacks. The analysis of notes found in various safe-houses confirms that terrorists make careful observations about the nature and level of security, both physical and procedural, at targeted companies.

Procedural Security Techniques

There are a number of procedures that can be implemented in order to increase security immediately, such as employee photo identification cards, card access to controlled areas, visitor controls and log books, computer security procedures, and delivery/tradesmen controls and logs for individuals and vehicles. Records should also be maintained for maintenance and cleaning crews, some of whom have after-hours access to offices and executive areas. Personally owned computers and computer media should be severely restricted, if not prohibited, at company offices. Strict control of executive schedules, home addresses, telephone numbers, and personal vehicle identification data is imperative. Addresses in many countries can be determined from telephone numbers.

Trash Disposal Security Techniques

Trash cover is a means of obtaining information by examining and analyzing corporate or personal refuse for exploitable information—both at the office and the executive residence. This is an effective procedure that has been used successfully by competitors, intelligence services, police, computer hackers, stalkers, and terrorists. Use paper shredders to destroy all sensitive and potentially useful information regarding company activities.

Consider the use of a small one or two-drawer security container or safe and mini personal shredder at executive residences for protection from browsing by domestic help or others who may have gained building access. The use of a personal shredder and safe can greatly reduce the potential for this type of exploitation.
Understand the exploitation potential of advertising, press releases, and the corporate posture.

Consider and evaluate the potential risk posed by the overt collection of open source information about company executives and business activities. Analyze the risk versus the benefits to be gained by the dissemination of information which, if necessary, can be controlled, timed, and managed.

Delay promotional activities during times when it is best to be as low key as possible.

Consider the advantages and disadvantages of publicizing the business' affiliation to a U.S. firm. Be aware that society page photographs from special functions and social and sporting events are sometimes collected by terrorist groups to aid in target selection and identification. This applies to family members as well.

Monitor Local Terrorism Indicators

Be familiar with dates of significance to terrorist groups, such as anniversary "trigger" dates, and know how to recognize the impact of a potential "trigger" event such as the onset of the Gulf War or death of a special group leader, etc. Be aware of incidents that have caused a reaction in the past. Remember that actions in other countries can result in local attacks and reprisals by transitional or other sympathetic groups as in the case of conflicts in the Middle East.

Establish a Terrorism Read File

Identify and list the principal terrorist groups of concern. Then obtain basic background information on these groups. Develop a list of key anniversary trigger dates for potential terrorist actions—times when some type of action may be reasonably predictable. Designate a staff member responsible for monitoring the local press for significant terrorist actions. Clip and save relevant news items.

Major demonstrations, safe-house raids, terrorist robberies, and police actions should be part of a watch list or target list of stories and reports for the collection effort. Take particular note of assassinations, kidnappings, and actions or threats directed against the business community. Robberies of payroll offices, banks, and other businesses can be an early indicator of pre-operational fund raising for future activities.

Generally, the type of news coverage in the local English language press for expatriate business people and tourists is not sufficient to accomplish this task. The local language press must be used. Usually a great deal of open source information is available. Articles should be clipped, dated, and filed. Translation is not necessary. Stories can be synopsized and translated later as required. Some newspapers publish year end summaries just after New Year's Day that list in chronological order all significant events from the past year—including terrorist actions. Articles such as these should be collected. Additionally, a local newspaper-sponsored almanac can be an excellent historical reference. All of this information can be extremely useful in following and documenting the local security situation, briefing visiting corporate security officials, and supporting requests for additional security measures.

Several general managers who have successfully implemented these suggestions have reported that visiting corporate security officials were "amazed" to see the extent local papers contained many vivid photos of bombings and assassinations of what was really going on in the city where their business was located. These general managers have found their terrorism read files to be extremely useful and persuasive.

The Potential Effect of the Word "American"

Be aware that the mere presence of the word "American" in a corporate title can attract attention and be part of the targeting process.

In Istanbul several local companies with the word American in their titles were bombed in short-notice, field-expedient targeting, at the start of the Gulf War. Several had no U.S. connection whatsoever. This was literally "telephone book target selection." No research was done beyond determining the name and address of the business.

Suspicious Activity Reporting Checklist

- Suspect Height:
- Weight:
- Sex:
- Race/Nationality:
- Hair (color and length):
- Clothing (hat, jacket, pants, shirt, footwear, etc.):
- Distinguishing features (glasses, mustache, or beard):
- Walks with limp: Scars: Birthmarks:

- Activity Time of sighting:

- Location:

- What was the suspect doing?

Any use of a camera, binoculars, telephoto lens, camcorder, short-wave radio, tape recorder or other devices, note taking, drawing/sketching, or hand signals?

- Vehicles Make and Year:

- License Plate Number:

- Type (two-door, four-door, other):

- Number of occupants:
- If departed, direction of travel:

- Vehicle Color:

- Did anyone else see the above suspect, activity, or vehicle? Yes, No; If yes, who:

- Full name of person making this report (please print and sign name):

Security Guard Selection Criteria

Security Guard protection typically comes from full time corporate employees or private security guard companies. In a foreign environment it is preferable that the security guard function be performed by a corporate employee as opposed to contracting through a private guard company. It may be useful to utilize these companies on a limited basis for their local expertise and language skills but critical information as all situations should be on a "need to know" basis only.

Experience has shown that the initial selection process is extremely important. Every effort must be made to find good candidates who have the potential to perform effectively. The following recommended profile outlines some of the experience and qualities recommended:

- Clean personal background including, medical, criminal and financial.

- Military background, preferably security or Special Forces.

- Law Enforcement background, preferably SWAT.

- Intelligence or Counter-Terrorism, military or civilian.

- Weapons and or explosives background.

- Athletic with Martial Arts background.

- Excellent physical condition.

The best candidates will ideally have an interest in a martial art such as Karate, Judo, or Tai Kwan Do. The discipline, fitness, and mind-set associated with these types of activity enhance performance. At a minimum, the candidate should be involved in some form of athletics. Martial Arts schools are one potential source for this type of individual since the instructors typically are very familiar with their students and their background.

In job announcements, stress the importance of physical fitness and that preference will be given to applicants with military or law enforcement experience. This experience is highly desirable because these individuals have already demonstrated their ability to follow orders, work hard, and achieve high standards.

In determining salary, check the local market and see what a police officer earns. Design an incentive for performance and include a strict probationary period. If guards do not perform well during probation, it is best to let them go.

Protective Window Film

Shards of flying glass can be lethal. Because of the potential danger of thrown objects or explosive blasts, all exterior, non-ballistic-resistant windows in office buildings should be treated with protective window film. While heavy wooden or metal shutters are an effective means of protecting windows and containing flying glass, the protection depends on the occupant keeping the shutters closed. That is not likely except in times of explicit danger. The best overall protection against the danger of flying glass is the application of protective window film to the inside of the glass. It will not prevent the glass from breaking, but will hold it in place if it is broken. More importantly, protective window film is in place and "working at all times".

Bomb curtains have been touted as effective against flying glass. As a general statement, however, they are heavy, expensive, and not particularly effective. They present the same weakness as shutters, in that an occupant may not keep them closed because they restrict light and ventilation. As a result, they are not recommended.

The U.S. Government generally recommends protective film that is a minimum of 4 mils thick (.004 inch, 1 mil is .001 inch). Reflective film is not recommended for this purpose, although some firms are experimenting with a new shatter-resistant, partially reflective coating.

Mylar is a well known trade name for one of the first protective window films made, but there are now a number of products available such as Armorcoat, Profilon, Protekt, Trugard, Scotchshield, and many others. Be sure to specify scratch-resistant film. Coatings thicker than 4 mils are available and are sometimes used in special applications such as jewelry store showcases, etc. Ten mil films have proven effective in stopping smash-and-grab robberies and offer a higher degree of protection against thrown objects such as Molotov cocktails. For best results, your company should try to find an experienced contractor to obtain the latest material and to do the installation.

For special, high-security situations, consider the use of ballistic-resistant transparencies or "glass" that can be obtained in various thickness' depending upon the level of protection required.

Ballistic-resistant glass is considerably more expensive than shatter-resistant window film.

Many of the companies that make protective coatings also produce specialty window films that are not shatter-resistant for energy control and increased privacy. These coatings can be used in vehicles as well as residences. Lightly tinted vehicle windows can make it difficult for passers-by or would-be suspects to identify passengers. Because these coatings are extremely thin, they must be professionally installed.

OFFICE SURVEY CHECKLIST

The Office Survey should include the names of key managers including but not limited to the General Manager, Security Manager, and Human Resource Manager along with their points of contact including addresses, telephones etc. Following are some suggested topics for inclusion in the Office Survey:

- Review of theft reports prepared by this site for a designated period of time.

- What corrective action has been taken as a result of previous incidents?

- Do theft reports reflect patterns, trends, or particular problems at this location?

- What does site management regard as the most prevalent or serious security problem?

- What is the Area Covered/Office Size?

- Does the site maintain items of value, such as works of art, paintings, wall hangings, etc.?

- What are the site's most valuable physical assets?

- Does the location have an employees' handbook or manual covering rules of conduct?

- Are employees aware of consequences of violating rules including possible discharge?

- Do these rules of conduct include theft of any type of company asset including information?

- Identify all off-site locations that should be included in survey, including warehouses.

- Are these locations protected against vandalism and theft?

- What is the police agency having jurisdiction over the site?

- Does the plant have a dedicated telephone line to this agency?

- Have they been called for assistance in the recent past?

- What has been their response?

- Do they normally include any of our perimeters in their patrols?

- If requested, would they?

- Are police emergency numbers readily available to all personnel?

- Is "incident specific" information available on what corporate office should be contacted?

- Is there a policy for reporting incidents to the police including theft, drugs, threats etc.?

Some police agencies have a Crime Prevention Unit that responds to invitations to speak on various topics (drugs, rape, etc.) or that may conduct limited security surveys.

PERIMETER SECURITY

Lighting Evaluation

- Is the perimeter adequately lighted?

- Does lighting aid or inhibit guards in the performance of their duties?

- Is lighting compatible with closed-circuit television (CCTV)?

- Does it cause monitor to "bloom" or distort?

- Is power supply adequately protected?

- Is lighting properly maintained and cleaned?

- Are sensitive areas including parking lots, entry areas, and stores, etc. adequately lighted?

- If an emergency occurred, is the site adequately lighted?

- Is the fence line adequately lighted?

- In appropriate areas, is glare projection lighting used?

Security Force

- Proprietary? If proprietary, what is method and source of selection of personnel?

- Contract? If contract, name of agency and telephone number.

- Are perimeter patrols conducted? How often?

- Is an incident log, including alarms/responses maintained? Reviewed daily? By whom?

- Are security personnel used for non-security related duties? Yes, what duties?

- Does site use photo ID cards? System? Who administers it?

If Compatible with access controls:

- Are all employees required to show photo ID card upon entry?

- Is duplicate copy kept on file?

- Are parking decals or other methods of registering employee vehicles used?

- Are privately owned vehicles permitted to park on site?

- If so, can an individual reach a vehicle without passing a guard?

- Does the site have a receptionist in place at all times?

- Are visitors required to register?

- Are they provided with an identifying badge?

- Are non-company employees escorted while on the site?

- Is visitor identification verified (e.g., vending company ID, etc.)?

Perimeter Protection

- If outside building walls form part of the perimeter, are all doors and windows secured?

- Can entry be achieved via the roof?

- Can hinge pins be removed from doors?

- Are all entry/egress points controlled when opened?

INTERNAL SECURITY

Lock / Key Control

- With whom does physical and administrative key control rest?

- Is a master key system in use?

- How many grandmasters/master keys have been issued?

- Is adequate control exercised over these keys?

- Is a cross-control system (name versus key number) in use?

- What type of numbering system is in use?

- Is the entire system, including blanks, inventoried on a regular basis?

- Are they stamped "Do Not Duplicate"?

- What level of written management authorization is required for issuance of keys?

- Identify personnel who are permitted to have keys to perimeter fence, doors.

- Are office/facility keys, particularly masters, permitted to be taken home?

- Are keys signed in/out in a daily log?

- Are locks rotated?

- How long has the present lock/key system been in use?

- Have keys been reported lost?

- What level key?

- What is policy when this happens?

- Is a record of locations of safes and their combinations maintained?
- Are combinations routinely changed annually?

- Are combinations changed when an individual no longer has a need to know it?

- Are safe combinations, if written, maintained in a secure place?

Alarms and Electronics

- What type, if any, electronic security system terminates at the site or at an outside central station?

- Has service/response been satisfactory?

- List alarms such as burglar, doors, windows, motion, duress, card access, CCTV, etc.

Theft Control Procedures

- Does the site have a policy of marking "all" property items susceptible to theft?

- Describe the extent of the program.

- Does it include die stamping or etching and painting?

- Are serial numbers of all items bearing them recorded?

- In the event of theft, is this information related to the police for inclusion in stolen property indexes, and for identification and return in case of subsequent recovery?

- Are trash receptacles periodically inspected to determine whether items of value may be removed from the site via them?
- Are all stores/office supplies, etc., attended when open?

- Is there a procedure for drawing supplies when no attendant is present?

- Are telephone records properly safeguarded to prevent unauthorized destruction?

- Is access to telephone switching equipment (the "frame room") restricted?

- Who performs custodial services - proprietary or contract janitorial people?

- Is access limited to the office area only?

- Are they bonded?

- Are they required to wear ID badges?

- Are they checked during the performance of their duties?

- Are they inspected by guards as they leave?

- Are the janitors' vehicles inspected on the way off the property?

- How is trash removed from the site?

- Are the vehicles used to remove trash inspected on the way off the property?

- Do the janitors have access to restricted or sensitive areas?

- Are they given office keys (masters)?

- Are they permitted to take these keys off the site with them?

- How much cash is kept on site?

- Is it handled at more than one location?
- How is cash supply replenished?

- Where is it kept during working hours?

- Where is it kept after hours?

- Where are blank payroll checks kept?

- Where are blank disbursement checks kept?

- Considering the neighborhood the site is located in, and the amount of cash on site, how do you assess your vulnerability to armed robbery or burglary? (Low) (Medium) (High)

Security of Proprietary Information

- Is there Proprietary and/or Limited data on site?

- If so, in what form?

- Is it properly marked?

- Is it stored in a secure location?

- Are the following locked at the end of the day: Offices, Filing Cabinets, and Desks?

- What is the office "destroy procedure" and file purging for Proprietary data?

- Does the site have a clean desk policy?

Personnel Security

- Are any background checks conducted prior to employment?

- Are personnel's previous employment dates verified?

- Are medical records properly safeguarded?

- Is security included in the new hire orientation?

- Is company property (credit cards, ID keys) retrieved during exit interviews?

Emergency Procedures

- Do you have a current bomb threat procedure?

- Who implements it?

- Does the procedure include a checklist for the switchboard operator?

- Is there a contingency plan for acts of violence?

- Is there a disaster plan?

- If personnel are required to work alone, are they periodically checked by someone to ascertain their well-being?

- What means do they have of calling for help in an emergency?

Office Computer Security

- Are terminated employees immediately separated from any computer?

- Is access to the data center controlled physically, electronically?

- Locked when not in use?

- Is output distributed via user controlled lock boxes?

- Is library maintained physically separate from machine room?

Threat Information

- Has liaison been established by your office with the American Embassy?

- Is the Embassy able to notify you of security threats concerning known terrorist groups active in the area?

- Is the Embassy able to notify you of any groups that harbor hatred for U.S. corporations, your company, its managers, and employees?

- Are you aware of key Anniversary dates that local population or terrorist groups celebrate?

- What tactics and activities are practiced or adopted by local terrorist groups that might affect your company, its managers and employees?

- Do you have sources that will inform you of any political controversy or labor disputes that might impact your operations?

- Will you provide corporate security with copies of information, which may be detrimental to the company, as received from the American Embassy as well as other sources including newspapers etc.?

FACILITY THREAT QUESTIONNAIRE

- Are there any known groups that harbor hatred for U. S. businesses, managers and employees?

- What terrorist groups are known to be active in the area?

- What tactics have these groups been known to use?

- What is the possibility of them changing tactics?

- Are there known groups that vocally oppose foreign capitalism or imperialism in the area?

- Are there any known groups that vocally or actively oppose the local government that the United States supports?

- Is there any current political controversy or labor dispute that we should be aware of?

- Are there any upcoming anniversary dates that the local population or terrorist groups celebrate?

- Have there been any previous hostage taking or kidnapping incidents, bombings, assassinations, strikes against U.S. businesses or the government, demonstrations, assaults, sabotage against corporate facilities or products, or occupation of corporate facilities in the area?

The Corporate Executive Survival Guide

- Have there been previous hostage taking or kidnapping incidents?

- How were the victims seized?

- What was the fate of the hostages?

- How much ransom was demanded?

- Was it paid?

- How were the negotiations handled?

- Does the host country prohibit negotiating with hostage takers or prohibit the payment of ransom?
- Do you consider the local police and intelligence services effective?

- What are the aims of the local criminals or terrorist groups?

- What tactics or type of activity by these groups would best further those aims?

- What is the identified groups' capability of carrying out planned activities such as ambush, hostage taking, kidnapping, execution, bombing, etc.?

- In the event of terrorist activity, what organizations, businesses, groups, or individuals would be the most likely targets?

New Office Building Considerations

Topography

Your site ideally should be situated at the high point, if any, of a land tract, which makes it less vulnerable to weapons fire, makes egress/ingress more difficult and easier to detect or observe any intrusions.

Site Location

Site should be located away from main thoroughfares and provide for the following:

- 100-ft. minimum setback between perimeter and building exterior whenever possible.

- Sufficient parking space for personnel outside the compound in a secure area within sight of the building, preferably, immediately adjacent to the compound.

- Sufficient parking space for visitors near the site but not on the site itself.

- Sufficient space to allow for the construction of a vehicular security control checkpoint (lock-type system), which would allow vehicles to be searched, if deemed necessary, and cleared without providing direct access to the site.

- Sufficient space to allow for the construction of a pedestrian security control checkpoint (guardhouse) to check identification, conduct a package check or parcel inspection or carry out visitor processing before the pedestrian is allowed further access to the site.

- Sufficient space for construction of a 9-ft. outer perimeter barrier or wall.

Environmental Considerations

Site should be located in a semi-residential, semi-commercial area where local vehicular traffic flow patterns do not impede access to or from the site.

Existing Office Building Considerations

The following security considerations for high-rise buildings are listed in order of preference as the availability of local facilities dictate:

- A detached (free-standing) building and site entirely occupied and controlled by you.

- A semidetached office building that is entirely occupied by you.

- A non-detached office building that is entirely occupied and controlled by you.

- A detached (free-standing) office building in which the uppermost floors are entirely occupied and controlled by you.

- A semidetached office building in which the uppermost floors are entirely occupied and controlled by you.

- A non-detached office building in which uppermost floors are entirely occupied and controlled by you.

- A detached (free-standing) office building in which the central floors are entirely occupied and controlled by you.

- A semidetached office building in which the central floors are entirely occupied and controlled by you.

- A non-detached office building central floors are entirely controlled and occupied by you.

- A detached (free-standing) office building in which some floors are occupied and controlled by you.

- A semidetached office building in which some floors are occupied and controlled by you.

- A non-detached office building in which some floors are occupied and controlled by you.

Common Office Site Requirements

Both new and existing office buildings should be capable of accommodating these security items:

- Floor load capacity must be able to maintain the additional weight of public access control equipment (ballistic doors, walls, windows), security containers, and disintegrates and shredders, if needed.

- Exterior walls must be smooth shell, sturdy, and protected to a height of 16 ft. to prevent forced entry.

- Building must be conducive to grilling or eliminating all windows below 16-ft. level.

The previously-listed criteria should be adopted to provide satisfactory protection for employees and visitors. If the site is found to be deficient in some areas, attempt to resolve those deficiencies by instituting security measures that will negate the deficiencies. Professional security and/or engineering assistance should be considered to address unique situations.

At a minimum, the following general security measures should be incorporated into planning designs:

- perimeter controls

- grillwork

- shatter-resistant film for windows

- public access controls

- package search and check

- secured area

- provisions for emergency egress

- emergency alarms and emergency power

Design Standards for Site and Building Security

This section establishes the minimum physical security standards to be incorporated in the design of facilities.

The objective is to provide protection for assets, personnel, property, and customers; ensure that consistent security measures are used at various locations; and ensure design integrity and compatibility of all elements of security with the architecture of the site.

Labor-saving and state-of-the-art security system components and assemblies should be used in all U.S. activities operating overseas, provided they can be maintained locally and there are spare parts available locally.

For manufacturing plant and laboratory facilities, security equipment such as closed-circuit television (CCTV) cameras and monitors, intercoms, card readers, and special glass protection, should be considered. Special care should be taken to verify the vendor's references, especially as they pertain to the quality of installation and service of security equipment. If the vendor maintains a central station for monitoring of alarms, a visit should be made to the central station to observe the professionalism of the operation. Design, purchase, and installation should be coordinated through your architect. Bear in mind, and make provisions for, the cost of maintenance on your security equipment. In some locations overseas, security equipment may be less expensive and more reliable than guards who receive relatively low pay and little training.

Security Design Objectives

In designing business or activity sites, roadways, buildings, and interior space, the following functional security objectives should be achieved:

Physical and psychological boundaries (signs, closed doors, etc.) should establish four areas with increasing security controls beginning at the property boundaries. The areas are defined as: (1) perimeter -- property boundaries; (2) exterior -- lobbies/docks; (3) interior -- employee space; and (4) restricted -laboratories, computer rooms, etc.

Vehicular traffic signs should clearly designate the separate entrances for trucks/deliveries and visitors and employee vehicles. Control points should be provided near the site boundaries where feasible. Sidewalks should channel pedestrians toward controlled lobbies and entrances.

Avoid having unsecured areas where there is no one nearby with responsibility for the function of the areas.

EXTERIOR PROTECTION

Perimeter Barrier

Perimeter security barriers are necessary to prevent unauthorized access. While it is clear that any barrier may be compromised with external aids, barriers will delay easy access and make it more possible to stop the trespasser.

If the threat is considered to be high at free-standing facilities, there should be a smooth faced perimeter wall or combination wall/fence, a minimum of 9 ft. tall and extending 3 ft. below grade. The wall or fence may be constructed of stone, masonry, concrete, chain link, or steel grillwork. However, if space limitations and local conditions dictate the need, any newly constructed wall should be designed to prevent vehicle penetration, and should use a reinforced concrete foundation wall, 18 in. thick with an additional 1-1/2 in. concrete covering on each side of the steel reinforcement, and extend 36 in. above the grade. This type of wall is designed to support three wall toppings: masonry, concrete, or steel picket fencing. The toppings should be securely anchored into the foundation wall. If a picket fence is used instead of a wall, the upright supports should be spaced at least 9 ft. apart so that the fence, if knocked down, can't be used as a ladder.

In addition, intrusion alert systems can be used to enhance perimeter security.

In cases where the above standards of construction are neither feasible, fiscally prudent, nor required by the threat, alternative methods offering comparable protection can be used. These alternatives should maximize the use of locally available materials and conditions to take advantage of existing terrain features or by the creative use of earth beams and landscaping techniques such as concrete planters.

Inside the perimeter barrier, the building should be set back on the property to provide maximum distance from that portion of the perimeter barrier which is accessible by vehicle. The desirable distance of the setback is at least 100 feet depending on the bomb resistance provided by the barrier.

At facilities with less than optimum barriers, or at locations where the terrorist threat or building location increases the vulnerability to vehicular attack, bollards, or cement planters can be used to strengthen the perimeter boundary. At walled or fenced facilities with insufficient setback, bollards or planters can be installed outside the perimeter to increase the setback of the buildings. In either case, design and placement of bollards or other anti-vehicular devices should be considered in the early planning stages. It doesn't make sense to have impenetrable gates connected by easily penetrated walls.

Vehicle Entrances

Vehicular entry-exit points should be kept to a minimum. Ideally, to maximize traffic flow and security, only two regularly used vehicular entry-exit points are necessary. Both should be similarly constructed and monitored. The use of one would be limited to employees' cars, while the other would be used by visitors and delivery vehicles. Depending on the size and nature of the facility, a gate for emergency vehicular and pedestrian egress should be installed at a location that is easily and safely accessible by employees. Emergency gates should be securely locked and periodically checked. All entry-exit points should be secured with a heavy duty sliding steel, iron, or heavily braced chain link gate equipped with a heavy locking device.

A device constructed to protect against a ramming vehicle attack. They are deployed in lines around a perimeter for anti-ram protection, or to provide supplemental control of vehicle traffic through permanent checkpoints when other means are not practical or effective.

The primary gate should be electrically operated (with a manual back-up by a security officer situated in an adjacent booth). The gate at the vehicle entrance should be positioned to avoid a long straight approach to force approaching vehicles to slow down before reaching the gate. The general technique employed is to require a sharp turn immediately in front of the gate.

In addition to the gate, and whenever justifiable, a vehicular arrest system can be installed. An appropriate vehicle arrest system, whether active, a piece of equipment designed to stop vehicles in their tracks, or passive, a dense mass, will be able to effectively arrest a vehicle with a gross weight of 15,000 pounds traveling at 50 MPH at a 90 degree angle.

Vehicle Control

Vehicle Checks

The following guidelines provide a basis for checking vehicles for explosive devices, or what is known as an improvised explosive device. These guidelines include some, but not all, of the techniques used by professional explosive ordinance disposal personnel.

Before touching the vehicle, conduct an external search as follows:

- Check the area around the vehicle. Look for bits of tape, wire, string, or time fuse that may have been left during the installation of an improvised explosive device.

- Look for marks on the ground, such as footprints, car jack or jack stand impressions. Depending on the slope of the parking surface, these marks may indicate unusual activity around the vehicle.

- Look for signs of forced entry around the doors, windows, trunk, and hood of the car. Fingerprints and smudges on the trunk, hood, door, or wheel covers may indicate a recent attempt to enter the vehicle.

- Look inside the vehicle, through the windows, for any obvious devices, packages or other items that do not belong.

- Look under the dashboard for protruding wires.

- Look on the floor for packages partially hidden under the front seat.

The most likely place to find a bomb, if the vehicle has been locked, is under the vehicle. Check for the following:

- Chunks of dirt on the ground that may have been dislodged from the undercarriage of the car during an attempt to place an explosive device.

- Loose wires or strands of wire that are clean (probably 22-24 gauge in thickness, similar to those used in a blasting cap).

- Check the top and both sides of all four tires.

- Look into the exhaust pipe for any inserted objects.

- All vehicles should be equipped with locking gas caps to prevent foreign objects from being dropped into the gas tank.

To check the inside of a vehicle that has been left unlocked:

- Look through the windows (see above) and then open a door other than the driver's side.

- Check the interior of the car in a logical sequence, generally starting on the floor and working up.

- Check under the floor mats for pressure-sensitive switches or any other items that should not be there.

- Look under the front seats and lift and inspect under the rear seats.

- Check the door panels for signs of tampering.

- At a minimum, always look under an unattended vehicle before entering for signs of an improvised explosive device that may have been left on the pavement or become detached from its mounting place. If, at any time during the inspection, a suspicious object is discovered, do not touch it. Immediately move away from the vehicle. Notify the police

The search techniques mentioned above are rather comprehensive and presented to inform and assist those individuals and businesses that are interested in understanding how to conduct a thorough vehicle bomb search

Primary Entrance Security Booth

Primary entrances to a facility should have a booth for security personnel during peak traffic periods and automated systems for remote operations during other periods

Capabilities:

- Electrically-operated gates to be activated by security personnel at either the booth or security control center or by a badge reader located in a convenient location for a driver.

- CCTV with the capability of displaying full-facial features of a driver and vehicle characteristics on the monitor at security control center.

- An intercom system located in convenient location for a driver communicate with the gate-house security control center.

- Bollards or other elements to protect the security booth and gates against car crash.

- Sensors to activate the gate, detect vehicles approaching and departing the gate, activate a CCTV monitor displaying the gate, sound an audio alert in the security control center.
- Lighting to illuminate the gate area and approaches to a higher level than surrounding areas.

- Signs to instruct visitors and to post property as required.

- Road surfaces to enable queuing, turnaround, and parking.

- Vehicles bypass control (i.e., gate extensions), low and dense shrubbery, fences, and walls.

Gate Requirements

Gates (when gatehouse is not manned) are controlled by card key or Central Security (reached via intercom).

At the vehicular entry-exit, a security officer booth should be constructed to control access. At facilities not having perimeter walls, the security officer booth should be installed immediately inside the facility foyer.

If justified by the threat the security officer booth should be completely protected with reinforced concrete, walls, ballistic doors, and windows. The booth should be equipped with a security officer duress alarm and intercom system, both enunciating at the facility receptionist and security officer's office. This security officer would also be responsible for complete operation of the vehicle gate. If necessary, package inspection and visitor screening may be conducted just outside of the perimeter security officer booth by an unarmed security officer equipped with walk-through and hand-held metal detectors. Provisions for environmental comfort should be considered when designing the booth.

Parking

Given the changing nature of security threats, parking should be restricted to the areas which provide the least security exposure. All parking within the perimeter walls should be restricted to employees, with spaces limited to an area as far from the building as possible. Parking for patrons and visitors, except for pre-designated VIP visitors, should be restricted to outside of the perimeter wall. If possible, parking on streets directly adjacent to the building should be forbidden. Wherever justifiable given the threat profile of your company, there should be no underground parking areas in the building basement or ground-level parking under building overhangs.

Lighting

Exterior lighting should illuminate all facility entrances and exits in addition to parking areas, perimeter walls, gates, courtyards, garden areas, and shrubbery rows.

Although sodium vapor lights are considered optimum for security purposes, the use of incandescent and florescent light fixtures is adequate. Exterior fixtures should be protected with grillwork when theft or vandalism has been identified as a problem.

Non-walled Facilities

In locations without perimeter wall protection, buildings should be protected with bollards, cement planters, or any other perimeter protection device. Such devices should be placed in a manner as to allow the maximum distance between the building and the roadway and/or vehicle access area. There may be local ordinances that make placement of these devices illegal or ineffective.

A positive and concerted effort should be made to contact local host country law enforcement or governmental authorities and request that they prohibit, restrict, or impede motor vehicles from parking, stopping, or loading in front of the facility. In high threat locations, if local conditions or government officials prohibit anti-vehicular perimeter security measures and your business is either the sole occupant of the building or located on the first or second floor, you should consider relocating to more secure facilities.

Facade

The building exterior should be a sheer/smooth shell, devoid of footholds, decorative lattice work, ledges, or balconies. The building facade should be protected to a height of 16 ft. to prevent access by intruders using basic hand tools. The use of glass on the building facade should be kept to an absolute minimum, only being used for standard size or smaller windows and, possibly, main entrance doors. All glass should be protected by plastic film. Consider the use of Lexan or other polycarbonate as alternatives to glass where practical.

External Doors

Local fire codes may impact on the guidance presented here. As decisions are made on these issues, local fire codes will have to be considered.

Main entrance doors may be either transparent or opaque and constructed of wood, metal, or glass. The main entrance door should be equipped with a double-cylinder dead bolt and additionally secured with crossbar or sliding dead bolts attached vertically to the top and bottom of each leaf. All doors, including interior doors, should be installed to take advantage of the door frame strength by having the doors open toward the attack side.

All other external doors should be opaque hollow metal fire doors with no external hardware. These external doors should be single doors unless used for delivery and loading purposes.

Should double doors be required, they should be equipped with two sliding dead bolts on the active leaf and two sliding dead bolts on the inactive leaf vertically installed on the top and bottom of the doors. A local alarmed panic bar and a 180-deg. viewing device should be installed on the active leaf.

All external doors leading to crawl spaces or basements must be securely padlocked and regularly inspected for tampering.

Windows

The interior side of all glass surfaces should be covered with a protective plastic film that meets or exceeds the manufacturer's specifications for shatter-resistant protective film. A good standard is 4-mil thickness for all protective film applications. This film will keep glass shards to a minimum in the event of an explosion or if objects are thrown through the window.

Grillwork should be installed on all exterior windows and air-conditioning units that are within 16 ft. of grade or are accessible from roofs, balconies, etc. The rule of thumb here is to cover all openings in excess of 100 in. square if the smallest dimension is 6 inches or larger.

Grillwork should be constructed of ½ inch diameter or greater steel rebar, anchored or imbedded (not bolted) into the window frame or surrounding masonry to a depth of 3 inches. Grillwork should be installed horizontally and vertically on center at no more than 8 inch intervals. However, grillwork installed in exterior window frames within the secure area should be spaced 5 in. on center, horizontally and vertically, and anchored in the manner described previously. Decorative grillwork patterns can be used for aesthetic purposes.

Grillwork that is covering windows designated as necessary for emergency escape should be hinged for easy egress. All hinged grillwork should be secured with a key operated security padlock. The key should be maintained on a cup hook in close proximity of the hinged grille, but out of reach of an intruder. These emergency escape windows should not be used in planning for fire evacuations.

Roof

The roof should be constructed of fire-resistant material. All hatches and doors leading to the roof should be securely locked with dead-bolt locks. Security measures such as barbed, concertina or tape security wire, broken glass, and walls or fences may be used to prevent access from nearby trees and/or adjoining roofs.
The overall design for perimeter security should consider using natural barriers, fencing, landscaping, or other physical or psychological boundaries to demonstrate a security presence to all site visitors.

All facilities should have some method of vehicle access control. Primary road entrances to all major plant, laboratory, and office locations should have a vehicle control facility operated by security personnel with automated systems for remote operation.

At smaller facilities, vehicle access control may be provided by badge-activated gates, manual swing gates, etc.

Site security should be able to close all secondary road entrances thereby limiting access to the primary entrance. Lighting and turn space should be provided as appropriate.

Parking

Security should be considered in the location and arrangement of parking lots. Pedestrians leaving parking lots should be channeled toward a limited number of building entrances.

Remote parking lots should be avoided.

All parking facilities should have an emergency communication system (intercom, telephones, etc.) installed at strategic locations to provide emergency communications directly to Security.

Parking lots should be provided with CCTV cameras capable of displaying and videotaping lot activity on a monitor in the security control center. Lighting must be of adequate level and direction to support cameras while, at the same time, giving consideration to energy efficiency and local environmental concerns.

Garages

For those buildings having an integral parking garage or structure, a complete system for vehicle control should be provided. CCTV surveillance should be provided for employee safety and building security. If the threat of car bombing is extant, consideration must be given to prohibiting parking in the building.

Access from the garage or parking structure into the building should be limited, secure, well lighted, and have no places of concealment. Elevators, stairs, and connecting bridges serving the garage or parking structure should discharge into a staffed or fully monitored area. Convex mirrors should be mounted outside the garage elevators to reflect the area adjacent to the door openings.

Physical Barriers

Bollards, landscape techniques, or other aesthetically designed barriers should be installed to impede vehicular access to lobbies and other glassed areas that could be penetrated by a vehicle (i.e., low or no curb, glass wall or door structure between lobby and driveway). Driveways should be designed and constructed to minimize or preclude high-speed vehicular approaches to lobbies and glassed areas.

Construction Activities

Landscaping and other outside architectural and/or aesthetic features should minimize creating any area that could conceal a person in close proximity to walkways, connecting links, buildings, and recreational spaces.

Landscaping design should include CCTV surveillance of building approaches and parking areas.

Landscape plantings around building perimeters need to be located at a minimum of 4 ft. from the building wall to prevent concealing people or objects.

Exterior Lighting

Facilities should have the capability of producing illumination on 100% of the building perimeter to a height of at least 6 ft.

For leased buildings, landlord approval of exterior lighting design requirements should be included in lease agreements.

Lighting of building exterior and walkways should be provided where required for employee safety and security.

Building Access

Building Entrances

The number of building entrances should be minimized, relative to the site, building layout, and functional requirements. A single off-hour's entrance near the security control center is desirable. At large sites, additional secured entrances should be considered with provisions for monitoring and control.

Doors

All employee entrance doors should permit installation of controlled access system hardware. The doors, jambs, hinges and locks must be designed to resist forced entry (e.g., spreading of door frames, accessing panic hardware, shimming bolts and/or latches, fixed hinge pins). Don't forget handicap requirements when applicable.

Minimum requirement for lock cylinders are "6-pin" pin-tumbler-type. Locks with removable core cylinders to permit periodic changing of the locking mechanism should be used.

All exterior doors accessing the security area should have alarm sensors to detect unauthorized openings.

Doors designed specifically for emergency exits need to have an alarm that is audible at the door with an additional annunciation at the security control center. These doors should have no exterior hardware on them.

Windows

For protection, large showroom type plate glass and small operable windows on the ground floor should be avoided. If, however, these types of windows are used and the building is located in a high-risk area, special consideration should be given to the use of locking and alarm devices, laminated glass, wire glass, film, or polycarbonate glazing.

For personnel protection, all windows should have shatter-resistant film.

Lobby

Main entrance to buildings should have space for a receptionist during the day and a security officer at night. The security control center should be located adjacent to the main entrance lobby and should be surrounded by professionally designed protective materials.

Rest rooms to meet the needs of the public should be provided in this area without requiring entry into interior space. Rest rooms should be kept locked in high-threat environments and the lobby-reception area should be a single, self-sufficient building entrance.

Telephones and Access controlled by the receptionist.

Consistent with existing risk level, the receptionist should not be allowed to accept small parcel or courier deliveries routinely unless they are expected by addressee.

Other Building Access Points

Other less obvious points of building entry, such as grilles, grating, manhole covers, areaways, utility tunnels, mechanical wall, and roof penetrations should be protected to impede and/or prevent entry into the building.

Permanent exterior stairs or ladders from the ground floor to the roof should not be used, nor should the building facade allow a person to climb up unaided. Exterior fire escapes should be retractable and secured in the up position.

INTERIOR PROTECTION

Building space can be divided into three categories: public areas, interior areas, and security or restricted areas requiring special security measures. These areas should be separated from one another within the building with a limited number of controlled passage points between the areas. "Controlled" in this context can allow or deny passage by any means deemed necessary (i.e., locks, security officers, etc.).

Corridors, stairwells, and other accessible areas should be arranged to avoid places for concealment.

Generally, restricted space should be located above the ground-floor level, away from exterior walls, and away from hazardous operations. Access to restricted space should be allowed only from interior space and not from exterior or public areas. Exit routes for normal or emergency egress should not transit restricted or security space.

Walls and Partitions

Public space should be separated from interior space and restricted space by slab-to-slab partitions. When the area above a hung ceiling is used as a common air return, provide appropriate modifications to walls or install alarm sensors. In shared occupancy buildings, space should be separated by slab-to-slab construction or as described previously.

Doors

Normally, interior doors should be of sufficient strength to prevent easy intrusion and equipped with good quality locking hardware. Keys to all doors should be carefully controlled and retrieval of keys should be noted by security personnel.

In shared occupancy buildings, every door leading to interior space should be considered an exterior door and designed with an appropriate degree of security.

Stairway doors located in multi-tenant buildings must be secured from the stairwell side (local fire regulations permitting) and always operable from the office side. In the event that code prevents these doors from being secured, the floor plan should be altered to provide security to your space.

Emergency exit doors that are designed specifically for that purpose should be equipped with a local audible alarm at the door and a signal at the monitoring location.

Doors to restricted access areas should be designed to resist intrusion and accommodate controlled-access hardware and alarms.

Doors on building equipment and utility rooms, electric closets, and telephone rooms should be provided with locks having a removable core, as is provided on exterior doors. As a minimum requirement, provide 6-pin tumbler locks.

For safety reasons, door hardware on secured interior doors should permit exit by means of a single knob or panic bar.

Other Public Areas

The design of public areas should prevent concealment of unauthorized Personnel and/or objects.

Ceilings in lobbies, rest rooms, and similar public areas should be made inaccessible, securely fastened or locked access panels installed where necessary to service equipment.

Public rest rooms and elevator lobbies in shared occupancy buildings should have ceilings that satisfy your security requirements.

Storage Requirements

Building vaults or metal safes may be required to protect cash or negotiable documents, precious metals, classified materials, etc. Vault construction should be made of reinforced concrete or masonry and be resistant to fire damage. Steel vault doors are available with various fire-related and security penetration classifications.

Elevators

All elevators should have emergency communications and emergency lighting. In shared occupancy buildings, elevators traveling to your interior space should be equipped with badge readers or other controls to prohibit unauthorized persons from direct entry into your interior space. If this is not feasible a guard, receptionist or other means of access control may be necessary at each entry point.

Cable Runs

All cable termination points, terminal blocks, and/or junction boxes should be within your facility.

Where practical, enclose cable runs in steel conduit.

Cables passing through space that you don't control should be continuous and installed in a conduit. You might even want to install an alarm in the conduit. Junction boxes should be minimized and fittings spot welded when warranted.

Security Control Center

If you have a security control center, it should have adequate space for security personnel and their equipment. Additional office space for technicians and managers should be available adjacent to the control center.

Your security control center should provide a fully integrated console designed to optimize the operator's ability to receive and evaluate security information and initiate appropriate response actions for (1) access control, (2) CCTV, (3) life safety, (4) intrusion and panic alarm, (5) communications, and (6) fully zoned public address system control.

The control center should have emergency power and convenient toilet facilities. Lighting should avoid glare on TV monitors and computer terminals. Sound-absorbing materials should be used on floors, walls, and ceilings. All security power should be backed up by an emergency electrical system.

Access Systems

The control center should be protected to the same degree as the most secure area it monitors. This type of system, if used, should include the computer hardware, monitoring station terminals, sensors, badge readers, door control devices, and the necessary communication links (leased line, digital dialer, or radio transmission) to the computer.

Alarm Systems

In addition to the normal designated access control system's doors and/or gates, remote access control points should interface to the following systems: (1) CCTV, (2) intercom, (3) door and/or gate release, and (4) power operated vehicle barriers.

Sensors should be resistant to surreptitious bypass. Door contact monitor switches should be recessed wherever possible. Surface-mounted contact switches should have protective covers.

Intrusion and fire alarms for restricted areas should incorporate a back-up battery power supply and be on circuits energized by normal and emergency generator power.

Control boxes, external bells, and junction boxes for all alarm systems should be secured with high-quality locks and electrically wired to cause an alarm if opened.

Alarm systems should be fully multiplexed in large installations. Alarm systems should interface with the computer-based security system and CCTV system.

Security sensors should individually register an audio-visual alarm (enunciator or computer, if provided) if located at the security central monitoring location and alert the security officer. A single-CRT display should have a printer- or indicator light. An audible alarm that meets common fire code standards should be activated with distinguishing characteristics for fire, intrusion, emergency exit, etc. All alarms ought to be locked in until reset manually.

Closed-Circuit TV (CCTV)

CCTV systems should permit the observation of multiple camera transmission images from one or more remote locations. Switching equipment should be installed to permit the display of any camera on any designated monitor.

To ensure total system reliability, only security hardware of high quality should be integrated into the security system.

Stairwell Door Reentry System

In multi-tenant high-rise facilities, stairwell doors present a potential security problem. These doors must be continuously operable from the office side into the stairwells. Reentry should be controlled to permit only authorized access and prevent entrapment in the stairwell.

Re-entry problems can be fixed if you provide locks on all stairwell doors except the doors leading to the first floor (lobby level) and approximately every fourth or fifth floor, or as required by local fire code requirements. Doors without these locks should be fitted with sensors to transmit alarms to the central security monitoring location and provide an audible alarm at the door location. Appropriate signs should be placed within the stairwells. Doors leading to roofs should be secured to the extent permitted by local fire code.

Special Functional Requirements

Facilities with unique functions may have special security requirements in addition to those stated in this book. These special requirements should be discussed with Corporate Security personnel or a security consultant. Typical areas with special requirements are product centers, parts distribution centers, sensitive parts storage facilities, customer centers, service exchange centers, etc.

PUBLIC ACCESS CONTROLS

Security Officers and Watchmen

All facilities of any size in threatened locations should have manned 24-hr. internal protection. Security Officers should be uniformed personnel and, if possible, placed under contract. They should be thoroughly trained, bilingual and have complete instructions in their native language clearly outlining their duties and responsibilities. If permitted by local law/customs, investigations or checks into the backgrounds of security officers should be conducted.

At facilities with a perimeter wall, there should be one 24-hr. perimeter security officer post. If the facility maintains a separate vehicular entrance security officer post, such a post should be manned from 1 hr. before to 1 hr. after normal business hours and during special events. Security officers should be responsible for conducting package inspections, package check-in, and, if used, should operate the walk-through and hand-held metal detectors. Security officers should also be responsible for inspecting local and international mail delivered to the facility, both visually and with a hand-held metal detector and explosive detector if possible before it is distributed. X-ray equipment for package inspection should be employed if the level of risk dictates.

At facilities with a perimeter guardhouse, the walk-through metal detector could be maintained and operated in an unsecured pass-through portion of the guardhouse. A walk-through metal detector is particularly recommended for a company with a high threat profile, especially if a security officer is spending a large percentage of time manually searching with hand-held metal detectors. In addition, this security officer could also be responsible for conducting package inspections. Any package storage, however, should be in shelves in the foyer and be under the direction of the foyer security officer or receptionist. Generally, all security screening and package storage will be carried out in the foyer.

Security Hard-line

Office areas should be equipped with a "hard-line" to provide physical protection from unregulated public access. Protection should be provided by a forced-entry-resistant hard-line that meets ballistic protection standards. These standards can be obtained from your corporate security personnel or a security consultant. When a security hard-line for public access control is constructed, the following criteria should apply:

Walls

For public access control purposes, exterior perimeter walls should be constructed of no less than 6 in. of reinforced concrete from slab to slab. The reinforcement should be of at least No. 5 rebar spaced 5 in. on center, horizontally and vertically, and anchored in both slabs. In existing buildings, the following are acceptable substitutions for 5-in. reinforced concrete hard-lines:

- Solid masonry, 6 in. thick or greater, with reinforcing bars horizontally and vertically installed.

- Solid un-reinforced masonry or brick, 8 in. thick or greater.

- Hollow masonry block, 4 to 8 in. thick with 1/4-in. steel backing.

- Solid masonry, at least 6 in. thick, with 1/4-in. steel backing.

Security Doors

- Fabricated ballistic steel wall, using two 1/4-in. layers of sheet steel separated by tubular steel studs.

- Reinforced concrete, less than 6 in. thick with 1/8-in. steel backing.

- Either opaque or transparent security doors can be used for public access control purposes. All doors should provide a 15-mint forced entry penetration delay. In addition, doors should be ballistic resistant.

- The public access control door should be a local access control door, meaning a receptionist or security officer can remotely open the door.

Security Windows

Whenever a security window or teller-window is installed in the hard-line, it should meet the 15-mint forced entry and standard ballistic resistance requirements.

Public Access Entry Requirements

No visitor should be allowed to enter through the hard-line without being visually identified by a security officer, receptionist, or other employee stationed behind the hard-line. If the identity of the visitor cannot be established, the visitor must be escorted at all times while in the facility.

Alarms and Intercoms

A telephone intercom between the secure office area, the foyer security officer, and guardhouse should be installed. In facilities where deemed necessary, a central alarm and public address system should be installed to alert staff and patrons of an emergency situation. Where such a system is required, the primary control console should be located in the security control center. Keep in mind that alarms without emergency response plans may be wasted alarms. Design, implement, and practice emergency plans.

Designated Secure Area

Every facility should be equipped with a secure area for immediate use in an emergency situation. This area is not intended to be used for prolonged periods of time. In the event of emergency, employees will vacate the premises as soon as possible. The secure area, therefore, is provided for the immediate congregation of employees at which time emergency exit plans would be implemented.

The secure area should be contained within the staff office area, behind the established hard-line segregating offices from public access. An individual office will usually be designated as the secure area. Entrance into the secure area should be protected by a solid core wood or hollow metal door equipped with two sliding dead bolts.

Emergency egress from the secure area will be through an opaque 15-mint forced-entry-resistant door equipped with an alarmed panic bar or through a grilled window, hinged for emergency egress. The exit preferably will not be visible from the facility's front entrance.

Emergency Exits

All facilities should have a means of emergency escape aside from the secure area exit. Positioned appropriately throughout the building should be sufficient emergency exit points to accommodate normal facility occupancy.

All emergency doors should be hollow metal doors (fire doors where appropriate) equipped with alarmed emergency exit panic bars.

Executive Offices

Any employee, but especially the executive, can be a target of terrorist or criminal tactics including forced entry, building occupation, kidnapping, sabotage, and even assassination. Executive offices can be protected against attacks.

The executive office should have a physical barrier such as electromagnetically operated doors, a silent trouble alarm button, with a signal terminating in the Plant Protection Department or at the secretary's desk, and close screening of visitors at the reception and security officer desks in the lobbies and again at the executive's office itself. The exact response to a trouble alarm should be examined by the Plant Protection/Security Department in consultation with the executive. Consideration should be given to whether employees should respond to the alarm or whether local police should be summoned. In some cases, it may be preferable to have the secretary place an intercom call to the executive to verify an alarm situation before an extraordinary response is initiated.

Secretaries should not admit visitors unless positively screened in advance or known from previous visits. If the visitor is not known and/or not expected, he or she should not be admitted until satisfactory identification and a valid reason to be on site is established. In such instances, Security should be called and an officer asked to come to the scene until the visitor establishes a legitimate reason for being in the office. If the visitor cannot do so, the officer should be asked to escort the visitor out of the building.

Unusual telephone calls, particularly those in which the caller does not identify himself/herself or those in which it appears that the caller may be misrepresenting himself/herself, should not be put through to the executive. Note should be made of the circumstances involved (i.e., incoming line number, date and time, nature of call, name of caller).

This information should then be provided to the Security Department for follow-up investigation.

Under no circumstances should an executive's secretary reveal to unknown callers the whereabouts of the executive, his/her home address, or telephone number.

The executive, when working alone in the evening, on weekends, or holidays, should advise Security how long he/she will be in the office and check out with Security when leaving.

General Office Security

Money, valuables, and important papers such as passports should not be kept in your desk. Thefts will occur in all offices, even during working hours. Some will be solved, most could have been prevented. The following suggestions will decrease the chance of further thefts:

- Don't tempt thieves by leaving valuables or money unsecured.

- If sharing an office or suite of offices, stagger lunch hours and coffee breaks so that the office is occupied at all times.

- If the office must be left vacant, lock the door.

- Locate desks in a way that persons entering the office or suite can be observed.

- Follow a clean desk policy before leaving at night. Keep valuables and company documents in locked containers.

- Confirm work to be done or property to be removed by Maintenance, outside service personnel, or vendors.

- Do not "hide" keys to office furniture under flower pots, calendars, etc. Thieves know all the hiding places. Do not label keys except by code.

Develop and Improve Employee Security Procedures

Make employees aware of how important it is to control information. Sensitize employees to handle inquiries, both in person and by telephone, with concern for the identity of the requester and the legitimacy of their "need-to-know."

Employees should be briefed on how to handle suspicious, probing calls and to whom to report such calls.

Office Security Countermeasures

American enterprises, particularly those in foreign countries, have been and will continue to be the subject of controversial political and economic issues that can turn their executives and offices into targets for terrorists and criminal actions. Countermeasures against these acts can and should be implemented in the office environment. The following list describes some of the measures that may be useful in improving personal security and safety at the office.

- Avoid working alone late at night and on days when the remainder of the staff is absent.

- The office door should be locked when you vacate your office for any lengthy period, at night and on weekends.

- Do not permit the secretary to leave keys to the office or desk.
- There should be limited access to the executive office area.

- Arrange office interiors so that strange or foreign objects left in the room will be immediately recognized.

- Unescorted visitors should not be allowed admittance nor should workers without proper identification and authorization.

- Implement a clean desk policy. Do not leave papers nor travel plans on desktops unattended.

- Control publicity in high-risk areas. Avoid identification by photographs for news release. Maintain a low profile.

- Janitorial or maintenance activity in key offices and factory areas should be supervised by competent company employees.

- A fire extinguisher, first-aid kit, and oxygen bottle should be stored in the office area.

- The most effective physical security configuration is to have doors locked (from within) with one visitor access door to the office area.

- Where large numbers of employees are involved, use the identification badge system containing a photograph.

- Upon the conclusion of meetings, staff personnel should inspect all guest rooms and function rooms to ensure that no documents, personal effects, or equipment have been left behind by participants.

Advice for Secretaries

A secretary has close knowledge of company business. He/she should maximize security, and the following measures should be reviewed with him/her:

- Be alert to strangers visiting the executive without an appointment and who are unknown to him/her.

- Be alert to strangers who loiter near the office.

- Do not reveal the executive's whereabouts to callers. Even if the caller is known, information should be on a need-to-know. As a standard policy, take a number where caller can be contacted. Do not give out telephone numbers or addresses.

- When receiving a threatening call, including a bomb threat, extortion threat, or from a mentally disturbed individual, remain calm and listen carefully. Each secretary and/or receptionist should have a threatening telephone call checklist which should be completed as soon as possible. A recommended checklist is in the following "Bomb Threat Plan".

- Keep executive travel and managers' travel itineraries confidential. Strictly limit distribution to those with a need to know.

- Observe caution when opening mail. "Things to look for" is included in the following "Bomb Threat Plan".

BOMB THREAT PLAN

Introduction

Establish a written bomb threat plan and bomb search procedures with clear instructions. Appropriate employees should be task with specific responsibilities.

Consider the installation of a telephone recorder for bomb threat calls. This can and should be done in such a way as to restrict access to the recorder and any tapes made.

Maintain a log of all bomb threats and other threatening phone calls. If a written threat is received, handle it as evidence, do not destroy possible latent fingerprints, and contact the police.

The mail handlers should have available established procedures in the event there are any signs of a bomb. It is also important not to accept packages from strangers until satisfied with the individual's identity and the nature of the parcel.

TELEPHONE THREAT GUIDE

Questions to ask

- When is bomb going to explode?

- Where is it right now?

- What does it look like?

- What kind of bomb is it?

- What will cause it to explode?

- Did you place the bomb?
- Why?

- What is your address?

- What is your name?

- Where are you calling from?

- Is this a prank?

- How do I know this is not a prank?

- May I talk to Hostage?

- If a Hostage Situation, is the hostage all right?

- If hostage situation, what do you want?

- Will you call back in 15 Minuets? IMPORTANT

- How can I contact you if I have trouble meeting your demands?

IDENTIFICATION OF CALLER:

- Sex of caller:
- Race:
- Age:
- Length of call:
- Number at which call is received:
- Time:
- Date:

DESCRIBE CALLERS VOICE

- Calm
- Angry
- Excited
- Slow
- Rapid
- Soft
- Loud
- Laughter
- Crying
- Normal
- Distinct

- Slurred
- Nasal
- Stutter
- Lisp
- Raspy
- Deep
- Ragged
- Clearing throat
- Deep breathing
- Cracking voice
- Disguised
- Accent
- Familiar - If voice is familiar, who did it sound like?

BACKGROUND SOUNDS

- Street noises
- Crockery
- Voices
- PA System
- Music

- House noises
- Motors
- Office machinery

LANGUAGE SKILL

- Well Spoken
- Educated
- Foul
- Irrational
- Incoherent
- Message read by caller

LETTER AND PARCEL BOMB GUIDE

Some mail devices may be recognized by visual inspection. Mail handling personnel should be alert to a number of recognition clues, the most common of which are detailed below.

Place of Origin: Note the postmark. This may be from a country directing a terrorist campaign or from an area associated with postal bombs. If the arrival of such mail is uncommon, it should be treated as suspect.

Senders Writing: Mail should be treated with caution if it features a foreign style of writing, not normally received, on the address. This should be considered in relation to above.

Excessive Postage: Mail with excessive postage and no return address should be viewed with caution.

Balance: A letter or package should be treated as suspect if it is unbalanced, has loose contents, or is heavier on one side than the other.

Weight: If a package or letter seems excessively heavy for its volume, it should be treated as suspect.

Feel: If an envelope has any feeling of springiness at the top, bottom, or sides, but does not bend or flex, be careful, this is a key sign of an explosive device. Warning- examine mail gently!

Protruding Wires: Mail devices are often loosened or damaged by rough handling. It is possible that a fuse, electrical wire, or connection may become loose and penetrate the wrapping or the envelope. Any such device is unstable and highly dangerous. It must not be touched.
Holes in the Envelope or Wrapping: An explosive mail device that has been handled roughly may show wire or spring holes in its outer wrapping. This, by itself or in combination with the other clues described, should alert mail handlers to a suspect device.

Grease Marks: Certain types of explosives leave greasy black marks on paper, a good indication of a suspect device. It can also mean that the explosive device has become old and unstable, making it extremely dangerous.

Smell: A smell suggestive of almonds or marzipan, or any other strange smell, including shoe polish is an indication of a suspect device.

Un-requested Deliveries: Un-requested deliveries, especially packages, should be screened and treated with caution. A book or thick brochure discovered upon opening a delivery should be reported to the security department or examined for any of the above clues. Any mail which raises the slightest suspicion should not be handled. Remember the catch phrase: TOUCHING TRIGGERS TRAGEDY. (It is of benefit to both parties if senders place their name, organization address, and telephone number on packets. Then, in cases of suspicion, they may be contacted for an explanation of contents.

Suspicious Packaging: If an envelope is taped down all around, instead of having a normal opening flap, it may contain a booby trap spring. Such letters should be handled very carefully and treated as suspect.

Letter Stiffness: Gentle handling can reveal whether an envelope contains folded paper or a device. The presence of stiff cardboard, metal or plastic should alert the handler to a possible suspect device.

Inner Enclosures: If, after opening a letter or package, the mail handler encounters an inner sealed enclosure whether or not it fits any of the above descriptions—the item should be treated as suspect.

VEHICLE TRAVEL SECURITY

Introduction

Threats of terrorism and kidnapping are serious problems involving all aspects of security management. Effective management dictates that available resources be used wisely and concentrated on security weak points. Terrorists are very quick to identify the security vulnerabilities of business, family, and pleasure travel. At their best, protection strategies dealing with vehicles and travel are perhaps the hardest to formulate, and the advantage tends to be with the terrorist. Current statistics indicate that the greatest danger from acts of terrorism occurs while the executive is traveling to or from the office and just before reaching his/her destination.

The inherent security problems of passenger vehicle travel are many. Vehicles are easily recognized by year, make, and model, and the trained terrorist can accurately assess any protection modifications and security devices. Using adequate resources, vehicles can be discreetly followed; therefore, making possible repeated dry runs of potential attacks with very low risk of detection. Under these conditions, different methods of attack can be formulated and tested until success is ensured. While traveling in a passenger vehicle, the executive has limited protection resources upon which to rely and often is dependent on fixed security manpower. This makes it easier for terrorist groups, which are geared to mobility, to ensure numerical superiority.

The attack potential against the executive in travel rests heavily on psychological instability and human weakness. The shock of surprise attack is greatest at points of changing surroundings, crossroads, and when entering or exiting vehicles. These are situations of constant change and points of activity where the executive has a tendency to be mentally off balance. Vehicles are often left in driveways, on streets, at service centers, and other isolated areas with no form of control or protection, allowing easy access to terrorists. Through illegal entry to the vehicle, the terrorist can gain a number of attack points; sabotage with the intent to maim and injure, sabotage with the intent of execution, and sabotage to ensure the success of future attacks. These psychological factors make the vehicle the ideal place to apply scare tactics, warnings, and gain initial control of the executive.

Even though travel problems provide the greatest number of security and psychological variables, there are actions and policies that can be developed to minimize the executive's risk and complicate the terrorist's plans. The basic travel policy can be divided into three areas: *(1) Normal Travel Procedures, (2) Vehicle Equipment, and (3) Vehicle Defense Strategy.* The following checklists will aid in formulating and evaluating an effective travel security policy.

Vehicle Equipment Checklist

- The executive vehicle designed to meet the terrorist or criminal threat in a high threat area should be a hardtop model with the following special equipment: (a) inside hood latch, (b) locked gas caps, (c) inner escape latch on trunk, (d) steel-belted radial tires with inner tire devices that permit movement even with a flat tire, (e) radiator protection, (f) disk brakes, and (g) an anti-bomb bolt through the end of the exhaust pipe.

- Positive communications can be ensured with a two-way radio or a car telephone.

- It is recommended that the executive vehicle designed to meet the terrorist or criminal threat carry the following safety equipment: (a) fire extinguisher, (b) first-aid kit, (c) flashlight,

(d) two spare tires, (e) large outside mirrors, and (f) a portable high-intensity spotlight.

- For additional protection, the vehicle should have an alarm system with an independent power source (an additional battery).

Travel Procedures Checklist

- The avoidance of routine times and patterns of travel by executives is the least expensive security strategy that can be utilized. The selection of the route should be at the discretion of the executive, not of a chauffeur. Always restrict travel plans to a need-to-know basis.

- Avoid driving in remote areas after dark and keep to established, well traveled roads.

- In high risk areas or when individuals are considered attractive targets, consideration should be given to executives and drivers being trained in anti-terrorism strategy and defensive driving. Establish responsibilities and develop contingency plans.

- There should be a simple duress procedure established between the executive and drivers. Any oral or visual signal will suffice (i.e., something that the executive or driver says or does only if something is amiss).

- Never overload a vehicle, and all persons should wear seat belts.

- Always park vehicles in parking areas that are either locked or watched and never park overnight on the street. Before entering vehicles, check for signs of tampering.

- When using a taxi service, vary the company. Ensure that the identification photo on the license matches the driver. If uneasy for any reason, simply take another taxi.

The Corporate Executive Survival Guide

- When attending social functions, go with others, if possible.

- Avoid driving close behind other vehicles, especially service trucks, and be aware of activities and road conditions two to three blocks ahead.

- Keep the ignition key separate and never leave the trunk key with parking or service attendants.

- Before each trip, the vehicle should be inspected to see that (a) the hood latch is secure, (b) the fender wells are empty, (c) the exhaust pipe is not blocked, (d) no one is in the back seat or on the floor, and (e) the gas tank is at least three quarters full.

- Establish a firm policy regarding the carrying and use of firearms. Local laws may prohibit firearms.

Defense Strategy Checklist

Always be alert to possible surveillance; if followed, drive to the nearest safe location, such as police stations, fire stations, or shopping center and ask for help. Carry a mini-cassette recorder in the car to dictate details of a suspect surveillance car such as color, make, model, license plate, description of occupants, etc. It is difficult to make such detailed notes while driving.

- Where feasible, drive in the in the inner lanes to keep from being forced to the curb.

- Beware of minor accidents that could block traffic in suspect areas; especially crossroads because they are preferred areas for terrorist or criminal activities as crossroads offer escape advantages.

- If a roadblock is encountered, use shoulder or curb (hit at 30-45-deg. angle) to go around, or ram the terrorist or criminal blocking vehicle. In all cases, do not stop and never allow the executive's vehicle to be boxed in with a loss of maneuverability.

- Blocking vehicles should be rammed in a non-engine area, at 45 deg., in low gear, and at a constant moderate speed. KNOCK THE BLOCKING VEHICLE OUT OF THE WAY.

- Whenever a target vehicle veers away from the terrorist vehicle, it gives adverse maneuvering room and presents a better target to gunfire.

Local Travel Guidelines

- Discuss travel plans on a need-to-know basis only. Telephone operators and secretaries should not advise callers and visitors when an executive is out of town on a trip.

- Remove company logos from luggage. Luggage identification tags should be of a type that allows the information on the tag to be covered. Use the business address on the tag.

- Do not leave valuables and/or sensitive documents in the hotel room.

- When sightseeing, observe basic security precautions and refrain from walking alone in known high-crime areas.

- Always have telephone change available and know how to use the phones. Learn key emergency phrases of the country to be able to ask for police, medical, etc. Joggers should carry identification.

- Men should carry wallets either in an inside jacket pocket or a front pants pocket, never in a hip pocket. The less money carried the better. Credit cards can be used for most purchases.

- The telephone numbers of the U.S. Embassy and company employee contact numbers should be carried with employees at all times.

- Always carry the appropriate documentation for the country being visited.

- When traveling, ask for a hotel room between the second and seventh floors. Most fire department equipment does not reach higher to effect rescue and ground floor rooms are more vulnerable to terrorist or criminal activity.

- American-type hotels usually offer a higher level of safety and security inasmuch as they offer smoke alarms, fire extinguishers, safety locks, hotel security, 24-hr. operators, English-speaking personnel, safety deposit boxes, and normally will not divulge a guest's room number.

- Choose taxis carefully and at random. Do not use non-licensed operators.

- Be as inconspicuous as possible in dress, social activities, and amount of money spent on food, souvenirs, gifts, etc.

- Stay in or use VIP rooms or security zones when waiting in commercial airports abroad. Minimize the amount of time spent in airports.

- Confirm arrivals at destinations with office and/or family. Use an itinerary when traveling.

Family and Company Cars

Selection of make and model: Purchase or lease a car that blends in well with the local passenger car environment. Remember - Low Profile!

Safety and Security Precautions

- Consider installation of burglar alarm on car consistent with risk level.

- Make sure gas cap, spare tire, and engine compartment are lockable in the interest of good safety and security.

- Always have the fuel tank at least half full.

- Keep vehicle(s) locked at all times.

- Never park your vehicle on the street for long periods of time.

- Keep your vehicle(s) housed in a garage.

- Make sure that you have both right and left side rear view mirrors. Visibility around your vehicle is critical.

- Do not leave registration papers in your car.

- If legal to do so, have your car license plate registered to a Post Office Box rather than to your home or office. List the P.O. Box to your office.

- Keep extra water and oil in the trunk.

- Do not use stickers or plates.

- Keep emergency equipment in the trunk, flashlight, flares, fire extinguisher, first aid kit, etc. personalized license

- If possible, install a communication device, such as a two-way radio or telephone in your car.

Auto Travel Countermeasures

Potential victims of kidnapping and assault are probably most vulnerable when entering or leaving their home or office.

- Never enter a car without checking the rear seat to insure that it is empty.

- Do not develop predictable patterns during the business day or during free time. For example, do not leave home or the office at the same time and by the same route every day.

- Do not have a standard tee-off time for golf, tennis, and hand ball, etc.

- If possible, exchange company cars, swap with co-workers occasionally.

- Know the location of police, hospital, military, and government buildings. Ascertain when they are open and which ones are 24-hour operations. These areas can provide a safe haven along normal transportation routes.

- Even the slightest disruption in travel patterns may disrupt a surveillance team sufficiently for them to tip their hand or abandon their efforts.

- Avoid trips to remote areas, particularly after dark. If it is essential to go into such an area, travel in a group or convoy and advise trusted personnel of your itinerary.

- Select well traveled streets as much as possible.

- Keep vehicles well maintained at all times, including a useable spare tire.

- Install additional rear-view mirrors so passengers may see what is behind.

- If chauffeur driven, consider riding up front next to the driver sometimes, in keeping with the low profile concept.

- Chauffeurs and high-risk personnel should be trained in offensive and evasive driving techniques.

- When driving, keep doors and windows locked.

- Be constantly alert to road conditions and surroundings, to include possible surveillance by car, motorcycle, or bicycle. All passengers should be vigilant.

- If surveillance or some other danger is detected, drive to the closest safe haven, such as police station, hospital emergency room, fire station, etc., lock your car and go inside. Advise authorities as appropriate.

- When traveling, pre-plan your route and one alternate.

- Be prepared for local environmental conditions (snow, rain, etc.).

- Never pick up hitchhikers.

- Whenever possible, drive to the center of the road, especially in rural settings, to avoid being forced off the road.

- Remain a safe distance behind the vehicle ahead to allow space for avoidance maneuvers, if necessary.

- Check side/rear view mirrors routinely.

- Carry 3 x 5 cards with important assistance phrases printed on them to assist with language problems.

- Always carry appropriate coin denomination for public phones. Practice use of public telephones.

- Report as appropriate all suspicious activity to the company security contact, embassy or consulate, or local police as soon as possible.

- Consider keeping a small hand-held cassette recorder in glove box at all times, descriptions of suspicious persons, activities, license plate numbers, etc., can be dictated while driving. It's impossible to make notes while driving or in stressful situations.

- Never leave identifying material or valuables in the vehicle.

Surveillance: If surveillance is suspected consider the following actions:

- Divert from originally intended destination, make a few turns to see if the suspect still persists.

- Immediately determine any identifying data that you can observe. (For example: make, color of car, license number, number and description of occupants.)

Remember; do not panic if surveillance is confirmed. Surveillance teams are normally neither
trained nor have the mission to assault the potential target.

Parking of vehicles:

- Always lock the vehicle, no matter where it is located.

- Do not leave the car in the care of a valet parking service such as hotel, restaurant or club.

- Require chauffeurs to stay with the car.

- Avoid leaving the vehicle parked on the street overnight.

- Never exit vehicle without checking the area for suspicious individuals. If in doubt, drive away.

James R. Doyle

VISITING VIP PROTECTION

General Principles

This section provides guidelines regarding security procedures to be implemented during visits of company executives. Implementation of these guidelines will reduce the executive's exposure to terrorist acts, criminal activity, and potential embarrassment.

It should be viewed as a tool to assist in organizing and planning visits by company executives or other key personnel.

Security Coordination

Security coordination guidelines should be used when a determination is made that the threat potential is minimal in view of the local security environment. Factors used in determining whether a minimal threat potential exists include:

- A stable local government.

- Effective law enforcement.

- No significant history of terrorist acts against multinational companies or their executives.

- No previous history of criminal or terrorist acts directed against company executives.

- No significant level of criminal activity (particularly violent crimes such as robbery, kidnapping, murder, and rape).

- No current adverse publicity against the company and no local group activity protesting company policies.

- Other risk factors applicable to the local environment.

A management-level employee should be Security Coordinator. The responsibilities consist of implementing the established security guidelines, coordinating all other security aspects of the visit, and serving as the visitor's main contact. The coordinator should be present at the airport, hotel, and event during arrivals and departures. He/she should ensure adequate security precautions are taken and be present at large public functions.

Air Travel

Travel in corporate aircraft is preferable because contact with the general public is limited, but use of commercial airlines is an acceptable alternative provided the airline involved is not considered a likely terrorist target. The following guidelines should be considered:

- When booking reservations, you should make no reference to the visitor's position.

- Personnel should be available at the airport to handle baggage and expedite customs clearances and local airport formalities, both on arrival and departure.

- A VIP room should be reserved at the airport for possible use in the event of a delayed departure by the aircraft.

- Time spent at the airport should be kept to a minimum.

- Public areas should be avoided, if at all possible.

- Use of public transportation to and from airports is not recommended.

- Distribution of travel itineraries should be restricted.

Aircraft Security

The following suggestions should be considered in the event that corporate aircraft are used:

- The hiring of contract security officers at major international airports to secure the corporate aircraft during stopovers is not necessary provided that the airport has a viable security system.

- The use of contract security officers on a 24-hr. basis is necessary in the event that the corporate aircraft uses a remote airfield with limited operations and minimal security or is parked in a remote area of a major airport.

Local Transportation

- The use of public transportation such a taxis, buses, and subways is not recommended.

- A four-door sedan should be available for use throughout the visit. Care should be taken to ensure that the vehicle is unobtrusive, so as not to bring undue attention to the visitor. The chauffeur or driver, if used, should be bilingual and knowledgeable of the local area and routes to be traveled.

Accommodations

- Hotel reservations should be booked at a first class hotel located in a low-crime area. Hotel management need not be contacted to provide unusual security or other arrangements for the visitor. A low-key approach is essential to ensure anonymity. Reference to the company or the visitor's position should be avoided.

- Visitors should be pre-registered to avoid being required to check in at the reception desk. The room key should be provided to the visitor immediately upon his or her arrival at the hotel or airport by personnel responsible for coordinating the visit.

- The guest room or suite should be located between the second and seventh floor of the hotel, preferably on a floor with a separate concierge. The room should be away from the public elevator lobby but near an emergency exit.

- Valuables should be stored in accordance with hotel safekeeping provisions.

- Use of a guest house or private residence is acceptable as long as it is not located in an isolated area.

Official Functions and Activities

- Coordinate all activities and visit sites before the visitor's attendance. The coordinator should obtain guest lists and detailed itineraries, determine emergency evacuation routes, and ascertain the purpose of the function.

- The coordinator should ensure that the function or activity does not subject the visitor to undue risk.

- Official company functions should be on an invitational basis and guests should be required to present their invitations at a reception desk staffed by company personnel before being granted access to the function. The receptionist should match the invitation to the guest list.

Liaison With Local Authorities

Prior to a visit by a VIP, you should make contact with the appropriate local authorities to advise them of the upcoming visit and to ascertain whether the current local security environment necessitates an upgraded security posture for the visit.

Information Packets

An information packet should be prepared before the visit and presented to the executive upon his/her arrival. Information provided should include:

- Emergency telephone contact list, including company personnel (home and office numbers), hospital, police, fire, emergency services, and company doctor.

- Maps of the area.

- Detailed itinerary.

- Availability of company transportation.

- Brief review of current security situation including curfews, government-imposed restrictions, description of high-crime areas to be avoided, and other relevant factors.

- Explanation of local currency (exchange rates and currency control laws or regulations).

- Details of visits by VIPs should be considered company confidential and distribution limited on a need-to-know basis.

- Media coverage, unless requested by the visitor, is unwarranted.

Unarmed Security Escort

An unarmed security escort should be used when a determination is made by management that the threat potential to the executive justifies this level of protection in view of the local security environment. Factors used in determining whether a moderate threat exists include:

- Stable local government.

- Effective law enforcement.

- Some history of terrorist attacks against multinational companies and/or their executives.

- No previous history of criminal or terrorist acts directed against company executives.

- Upswing in criminal activity, particularly violent crimes with some history of criminal Kidnappings for financial gain.

- Some current adverse publicity against the company and poten-tial for nonviolent groups to protest against company policies during the executive's visit.

Armed Protective Security Detail

A protective security detail should be used when a determination is made by management that the threat potential to the executive is high in view of the local security environment. Factors used in determining whether a high threat exists include:

- Unstable or unpopular local government, with terrorist groups actively attempting to bring about its overthrow.

- Ineffective or corrupt law enforcement agencies unable to reduce criminal activity and bring the terrorist problem under control.

- Significant history of terrorist attacks against multinational companies and/or their executives, including bombings, assas-sinations, and kidnappings.

- Recent history of criminal or terrorist acts or threats against company facilities and/or their executives.

- Widespread criminal activity reaching all elements of local society with emphasis on violent crimes.

- Considerable adverse publicity against company policies and organized local groups that have been leaning toward violence and are planning to protest company policies during the exec-utive's visit.

- Other factors appropriate to the local environment. Asking the U. S. Embassy or Consulate for pertinent threat information is a good idea.

High-threat potential means a significant risk to the well being of the executive. You should strongly recommend against a visit by the executive if a high risk exists. By definition, this category will apply to a limited number of locations, but might vary based on the local situation at a particular point in time. For example, a potential visit might be deemed a moderate risk one month and high risk another because of changes in the local environment.

High Risk Professional Body Guards

- Professional bodyguards dressed in plain clothes and equipped with weapons and two-way radios should accompany the executive at all times.

- At least one bodyguard should remain in the direct vicinity of the executive whenever potential public contact is envisioned.

- Security personnel should conduct advance surveys of all sites to be visited and be on the scene throughout the executive's visit to the location.

- Security personnel should be assigned to the hotel or residence on a 24-hr. basis to ensure that unauthorized individuals do not enter the room or suite.

- Cleaning staff should be escorted whenever they enter the accommodations.

- The room or suite should be periodically checked to ensure that contraband such as a bomb or electronic devices have not been introduced into the area.

- An escort car or cars should be used on all vehicular movements by the executive to provide a response capacity in the event of an attack or vehicular mishap or breakdown. The escort car or cars should be staffed by at least two security professionals.

- The executive's vehicle should be driven by a security professional trained in evasive or defensive maneuvers.

- The vehicle should be inspected before use to ensure that explosive devices have not been installed on the vehicle or that the vehicle has not been otherwise tampered with by unauthorized individuals. Use of an armored car, if available, is recommended.

- Public exposure should be limited to the minimum necessary for the executive to complete his or her assignment.

VIP Group Activities Guidelines

The exposure created by a number of executives gathering at a single location necessitates some degree of increased security. The following is a list of some general guidelines for use in such group activities:

- The suites should be inspected before occupancy to ensure that no contraband or unauthorized individuals are located in the rooms.

- Security should be provided for corporate aircraft over-night at the local airport. Such security may be provided by off-duty uniformed and armed police officers or contract security guards.

- The hotel activity boards should make no reference to the company. Publicity and press coverage should be minimized. A low profile is strongly recommended. Anonymity is a powerful ally of a traveling executive.

- If possible, hotel guest rooms occupied by company personnel should be located in one section of the hotel. Consideration should be given to hiring a security officer to patrol the hallway in the vicinity of the guest rooms and function rooms during hours of darkness or even on a 24-hr. basis.

- Access to functions should be controlled to prevent an unauthorized individual from gaining access to the meetings or functions. This can be handled by assigning a member of the meeting staff to serve as a receptionist outside the door. Access can be granted either by personal recognition or by checking identity cards.

- Information packets provided to participants should include the name and telephone number of the staff person responsible for security. Staff personnel should be provided with an emergency contact list, including the telephone numbers of the nearest hospital with an emergency room, ambulance service, police department, and fire department.

- Consideration should be given to leasing pagers to ensure that staff personnel can be rapidly contacted in the event of an emergency.

RESIDENTIAL &DEPENDENT SECURITY

Introduction

The following general guidelines will help employees and dependents living in foreign countries to reduce their personal vulnerability to terrorist acts.

To protect general residential security:

- Be alert for any signs of unusual activity that could indicate that the residence is under surveillance. The detection of potential threats is one of the most important safeguards for residential protection.

- Do not carry car and home keys on the same ring, and do not mark residence key rings with address or other identification.

- Avoid the use of identifying or descriptive titles or designators on gates, doors, or bells indicating personal status.

- Never provide residence addresses to unknown individuals.

- Locate the nearest phone if the residence does not have a phone, make arrangements for its use in any emergency situation, and advise all members of the household including the servants of its location, and provide this phone number to the office staff.

- Never react to an emergency call alleging an accident or injury to a member of the family until the emergency is verified through a secondary source, e.g., hospital or police station.

- Assume a low profile in the neighborhood, avoid becoming involved in disputes with local citizens or neighbors, and if others initiate a dispute, leave the scene as quickly as possible and report the matter to the proper authorities.

- Leave an interior light and a radio on when leaving the residence at night to give the impression that someone is at home.

- Arrange to have the neighbors pick up all routine deliveries when leaving the residence for an extended period of time.

- Record all valuable belongings by serial number and full identification marks where possible.

- Be particularly alert when entering or leaving the residence during the early morning or late evening hours, and be suspicious of anything that appears abnormal or unusual.

- Make it a practice to observe the streets and areas around the residence when either leaving or returning. If anything suspicious is noted, do not attempt to leave or enter, as the case may be, and immediately alert the proper authorities for assistance.

- Closely examine all received mail, particularly if it is unsolicited, and if in doubt, call the U.S. security officer or local police for assistance.

- Have all repairmen call by appointment and carefully check all identification. Do not leave them alone in the home.

- Be alert for any suspicious persons working around the residence, e.g., public utility crews and road repair personnel, particularly where they can observe the residence. Report all such suspicious activities to the local police and to the company security officer.

- Attempt to find more than one shop which provides the necessary convenience services to avoid having to frequent the same place routinely or on a scheduled basis.

- Do not provide strangers or unknown callers information about family or office associate activities unless they have a valid need to know.

- Be alert for sudden, unexplained absences of local nationals in areas that they normally frequent.

- Never carry a personal weapon unless prior official approval has been granted, the required local documentation has been obtained, and accredited training has been taken in the proper and safe use of the weapon.

- Prepare and issue to each family member a card or slip of paper containing pertinent medical and emergency contact instructions to be used if they become involved in an accident, terrorist incident, or are unable to provide a verbal response. Emphasize the need to retain this information on their person at all times and periodically update it.

RESIDENTIAL PERIMETER SECURITY

For security measures pertaining to perimeter areas, ensure that:

- Existing perimeter walls and fences are kept in good repair and all doors, gates, and other openings are locked at all times.

- Adequate perimeter lighting is installed around the residence and operating during non-daylight hours, and such exterior lighting provides enough illumination to permit identification of visitors;

- Ornamental or decorative shrubbery placed near the residence is trimmed and well maintained to prevent its use for concealment of persons or objects;

- Where and when feasible, watchdog(s) are used inside and/or outside to act as an alert and or deterrent; and the local police are alerted that the residence is occupied and determine the best and most expeditious method of notifying them in an emergency.

RESIDENCE PHYSICAL SECURITY

Since proper physical security measures can provide a great degree of protection, ensure that:

- All exterior doors are equipped with good quality locks, preferably the vertical deadbolt type, and all exterior doors are locked at all times.

- Exterior doors are solid wood construction and fitted with a viewer to permit the observation of visitors on the opposite side.

- Glass areas of exterior doors are protected by metal grills, bars, or strong screens and those doors with glass fixtures have double-face key locks to prevent entry by breaking out the glass and reaching inside to operate the thumb latch.

- Keys are not left in door locks.

- Spare keys are not hidden outside the home.

- All door locks are changed upon occupancy of a new residence, and strict accountability of all keys are maintained.

- All locks are replaced or re-keyed when keys are lost or mislaid.

- Deadbolts are activated when locking all doors, even when in the home.

- All outside exterior fuse and switch boxes are locked.

- All entrance doors and windows are locked when leaving the residence.
- Window grills, bars, or heavy screens are installed on all windows on the ground floor, assuring adequate alternate means of emergency escape from the residence.

- Windows adjoining trees or other buildings are protected, including provisions for alternate avenues of escape.

- All windows are protected on the inside with Venetian blinds and drapes, and such protective/decorative devices should be closed after dark.

- Drapes and blinds are arranged so that interior movements cannot be observed from the outside.

- All residents stay away from windows and close blinds or drapes if a civil disturbance and/or riot occurs.

- All home windows are checked and locked before retiring for the night.

- Valuable items are not displayed in areas where they can be easily observed from outside.

- A safe-haven strong-room within an interior area of the residence is selected and established to provide the maximum amount of security.

- Instruct all family members to alert the rest of the family and proceed to the safe-haven or at the first sign of a disturbance.

DEPENDENT CHILDREN SECURITY

Since dependent security is of the utmost importance, parents must:

- Know where children are at all times and be especially aware of their social activities and the facilities they frequent.

- Escort children to and from school and school buses.
- Instruct school authorities that, under no circumstances, are the children to be picked up by persons other than family members or other authorized individuals.

- Instruct children to report to parents any incidents of an unusual nature, e.g., molestation's and offers of transportation.

- Know the whereabouts of all family members at all times.

- Keep each other informed of whereabouts, itineraries, and expected time of return.

- Caution all dependents to be alert for person watching or observing either the residence or its occupants; and avoid the establishment of family patterns where possible.

SERVANT SECURITY

Since servants can play an important role in the family's safety and security, employees should:

- Verify the background and check references of all servants through the local security officer.

- Brief servants frequently on security precautions they are expected to exercise.

- Instruct servants to:

- Prevent strangers or unauthorized visitors from entering the home without specific approval.

- Identify all callers before opening doors.

- Reject packages from unknown callers.

- Obtain as much identifying information as possible regarding individuals attempting to deliver any unknown package.
- Avoid giving the impression that they are at home alone.

- Inform callers that the occupants are busy and determine the identity and purpose of the caller, advising them that the occupants will contact them later.

- Provide no information over the phone or to visitors regarding the residence or its occupants.

- Avoid discussing the activities of the family with friends or acquaintances, and report the presence of any suspicious persons or objects observed in or near the residence.

- Do not make confidants of the servants. Tell them only what they need to know regarding your plans and intended movements.

- Re-brief all servants periodically on security instructions related to the home, its occupants, and their responsibilities.

SOCIAL AND RECREATIONAL ACTIVITIES

To ensure better personnel protection and/or safety during social and recreational activities:

- Prepare invitations when hosting a large social gathering in your home and notify guests that the invitation will be collected upon arrival as a control mechanism to prevent the admission of uninvited or unknown "guests".

- Conduct security checks, if possible, on any temporary domestic help retained for social functions.

- Become acquainted with the neighbors and form a block warning system whereby anyone will notify local police if they observe suspicious persons or activities in the neighborhood or around a residence.

- Periodically discuss with family members the possibility of suspicious activities during social functions and review planned responses with them.

- Limit family social activities and set curfews for dependents contingent on the local situation.

- Do not enter an elevator already occupied by a stranger or suspicious-looking person during late hours and in isolated areas.

- Try to stand next to the control panel and be ready to press the alarm button if necessary, when riding in an elevator.

- Be familiar with local language phrases needed to summon help.

- Provide each family member with emergency telephone numbers and the proper local coinage for the commercial phones, if necessary.

- Vary arrival and departure times to regular daily or weekly social events when possible, even though it may be inconvenient.

- Do not discuss social or recreational activities in public places.

- Refuse to accept transportation from unknown persons.

- Use only approved recreational facilities where safety and protective features are provided.

PERSONAL PROTECTION DURING LOCAL TRAVEL

When traveling, personnel should observe the following protective measures to reduce the possibility of being exposed to a dangerous situation or the risk of a security breach:

- Avoid carrying large sums of money; however, carry a reasonable amount of local currency concealed for emergency use.

- Carry the routine Identification any traveler would have, i.e., passport, credit cards, and driver's license.

- Do not carry on your person or in your luggage any passes, credentials, telephone numbers, or other identification that would possibly identify you with an intelligence agency or the Department of Defense.

- Cooperate with duly designated officials when they are conducting routine screening procedures before boarding transportation vehicles.

- Avoid behavior that would attract attention if involved in an aircraft hijacking, detained, or questioned while en-route.

- Respond to questioning in a polite, civil manner while maintaining common sense, good cover, and security.

- Move through the inspection and check-in procedures in commercial transportation terminals as soon after arrival as possible, and spend all waiting time in security controlled areas.

- Attempt to select a seat near an exit when traveling on public transportation.

- Avoid flashy, ostentatious display of personal effects while traveling.

- Remain alert to immediate surroundings at all times when driving a vehicle, drive defensively, and be prepared to respond to situations that could influence the safety of the vehicle and its occupants.

- Do not publicize travel plans.

- Advise a family member or friend of intended route(s) of travel and approximate transit time(s) when leaving home for a social event or local trip.

- Establish routine check-in procedures with family or friends and follow them precisely.

- Avoid going anywhere alone when possible, travel only on busy, well-lighted thoroughfares, and avoid isolated back-country roads.

- Know where the dangerous areas in city are located and avoid them.

- Remain in a lane that prevents the car from being forced to the side of the road, and allow alternate routes of escape.

- Keep all vehicle doors locked and windows rolled up to within 2 inches of the top when traveling to prevent unexpected entry by individuals.

- Lock unattended vehicles and attempt to park them off the streets at all times.

- Inspect the interior and exterior of a vehicle before entering even if it has been locked and look for any suspicious objects or unexplained wires inside or underneath.

- Vary pick-up points when using texts if possible, and instruct the driver on the route to take if familiar with the area.

- Regardless of the mode of transportation, prepare an itinerary for office or family use that includes dates of travel, transport vehicle identity, arrival and departure times, contact instructions, and phone number and name of person to be notified in an emergency.

- Keep personal vehicle in good running condition and know its capabilities and limitations.

- Rotate use of official vehicles among all station personnel to reduce identifying individuals with a particular car.

- Use local license plates if possible, and avoid any distinguishing markers or decals.

- Advise all vehicle occupants to observe traffic, suspicious vehicle(s) behind you, and/or a vehicle containing several persons parked near intersections.

- Maintain a safe distance between your vehicle and the car in front to avoid or pass it without being blocked if it should suddenly stop.

- Inform someone of your route and destination when traveling late at night or visiting remote and strange areas.

- Avoid any observed or known civil disturbances or potential demonstration locations, even if the travel direction or route must be drastically changed.

- Conduct area familiarization studies of the establishments frequently visited, and pre-select and memorize the locations of available safe-havens such as police or other security force posts along all routes of possible travel.

- Try to keep the gas tank in your personal vehicle full at all times.

- Do not pick up strangers regardless of the circumstances.

- Fasten seat belts at all times (driver and all vehicle occupants) when the vehicle is in motion.

- Avoid establishing routine schedules.

If you are planning personal travel, the following tips could help you have a safe and secure trip:

- Utilize traveler's checks or credit cards, rather than carrying large amounts of cash; however, when you leave a place of business after using a credit card, do not leave the carbon record of your charge behind. Not only does the receipt help you keep track of your funds, but a recent development has shown that people are copying the account number from the discarded carbons for these charge receipts and then ordering airline tickets or other merchandise, and charging it to the copied account.

- Plan for any language barriers and know some of the language commonly spoken wherever you are traveling.

- Learn to recognize the uniforms of local law enforcement officers.

- Dress inconspicuously.

- Avoid meeting strangers in unknown or isolated areas.

- Do not depend on the hotel room door lock for protection, whether in the room or not. For extra protection, use a chair, drawer, rubber wedge, or portable travel lock.

- Lock balcony doors or any windows in a hotel that are accessible from outside.

- Locate the fire exits, be able to recognize the fire alarm signal, and plan actions in the event of a hotel fire. If escape is not possible, fill the bathtub with water and be prepared to wait out the fire in the bathroom.

- Carry all luggage in the auto trunk.

- Bring all luggage into the hotel room each night.

- Use a reliable travel agency, club or association to obtain information about the destination and what should be done or avoided while there.

- Be cautious when shopping because charge accounts, check cashing, or package delivery will probably not be available. Carry the most valuable package closest to the body.

- Lock suitcases and do not over-pack if using public transportation.

- Store luggage in a coin-operated locker during a layover

- Use only authorized baggage handling personnel for assistance with your luggage.

- Determine taxi fares before using a taxi service.

- Lock camper or motor-home doors even while driving.

- Notify rangers, park police, or other nearby campers of selected campsite.

- Use the auto horn as an emergency alarm if required.

- Be especially dubious of unwarranted attention and offers of friendship from strangers in resort areas.

- Take precautions against pickpockets in a crowd.

- Go sightseeing with a group and be cautious of suggestions of places to go and things to do.

RESIDENCE PROTECTION WHILE TRAVELING

- Before leaving home for any travel, make the following preparations:
- Ask a neighbor to park a car in the driveway from time to time, possibly leaving it there overnight.

- Do not let newspapers and mail accumulate, but do not cancel them. Have a neighbor pick them up. If the newspaper office or the post office is notified, a large group of people are aware that you will be gone.

- Invest in three or four automatic timers, and set them so that lights go on and off in the living room, bathroom, and bedroom. It is especially effective if these timers are set to operate in sequence. Remember that lights left on all night are a sure sign that someone is away.

- Attach a timer to a radio or TV. Silence makes a house appear empty.

- Have someone mow the lawn regularly.

- Make certain all windows and doors are secured before leaving. Since an empty garage advertises the owner's absence, close and lock the garage door.

- Leave a house key with a trusted neighbor, as well as a phone number for any emergency.

- Do not leave a key under the doormat, in the mailbox, or on the door sill. The burglar knows all those places.

James R. Doyle

SECURITY GUDELINES FOR FAMILIES

Introduction

The objective of this book is to provide a diverse selection of security measures for consideration by employees and their families living outside the United States. Obviously, the security precautions described herein should be implemented consistent with the level of risk currently existing in the foreign country of residence.

Diverse political climates, local laws and customs, and a wide range of other variables make it impossible to apply standard security precautions worldwide.

Levels of risk can change very rapidly, sometimes overnight, triggered by internal or external incidents or circumstances. It is advisable, therefore, to monitor continually the political climate and other factors which may impact the level of risk. Remember that establishing a family residence abroad requires much more security planning than a short-term visit to a foreign country for business or pleasure.

It is essential that security precautions be dynamic, not static, in order to respond effectively to the ever-changing level of risk. The adoption of a static, inflexible security posture is indicative of a disregard for the climate of risk and will almost certainly result in a lack of preparedness.

Residential Security Planning

Begin to develop a tentative Residential Security Plan for yourself and all members of your family before leaving the U.S. Update your plan regularly as circumstances dictate.

One single concept, more than any other, should permeate all planning activities, namely "LOW PROFILE." In other words, DO NOT draw attention to yourself as an American by driving a big American car, subscribing to U.S. magazines, etc.; blend in to local environs.

There is a great deal of professional help available for the family moving overseas. Major Multinational corporations have large International Departments and Corporate Security Departments which may serve as valuable resources for Residential Security Planning. Libraries have an abundance of current reference materials on working and living abroad.

Obtain a current political profile of the country to which you will be moving to aid you in assessing the level of risk. Corporate Security Directors of large multinational companies can identify a number of commercial organizations which publish political profiles of most countries as well as periodic updates.

You and your family should study the culture and customs of the country you are about to enter. Use library sources and reference works.

Assessing the Level of Risk at Foreign Sites

The following factors must be taken into consideration when evaluating the seriousness of the personal risk to your family when contemplating a move abroad:

1) A risk assessment of the location to which you will be moving.

2) The profile of the company for which you work. Highly visible defense contractors may not be welcome in some parts of the world.

The threat assessment designators below were formulated by the Department of State Threat Analysis Division in the Diplomatic Security Service. The level assigned to a particular country is the result of the political/ terrorist/criminal environment in that country.

High - The threat is serious and forced entries and assaults on residents are common or an active terrorist threat exists.

Medium - The threat is moderate with forced entries and some assaults on residents occurring, or the area has potential for terrorist activity.

Low - The threat is minimal and forced entry of residences and assault of occupants is not common. There is no known terrorist threat.

Location of the Residence

Every residence to some extent provides protection against criminal intrusion, because most of them have certain built-in security devices. However, no residence is totally secure and each faces some risk of crime. It is the occupants of the residence, however, through their security attitudes and awareness, who contribute the most to their overall security.

The first step in the residence selection process should be choosing a safe neighborhood. The local police, U.S. Embassy, other American residents, and other sources, will facilitate this process.

During the neighborhood selection process, particular attention should be paid to the condition of the streets, e.g., paved or unpaved, maintenance condition, wide or narrow, one-way or two-way traffic (two-way is preferred). Parked and/or double-parked vehicles could impede access to, or egress from, the residence. Density of pedestrian traffic could create security hazards. Dense vehicular and/or pedestrian traffic facilitates retention of anonymity of criminals.

Examine the quality of lighting at nighttime; determine pedestrian and vehicular traffic patterns, parks, playgrounds, recreation areas, the existence of public or commercial enterprises intermingled with residential dwellings, fire hydrants and police call boxes. Attention should also be given to the routes into and out of the neighborhood.

The type of residences in the area will give some idea of the income level of the neighborhood. Families with similar income levels tend to share similar lifestyles and security concerns.

Note the overall security precautions that are taken in the neighborhood, such as barred windows, security fences, extensive lighting, large dogs, and security guards. Such visible precautions may indicate a high level of security awareness or a high crime area. Ensure you properly interpret reasons for same by checking the crime levels with local police.

Access Routes - Statistics of kidnappings and assassinations have shown that the vast majority occur close to the residence when the victim is leaving or returning home. It is essential that access routes to and from the residence provide sufficient alternatives which do not lock you into predictable patterns. Specifically, it is essential that dead-end streets or narrow one-way streets be avoided.

Parking - Underground parking, unless tightly controlled, should be avoided particularly in high threat areas and in multi-story buildings. Ideally, a garage that can be locked is the most suitable means of securing vehicles at single family dwellings. Carports and driveways within fenced or guarded areas will also normally suffice. Parking the car on the street should be avoided.

In the interest of retaining a low profile, it is not always advisable to be identified with certain controversial companies, such as munitions or defense contractors.

Avoid residences that are susceptible to clandestine approach and concealment due to shrubbery and trees. Consider residences located near friends or co-workers, so that you can car pool during high-stress periods.

Selection of Residence Type

Given a choice between apartment or single dwelling living, an apartment offers greater protection against criminal intrusion. An apartment, especially one above the second floor, presents a more difficult target, provides the tenant some degree of anonymity, provides the benefit of close neighbors, and is almost always easier and less expensive to modify with security hardware. In the event of an emergency and loss of communications, neighbors can often be relied upon to come to another tenant's assistance. At the very least, they can notify the authorities.

Apartments on the first or second floors should be avoided because of their immediate and easy accessibility from the street level or from trees, tops of large vehicles, or porch roofs. Foreign objects can easily be introduced to first and second floor apartments from the outside area accessible to the public.

Although an apartment above the second or third floor is preferred, do not select apartments on floors above the fire fighting and rescue capabilities of the local fire department. Even the most sophisticated fire and rescue equipment has limitations. In most countries it would be well not to live above the seventh floor.

It is important that access to the lobby of the apartment building be tightly controlled by a doorman or an electronic system such as card key readers or CCTV.

Surveillance of a particular target is sometimes more difficult in an apartment building because of multiple tenants.

The private or single dwelling allows the occupant greater opportunity to establish more rigid access control to the property. However, since single dwelling residences are seldom designed or built with security as a major consideration, it is usually more difficult to achieve good security.

After Moving In The Residence

Take your passport to the U.S. Embassy or Consulate and register as soon as possible following arrival in a foreign country.

All countries abroad where Americans are permitted to conduct business have a U.S. Embassy or American Interests Sector of a friendly embassy in the capital city of that country. In other major population centers there is often times a U.S. Consulate.

Registration greatly facilitates emergency evacuation from the country of residence, if it becomes necessary.

When you have finally moved into your new residence, make an immediate effort to familiarize yourself with your new surroundings. Walk around the neighborhood and drive around the area to get a good idea of where you are located. Note the layout of the streets. Make a mental note of one way streets. Drive around at night. Streets and buildings look much different in the dark with artificial light.

Get acquainted with at least one neighbor as quickly as possible. You may need a neighbor in an emergency or for a temporary "safe haven" in the event of a burglary or other type of incident.

Learn the location of the nearest hospital and police station. Drive the route to the hospital in daylight and at night. Go directly to the Emergency Room entrance so no time is lost if you really have to use the facility. Check on traffic conditions during rush hours and at other times.

Determine how long it will take you to reach the Emergency Room at various times during day and at night.

American Embassies and Consulates can advise any American citizen or business representative on possible terrorist threats in foreign countries. However, it must be noted that officials must limit their assistance to security services of an advisory nature. As mentioned at the beginning of this book it is incumbent on each individual to assume a high level of personal responsibility and not rely on any one source for security. The American Embassy or Consulate typically, can provide the following information:

- The nature, if any, of the general terrorist threat in a particular country.

- Whether private American citizens or companies have been the target of terrorist threats or attacks in the recent past.

- Specific areas in cities or countryside that are considered dangerous for foreigners.

- Recommended host government contacts, including police officials; local employment requirements for private security services.

- Methods and agencies available for security and background checks on local employees.

- Local laws and regulations concerning ownership, possession, and registration of weapons.

- Local government laws, regulations, and policies on paying ransom or making concessions to terrorists.

In the case of a terrorist action against an American citizen or company, the embassy or consulate can:

- Facilitate communication with the home office and the family of the victim if normal channels are not adequate.

- Help establish useful liaison with local authorities.

- Provide information and suggest possible alternatives open to the family or company of the victim.

- The U.S. Government, however, cannot decide whether or not to agree to terrorist demands. Such a decision can be made only by the family or company of the victim, but it should be in conjunction with the appropriate authorities.

The official U.S. Government policy, as publicly stated, is not to make any concessions to terrorist demands and, while such policy is not necessarily binding on the private sector, the private sector is well advised to review its proposed action in time of crisis with the Embassy or Consulate.

Unlike some U.S. Government employees who enjoy diplomatic immunity while living and working in the host country, U.S. private sector employees and their families are subject to all laws of the host country. It is well to remember that the constitutional safeguards enjoyed by all Americans in the U.S. do not apply to the actions of foreign governments.

Obtain emergency fire and safety equipment as soon as possible, including but not limited to fire extinguishers, first-aid kits, blankets, matches and candles, flashlights and battery operated radios with spare batteries. Consider storing a seven day supply of canned food, juices, water and staples for all members of the family. Supplies should be stored for emergency use and inspected on a regular basis.

Family members and domestic employees should be trained and tested on the use of each item of emergency equipment.

Once an emergency strikes, it is too late to go looking for a "friendly face. Know beforehand where you will turn for help. Familiarize yourself with the identities of nearby neighbors, their servants, and their vehicles. This will facilitate the identification of a stranger or an unauthorized individual in the area.

Investigate the possibility of participating in an alert/calling list in event of emergencies. If such a list does not exist, create one.

Be cognizant of host country fire regulations and telephone numbers. Determine if the emergency number has someone on the other end who can understand you if you do not speak the local language. Arrange alternate emergency numbers which can forward your call in the local language if necessary.

It is highly recommended that an "Employee and Family Profile" form be filled out for each family and updated at least once a year. Keep one copy at home and one at the office with supervisor or person responsible for security. Include current photos of each family member.

Perimeter Security

Generally, there are two lines of defense for a residence, the outer and the inner perimeter. The outer ordinarily is a property line in the case of a single residence, or the outer lobby door in an apartment or high-rise condominium. A third, or remote outer perimeter, may exist if your home or apartment is situated in a private compound or club environment.

Outer Perimeter

Any perimeter barrier, even if it is only a symbolic hedge, serves as a deterrent. An intruder must commit an overt act in crossing the barrier and run the risk of being seen. Therefore, it is recommended that, where possible, a single family dwelling overseas have a perimeter barrier.

The type barrier employed should be carefully considered as each has its advantages and disadvantages. Different type barriers include:

- Hedges and Natural Growth Material - This type of barrier is useful in marking the property line. However, unless they are thick and covered with thorns or pointed leaves, they can easily be breached.

- Picket and Chain Link Fences - Advantages include view of outside area by resident, while not providing a hiding place for a potential intruder. Residual benefit is restraint for watchdog.

- Solid or Block Fences/Walls - Although a solid wall limits the occupant's observation out of the compound and could provide concealment for an intruder, it is usually the most secure perimeter barrier.

The perimeter barrier is no stronger than the gate. A solid wooden gate is appropriate for a hedge or picket fence, a chain link gate is appropriate for hedge, a picket fence or a chain link fence, and solid wooden or metal gate is appropriate for a sold fence/wall. The gate should be well anchored with hinges on fence or wall, swing outward inside, and be provided with keys to locks. Shrubbery around a single detached dwelling should be trimmed in such a way that it does not provide a hiding place.

Consider installation of a contingency or emergency exit through the rear of the property, to be utilized only in high risk situations.

Inner Perimeter

Grills - All building exterior openings over 96 square inches in size on the ground floor or accessible from trees, vehicle tops or porches should be grilled. Bars of solid steel, flat or round stock, spaced five to seven inches apart, with horizontal braces 10-12 inches apart to provide adequate rigidity, and securely imbedded on all sides to a depth of at least three inches into the adjacent wall/frame, should be installed. Use clip anchors or bend the end of the bars when grouting them into the wall. Otherwise, where possible, the bars should extend through the wall and be secured on the interior.

Shatter resistant film, a high quality clear plastic sheeting glued to windows, is recommended and should be applied to windows and doors before the grills are installed. Decorative grills should be so designed that the protection afforded is equal to the conventional type grills. Wherever possible, grillwork should be installed on the interior of the opening.

At least one grill in each section of the sleeping quarters should be hinged and equipped with an emergency release to permit emergency exit in the event of fire. Houses with a single corridor access to all sleeping quarters should have an iron grill gate to control the bedrooms at night time. This grill gate would constitute an inner perimeter protection for the sleeping quarters. Where grillwork is required, *a complete early warning fire detection and alarm system must be installed.*

Locks and Key Control Locks are described in several ways and these various descriptions tend to confuse the layman. For example, they are described by their use (primary or auxiliary), by their locking mechanism (pin tumbler, wafer disc, lever, magnetic, cipher, etc.), by the type of cylinder (single or double), or by the type of mounting (key-in-the-knob, mortised, rim, etc.).

All primary residential entry doors should be equipped with both a primary and auxiliary lock. Additionally, each entry door should have a 190 degree optical viewer or equivalent.

Primary locks are the main lock on a door and are identified by the fact they have handles. These locks are usually key-in-the-knob or mortised type locks with the locking hardware located in a cavity in the door. Unless they have a latch or bolt that extends into the door jamb 5/8 inch to one inch, they do not provide sufficient protection.

Auxiliary locks usually are deadbolts which are mortise or rim/surface mounted, located on the inner door and door frame surface, and do not have handles. This type lock does not have to be keyed and may be nothing more than a sliding deadbolts. The exception to this rule is where there is a window or side light within 40 inches of the lock.

Change all exterior locks, including garage door and mail box lock (if in an apartment) prior to moving into new residence abroad, in either a new or used home. It is possible to change only the lock cylinder or to re-pin the cylinder on good quality locks without changing the complete locking device.

Exterior doors with or near glass panels should be equipped with dead bolts which are key operated on both interior and exterior. It is advisable to place an extra key for this type lock in a concealed area in the immediate proximity to the inside lock in case of emergencies. All residents should be aware of its location. Never leave the key in the inside lock for personal convenience.

Lock all fuse boxes and electrical panels located on the exterior of the residence.

Maintain strict key control on all exterior locks. Never hide an exterior door key outside the house. Sophisticated burglars know all the hiding places.

Install an intercom between primary entrance and the inside foyer or protected area. In apartments and homes the intercom should be backed up with a peep hole in solid core door with an angle of visibility of 190 degrees.

Remove all name identification from your gate and doors. Avoid displays which identify YOU as an American.

Burglars/terrorists are always on the alert for an easy way to enter a residence. Doors, windows, and garages should be closed and locked at all times when the residents are away from home, no matter how short the time. If there is any doubt about accountability of keys to a home, have the lock cylinders replaced or re-pinned. Keys should be controlled and only given to mature family members or trusted friends. When domestic employees are given a key, it should only be to the primary lock of one entry door. They should never be given keys to both the primary and auxiliary locks. This ensures that the occupants can always secure the residence in the evenings or when the domestic staff is absent. Insure that access to the residence is not permitted through domestic employee's quarters.

Have qualified locksmith install effective locking devices on sliding glass doors which are highly vulnerable. Avoid using louvered or jalousie windows which are a very easy mark for even the most inexperienced burglar.

Any padlocks used for residential security should always be stored in the locked position. Sophisticated burglars sometimes will replace a padlock with a similar one to which they alone have the key.

Electronic garage door openers have advantages and disadvantages and, therefore, should be installed with discretion. A security advantage, in addition to the convenience, is that it is not necessary to leave the security of your locked car to enter and lock your garage behind you. The disadvantage is that such devices can often be compromised by a variety of inexpensive transmitters. If installed, insure maximum protection is installed on door between garage and interior of house. Discuss with competent locksmith.

Intrusion Alarms and Security Lighting

Intrusion or alerting devices are any means by which a resident and/or the local police/security force are made aware of the attempted or forcible entry of a residence. This includes alarm systems, guards, dogs, noisemakers, and communications systems.

Alarm Systems - Basically, alarm systems perform two functions: they detect an intruder, and they report the intrusion. However, for the purpose of residential security use overseas, an alarm system in a residence should be considered as a deterrent device. In areas abroad where forced entry of a residence is commonplace, or where an active terrorist threat is present, the use of a good residential alarm system is highly recommended.

Minimum desired alarm system features are:

- Capable of operating on the local electrical current and have a rechargeable battery backup.

- Relatively easy to install and trouble-shoot. Many local electricians may not be capable of installing or repairing a complex alarm system.

- Equipped with a time delay feature to allow the occupant to arm or disarm the system without activating the alarm.

- Capable of being wired with a fixed or mobile panic switch, a device which permits manual activation of the alarm system. Panic switches should be installed in the safe haven, in the living portion of the residence and outside as well for use by residential guards.

- Security lighting should be an integral part of the intrusion system.

Lighting - Most intruders will go to great lengths to escape visual detection. Therefore, they will normally strike at a residence that appears vacant or is dark.

Outdoor lighting can be a major deterrent against criminal intrusion. Properly used, it can discourage criminal activity and aid observation.

The important elements of protective outdoor lighting are coverage and evenness of light. It is possible that in some residential settings existing street lighting, along with one or two porch lights, will furnish sufficient lighting. However, it may be necessary to install additional lighting in order to achieve the degree of security desired. If outdoor lighting is to be used as a protective measure, all accesses to vulnerable areas of the property and house should be lighted.

Lighting should be placed in such a manner that it covers the walls of the residence and the ground area adjacent to the perimeter walls. Also, it should illuminate shrubbery and eliminate building blind spots.

If security lighting is deemed advisable in your location, it should consist of two independent systems. Cosmetic or low level tamper-resistant fixtures installed in the eaves or overhangs for continuous perimeter illumination, and emergency floodlights tied to the alarm system so that they will turn on automatically when the alarm is activated. A manual switch should be installed in the living quarters of the single-family residence, so that they may be turned on independent of the alarm system.

It is a good idea to connect the cosmetic lighting to a photoelectric cell which automatically turns them on at dusk and off at dawn. They should be connected to a dimmer, so that the light level can be adjusted to the extent that it would discourage an attack on the house by burglars but at the same time would not be offensive to the neighbors.

Insure that all lighting systems are installed in compliance with local codes.

Consider installation of diesel powered auxiliary generator which turns on automatically when electric power fails. Turn on at least once each quarter to insure it's in good working order. "Mushroom" lights, which are installed along the foundation of the house and cast a light up the side of the structure are easily compromised and should be avoided.

James R. Doyle

Extended Absences From the Residence

Extended absences present the burglar with his easiest opportunity to target a residence. There are many indicators to a burglar that a residence is unoccupied. For example, discussing the planned absence in the office or in the neighborhood, forgetting to cancel deliveries, leaving the home unlighted and the blinds or drapes drawn, and closing the shutters.

While residents are away, automatic timers or photoelectric switches should turn on inside lights, a radio, or even an air-conditioner to create the illusion that someone is home.

Invite a reliable neighbor to park a car in your driveway at times during your absence, especially at night.

Ask close friends or neighbors to look after the home and turn on and off different lights, put out trash as usual, etc.

In many foreign locations it is advisable to have trusted domestic employees remain in the residence during extended absences.

If you live in a single-family house or if the servants are on vacation, you could hire a guard but do not give him access to enter the house. He should only patrol the garden area which encircles the house.

Hook up of a telephone answering device which serves to defeat the telephone call that is made by the terrorist/criminal to determine if someone is home.

Domestic Hires - Screening and Responsibilities

Domestic employees can either be a valuable asset to residential security or a decided liability. The chances of obtaining the services of a reliable servant can be improved by hiring one employed and recommended by a friend, acquaintance or neighbor.

Prospective applicants should be required to produce references and should be interviewed thoroughly.

It is wise to personally check with references to confirm their existence and obtain information concerning the reliability, honesty, attitudes and work habits of prospective applicants.

In some countries, the authorities will conduct background investigations upon request.

In some foreign countries, it is an accepted practice to request full personal data from applicants for employment. This data should be copied from either a National Government ID card or a passport.

Do not accept the person's word as to their name and date of birth without an authentic government document to back up their claim.

Obtain the following information:

- Government Identity Card or passport, etc., for number, date of birth, nationality, full names, valid date, place of registry.

- Letters of reference: Be sure you know who wrote it and what it says. (Usually written in local language.)

- Obtain the address of the former employer and the company he represented.

- Good domestic employees are generally referred by your predecessor, although this is not always the case.

This entire procedure should only require a few days if you utilize good contacts with competent police recommended by the embassy, consulate or your predecessor. If you are unable to establish good contacts, contract the job out to reliable investigative consultants.

SERVANT CAUTIONS

Do not permit domestics of untested integrity and reliability in your home. If you must engage a cook or house servant before investigation is completed, do not entrust keys or an unoccupied house to the employee in question.

When you have hired a servant, record his/her complete name, date and place of birth, identity card number, telephone number, and address as well as the names of spouse, parent or close relative.

Domestic help should be briefed on security practices. It is critical that they be rehearsed and re-briefed from time to time to refresh their memory and to update previous instructions. Domestic staff should be briefed on visitor control, how to report suspicious or unusual activity, proper telephone answering procedures, and admittance of maintenance men to the residence. They should also be made aware of emergency telephone numbers. They should be able to reach the man or woman of the house by phone to report critical situations at the residence.

Domestic employees should be trained to answer the door rather than members of the household. They should not be allowed to admit visitors without specific approval. When visitors, repair or services personnel are expected, domestic employees should be informed of their probable time of arrival and identification and should not unlock or open the door until they have been properly identified.

Domestic employees should never give a caller the impression that no one is home, nor should they tell when the occupants are expected. They should be directed to reply that occupants are "Unable to come to the phone right now but will return the call, if the caller will leave his name and telephone number."

Domestic employees should not be allowed to overhear family plans and official business. Sensitive and confidential letters such as those dealing with business strategies, hiring or firing practices, employee disciplinary matters and other matters which are closely guarded at the office, should be equally guarded at home. Travel itineraries, purchasing negotiations and bids, labor negotiation strategies, pricing and marketing information, to name but a few, are other examples of official business which should not be shared with domestics in any form, written or oral, and documents relating to same should not be left unsecured about the residence.

Terrorists or burglars do not always break in; sometimes people let them in. Family members should be wary of salesmen, or unexpected visits from repairmen or utility company representatives, even if they are in uniform. Ask to see their credentials or call their office to verify their bona fides. If a stranger asks to use the telephone, do not let him in. Make the call for him. Do not hesitate to be suspicious if the situation warrants it. An intercom system can be used to determine a stranger's business before he is allowed access to the residence.

Frequently brief all domestic hires, such as maids, cooks, gardeners, handymen and chauffeurs, on security precautions. Be very specific in making clear what you expect of them. It is advisable to select one member of the domestic staff and make him/her responsible for the actions of others.

Instruct the domestic help to report to the man or woman of the house the presence of strangers in the neighborhood. Virtually all kidnappings and terrorist assaults have indicated that the perpetrators had an intimate knowledge of the victim's habits developed through sur-veillance prior to attack.

Do not allow domestic help to invite anyone into your home without prior approval.

All domestic employees should be given a copy of the following security instructions translated into their native language. All of the instructions apply to maids, and most apply to janitors, gardeners, and other domestic help. These employees should be alert to suspicious individuals around your residence. The importance of reporting any unusual inquiries or activities promptly should be emphasized. Vehicle license numbers and accurate descriptions should be obtained whenever possible. The Suspicious Activity Reporting Checklist can be used for this purpose.

- Keep exterior doors closed and locked during the day.

- Close and lock all exterior doors at night.

- Close and lock windows and shutters, and roll down window coverings at night.

- Do not admit strangers, peddlers, inspectors, survey or census takers, or investigators you do not know, even if they are in uniform or display credentials. Tell them to call your employer or contact the company office. Do not open the door to these people.

- Do not admit repair people unless you have been told by your employer to expect them.

- Do not accept packages unless you have been told by your employer to expect such a delivery.

- Do not give information of any kind about this family on the telephone unless you are absolutely certain the caller is a friend. Do not identify the family's street address or telephone number to unknown callers.

- If you receive any anonymous calls or threats, or if you observe anything unusual or suspicious in the vicinity of this house, report it to your employer.

- Make a note of the license number of any suspicious vehicle parked near this house and give the information to your employer.

- If any strange objects or packages are discovered in the house or yard, leave them alone and inform your employer at once. If your employer is not available, call the police.

Residential Telephone Security

One can never be sure of the true identity of a person on the other end of a telephone line. For this reason, it behooves all of us to exercise the following telephone security precautions:

- Do not answer the telephone by stating the name of the family.

- If a caller inquires, "To whom am I speaking?" respond with a question like, "Who are you calling?"

- Do not give the residence telephone number in response to wrong-number telephone calls. If the caller asks, "What number did I reach?" respond with another question like, What number are you calling?"

- Report repetitive wrong-number telephone calls to the telephone company, the person in charge of Security at your company, if there is such a person, and to the police as appropriate.

- Be suspicious of any caller alleging to represent the telephone company and advising that the telephone service may be interrupted.

- Be skeptical of telephone calls from strangers advising that a family member has been injured or has won a prize, or making any other assertion that is followed by a request for the family member to leave the home immediately. Verify the telephone call by looking up the number of the caller in the directory, check it against the one given by the caller, and then call the number to verify the information given.

- Children should be advised not to converse with strangers on the telephone for any reason. When an adult is not present, a child will occasionally answer the phone. Children should be instructed to tell callers in such circumstances that the adult being called is not available to come to the phone, rather than reveal that the adult is absent from the home.

- When practical, home telephone numbers should be unlisted and unpublished.

- Do not list home phone numbers in company directories unless circulation is highly restricted.

- Family members and domestic help should not divulge personal information or travel plans over the telephone to anyone without specific authority to do so.

- Avoid party lines.

- Consider use of answering devices for ALL incoming calls in order to be selective in which calls you choose to answer.

- Report ALL suspicious activity to your security contact at the company or the local police.

- Locate the nearest public telephone to your home and inform the family and household members of its location for their use in an emergency. Also, locate the nearest non-public telephone to your home to which you have access, perhaps a friendly neighbor's phone, for the same reason.

- All family members should carry the phone number of one or more trusted neighbors who have a clear view of your home, either front or rear.

- An extortionist may call you at your office and claim that family member(s) are being held at gun point at your home and, unless a sum of money is paid to a third party or placed at a designated location, they will be harmed. A telephone call to a neighbor who has a clear view of your home may, by simply looking out the window, determine that your family is in no jeopardy at all and thereby determine with reasonable certainty that the call is a hoax.

- If a strange vehicle is parked in the driveway, the police should be notified as appropriate.

- Emergency telephone numbers of police, fire, medical and ambulance service should be available for quick reference at each telephone in the home. Check accuracy of list every six months or so.

- You and family members should practice the use of public tele-phones.

- If available and legal in the country, maintain a set of portable two-way radios - one in your own home and one in a neighbor's home in the event wire communications are severed. Telephone service in many foreign countries is highly unreliable.

In certain emergencies, it may become necessary on short notice to locate and account for all members of the family. Make it a habit to know generally where family members will be every day. Make a list of phone numbers of all places frequently visited by family members such as neighbors, friends' homes, clubs, beauty salons, barbers, favorite restaurants, schools, etc. All family members should carry a copy of the list and a copy kept at home for domestics and one at the office. Update regularly.

Residential Mail

Businessmen should discourage the delivery of mail to their private residence. Either rent a Post Office Box registered to your office or have your personal mail delivered to your office.

Family members and domestic help should accept no mail parcels or other unexpected deliveries unless they are sure of the source.

Don't open the door to accept strange deliveries. Packages should be left by the door. Wait a considerable time before opening the door to retrieve the package.

If a delivery man requires a signature, have him slide receipt under the door.

Continuously remind yourself and others in the household to be suspicious of all incoming mail and parcels and to remain alert for the following danger signs:

- <u>Appearance</u>

    Is it from a strange place?
    Is there an excessive amount of postage?

Are there stains on the item?

Are wires or strings protruding or attached to the item in an unusual location?

Is the item marked conspicuously receiver's name: i.e., Personal Smith, Confidential for Mr. Smith?

Is the spelling on the item correct?

Does the letter or package contain an inner letter or package addressed to a particular individual or tied with a string, tape, wire, rubber band, or any compression item?

Do the return address and the postmark differ?

- <u>Weight</u>

    Is the item unusually heavy or light?

    Is the item uneven in balance or lopsided?

- <u>Odor</u>

    Do the items smell peculiar? Many explosives used by terrorists smell like shoe polish or almonds.

SUSPICIOUS PACKAGES

If any parcel is at all suspicious, STOP further handling, place item against exterior corner of room. DO NOT IMMERSE ITEM IN WATER. This may make paper soggy and cause spring-loaded device to detonate. Open windows and evacuate the immediate area. Call appropriate authorities.

Banking and Charge Accounts

Checking accounts, charge accounts and loan applications create audit trails which divulge more about you and your family than you may wish to be known. Purchasing habits can reveal much about the value of household goods and personal valuables that are kept in your residence and which might become attractive to potential thieves. It may be prudent to utilize major U.S. credit cards as opposed to writing checks on local banks, in order to reduce the audit trail your financial transactions can leave.

When requested to write a phone number on checks or credit card slips, use the office number and have family members do the same.

DO NOT imprint your home address or phone number on personalized checks.

Residential Trash Security

Trash containers have been proven to be excellent sources of intelligence for curiosity seekers and terrorists. Employees should not discard in residential trash private papers, letters, drafts of outgoing correspondence, bills and invoices, canceled checks, or any other type of materials which might result in embarrassment or compromise to the security of any member of the household.

Trash receptacles should be stored inside the residence or outside in a secure shed, to preclude easy access by the curiosity seeker or the placement of dangerous objects.

Quality of Law Enforcement Protection

Police Capability - Assessment of police protection available to a given area is necessary. Determine if the police have sufficient officers and means of transportation and communication to respond to residential crimes in a timely manner. Every effort should be expended to establish quick, dependable communication links to the local security or police force to insure their effective response in an emergency. You should be aware of the attitude of the government, police and the general public towards other nationals, particularly Americans. A strong anti-American attitude may be cause for diminished police responsiveness.

Where police capability is in doubt, the use of a private guard service should be considered. However, the use of guards is costly and the quality of guards varies significantly from area to area. Most guards are poorly trained and ineffective. However, if the guard can at least alert the resident to an attack on the residence by tripping a "panic" switch, sounding a horn, or blowing a whistle, he has done his job.

All guards should be subjected to a security check. As much as possible should be known about the employed guards, particularly where and how effectively he has worked previously. At a minimum, guards should be physically capable of performing their shift duties during the normal work day. They should be provided with the following: written guard orders (both in English and native language), a uniform, a communication or alerting device, e.g., air horn, whistle, alarm panic switch, two-way radio, etc., a flashlight, and a defensive weapon such as a club or a chemical deterrent (mace). In rare instances where the threat warrants and local laws and customs allow, a side arm should be considered provided the guard is fully trained in its use.

Firearms in Foreign Countries

Firearms restrictions and/or requirements differ from country to country. Persons assigned overseas should contact the local police authority to ascertain the law of the land concerning private ownership of weapons.

If authorized by the host country, weapons must be maintained and used in accordance with the local customs and laws. Host country licenses must be obtained when required. Training and safety should be prime considerations if a weapon is to be maintained in the home.

Illegal importation of a firearm is a serious criminal offense in many countries.

Children's School

When children are to be picked up at school by other than immediate family members, there should be an established procedure coordinated with school officials to assure that they are picked up only by authorized persons.

Children should be instructed in observing good security procedures such as traveling in groups, refusing rides with strangers, avoiding isolated play areas, keeping parents informed as to time and destination, reporting all strange events and attempted molestation's and how to get help or call the police.

In many overseas locations it is economical to contract with a taxi company/driver to pickup and drop off students at school and home. Insist on the same driver every day and instruct children not to ride with a strange driver. In other locations car pooling may be practical.

Coups d'etat – *Coups D'etat* is defined as "a sudden overthrow of a government by a usually small group of persons in or previously in positions of authority".

The following actions should be considered in the event of *Coups d'etat*:

- Establish and maintain contact with the U.S. Embassy and any designated officers. Each post abroad formulates an Emergency Action Plan unique to its location, to deal with a coup d'etat and an attempted coup.

- DO NOT automatically pack and leave the country on your own initiative. Most coups only last a few days and are usually preceded by some type of advance warning, such as demonstrations, and therefore, often times can be anticipated. Contact the U.S. Embassy for guidance BEFORE taking drastic action.

- Monitor local news media, TV, radio and newspapers for any evidence of anti-American activity, since such activity will have an impact on the Embassy's Emergency Action Plan.

- In certain locations, for example in some third world countries, where the political climate is right for coups and coup attempts, it is recommended that adequate supplies of non-perishable foods and drinking water be stockpiled in your home to sustain your family for an arbitrary period of time (days or weeks) consistent with the existing threat.

- Maintain regular (at least daily) contact with the Embassy during such periods of high stress.

- Develop alternate routes of evacuation from your residence to be used in the event of fire or other emergency where rapid evacuation would be necessary.

- Be prepared. Have bag packed for each family member in the event you have to leave on short notice.

- Appropriate amounts of currency and traveler's checks should be isolated and kept on hand.

- Keep airline tickets (without reservations) on hand for each family member.

- Maintain current passports and, visas for a "safe haven" country.

- Prepare a list of telephone numbers for transportation companies, should emergency evacuation be necessary, i.e., taxi, airlines, private limousine service, etc. Place near the office and home telephones.

- Consolidate important personal records/files for easy access and transportation.

- Have more than one (1) evacuation plan.

- Have in place a pre-planned telephonic pyramid contact system, to insure the American population in the host country is aware of what is happening. A pyramid contact system is one in which each person called with information is required to call two or three others to relay the same information.

Social Activities

During social gatherings, conversations with citizens of host country, especially with reference to political, racial, economic, religious and controversial local issues, should be closely guarded and as non-committal as possible.

Where possible, employees in high threat areas should avoid social activities which have a set place and schedule, such as the same church service every Sunday morning, shopping at the same store every Saturday, and attending well publicized American citizen functions.

Spouse and Dependent Activity

The following suggestions should be considered to enhance security:

- Each family member should be familiar with basic security procedures and techniques.

- All family members should know how to use the local telephones, both public and private.

- Family members should not reveal information concerning travel or other family plans; they should be cautious in answering such questions over the phone, even if the caller is known, to guard against the possibility of taps or other leaks.

- Family members should avoid local civil disturbances, demonstrations, crowds, or other high-risk areas.
- Children, in particular, should be on guard against being approached or questioned by strangers. It is safer to drive them to school than to let them walk. If they must walk, they should not go alone. Adult escorts are preferable, but even groups of children offer some deterrence. Although children must attend school on a particular schedule, parents are encouraged to vary

departures, arrivals, and routes to the extent possible. Use of carpools, especially if scheduling is on a random basis, also breaks down patterns of movement and enhances security.

- The location of family members should be known at all times. Causes of delays or unforeseen absences should be determined immediately. Family members should be encouraged to develop the habit of checking in before departure, after arrival, or when changing plans.

- Shopping or family outings should not conform to a set pattern or routine.

Watchdogs

A dog's extremely sensitive and discriminating senses of smell and hearing enable it to detect quickly a stranger who is not normally present in the residential area. The well-trained dog will normally bark ferociously when approached by an intruder.

Dogs should be well trained to react only to the introduction of strangers into the residence area, to stop barking on command from the owner, and to accept food only from its master.

Sophisticated burglars can neutralize the most ferocious of watchdogs by tossing it a meat patty laced with Demerol or other drug, which will put the dog to sleep for several hours.

There are some potential liabilities associated with the presence of an animal whose role is to deter, discourage, and rout criminal intruders, particularly if the animal does not discriminate well between friend and foe.

Recreation and Exercise

In order to establish a potential target's routine and evaluate the level of security awareness, terrorists usually watch their intended victims for some time before they attack. Therefore, persons in high threat areas should consider whether or not to participate in recreational/exercise activities which have a set place and schedule such as: bowling, little league sports, golf, tennis, jogging, walking, etc.

If you decide to participate in these sports, you should select jogging paths, tennis courts, golf clubs and all out-of-door activity locations with great care. For example, do not indiscriminately jog through a park with which you are not totally familiar. Use densely populated areas, if possible.

Illicit Drugs

Despite repeated warnings, drug arrests and convictions of American citizens are still on the increase. If you are caught with either soft or hard drugs overseas, you are subject to local and not U.S. laws. Penalties for possession or trafficking are often the same.

The laws governing the use, possession, and trafficking in illegal drugs vary widely throughout the world, as do penalties for violations of those laws. One may be legal in one country and may constitute a serious criminal offense in another. It behooves all U.S. Citizens living abroad to familiarize themselves with selected laws of the host country, especially those relating to illegal drugs.

The Administrator of the Drug Enforcement Administration, U.S. Department of Justice, has emphasized the seriousness of violations of illegal drug laws abroad and resultant penalties:

"Possession and use of illegal drugs overseas is no casual matter. Unlike the United States, in many countries trafficking and even possessing drugs for personal use are extremely serious offenses. You may have no rights at all - no bail, no speedy trial, no jury trial - the penalties can be severe and the prisons can be frightening. <u>You are subject to the criminal sanctions of another country. In at least two countries I know of, the penalty includes death and the U.S. State Department will not be able to help you.</u>"

It is important that this warning be emphasized to all family members living abroad, especially to teenage children and young adults.

In the case of prescription medications, it is advisable to leave all medicines in their original labeled containers if you require medication containing habit-forming drugs or narcotics. You should also carry a copy of the doctor's prescription. These precautions will make customs processing easier and also will ensure you do not violate the laws of the country where you plan to live or are currently residing.

RESIDENCE SECURITY EVALUATION WORKSHEET

The following questions should be considered in developing this worksheet:

- Do you know and have you posted near the telephone the number of the nearest police station?

- Do you know how to report a fire and your dwelling location in the local language?

- Do you and your family have an emergency escape plan with alternate emergency escape routes?

- Have you practiced this emergency plan?

- Have you instructed your family and servants regarding the admission of strangers, no matter how authentic their credentials may appear?

- Are you, your family, and servants alert in the observations of strange vehicles or persons who may have you under surveillance or may be "casing" your residence for a burglary?
- Have you verified the references and good health of your servants?

- Do you know the location and telephone number of the nearest police, fire department, and hospital?

- Do you have any type of fire extinguishers?

- Do you know the type of fire on which to use your extinguisher?

- Has your fire fighting equipment been inspected or recharged within the past year?

- Does every member of your family and domestic staff know now to use your fire fighting equipment?

- Do you keep your cash and small valuables in a safe storage place?

- Do you have a list of the serial numbers of your watches, cameras, typewriters, computers, radios, stereo, etc.?

- Do you keep an inventory of all valuable property?

- Do you have an accurate description (with photographs) of all valuable property, which does not have serial numbers?

- Do you avoid unnecessary display or publicity of your valuable items?

- Have you given your family and servants instructions on what they should do if they discover an intruder attempting to break in or already in the house?

- Have you told your family and servants to leave the house undisturbed and call the police if they find a burglary has been committed?

- Are all your first floor windows protected?

- Are unused windows permanently closed and sealed?

- Are your windows properly and securely mounted?

- Can window locks be opened by breaking the glass?

- Do you keep your windows locked when they are shut?

- Are you as careful with securing windows on the second floor or basement windows as you are with those on the ground floor?

- Have you locked up your ladder or relocated trellises that might be used as a ladder to gain entry through a second-story window?

- Do you have sliding glass doors and if so, do you have a rod or "Charlie Bar" to place in the track?

- Do you lock your garage at night and when you are away from home?

- Are all garage doors and windows equipped with adequate locks and are they in good working order?

- Are tools and equipment left in the garage where a burglar might be able to use them in gaining entry to your residence?

- Do you use heavy-duty sliding deadbolts on your most used doors as auxiliary locks?

- Can all your doors including porch, balcony basement, terrace and roof be locked securely?

- Are all your locks in good working order?

- Does anyone other than your immediate family have a key to your residence (i.e. previous tenants, owners, servants, friends)?

- Are all unused doors permanently secured?

- Are all locks securely mounted?

- Do you hide a spare key to your main entrance under a door mat, in a flower pot, or some other nearby, but obvious, spot?

- Do you answer the door partially dressed?

- Do you have a peephole or interview grille in your main door?

- Do you answer the door without first checking to see who has rung the bell or knocked?

- Do you lock your padlocks in place when the doors are unlocked (garage, storage room, unused servants' quarters, etc.)?

- Are padlock hasps installed so that screws cannot be removed?

- Are hasps and staple plates mounted so that they cannot be pried or twisted off?

RESIDENTIAL EXTERIOR

- Do garden gates lock?

- Are gates kept locked and the keys under your control?

- Is the gate bell in working order?

- Are stairways lighted?

- Are walls of sufficient height to deter thieves?

- Are exterior lights adequate to illuminate the residence grounds particularly around gates and doors?

- If butane gas is used, are the bottles secured in a safe place?

- Are there any poles, boxes, trees, or outbuildings that would help an intruder scale your wall or fence?

BUILDING DOORS

- Are the exterior doors of solid wood or metal construction?

- Are locks on your exterior doors of the cylinder type?

- Are they the dead locking (jimmy proof) type?

- Can any of your door locks be opened by breaking a glass or light wood panel next to the lock?

MISCELLANEOUS DEPENDENT CONCERNS

- Have children and employees been briefed on security requirements (locked windows & doors, no admittance of strangers, no acceptance of packages, etc.)?

- Do occupants have a firearm in the home? Is it protected (trigger lock, disassembled, etc.) from, children?

- Have occupants been trained in its use?

- Do the occupants, including older children & domestic employees, know how to use extinguishers?

- Is there a smoke detector in the dwelling?

- Are smoke detectors properly installed?

- Are smoke detector batteries replaced at least once a year?

- Are smoke detectors tested periodically?

- Does the dwelling have an operational emergency radio, with an outside antenna?

- Do the occupants, including older children and domestic employees, know how to use the radio?

- Are emergency phone numbers (post, fire, police, and ambulance) kept near the phone?

- Has a background check been conducted on domestic employees?

SAFEHAVEN

- If a safe haven is recommended, can one be accommodated?

- Does the safe haven have a solid core, metal, or metal-clad door?

- Is the emergency radio kept charged and available in the safe haven?

- Are toilet facilities available in the safe haven?

- Is there an emergency egress from the safe haven?

- Does the dwelling have at least one 5 lb. or 10 lb. ABC general purpose fire extinguisher located in the kitchen?

- Does the dwelling have at least one 2 1/2 gallon

- Are water type fire extinguishers located in the safe haven?

- Are fire extinguishers checked periodically?

ALARMS

- Are all entrance doors alarmed?

- Are all non-grilled windows within access of the ground, balconies, trees, etc. alarmed?

- Does the alarm have an external alerting device, such as a bell or siren?

- Is the alarm linked by transmitter to a central monitor station?

- Does the system have panic buttons placed at strategic locations around the residence?

- Do the occupants test the alarm periodically?

- Are exterior hinges protected?

- Does each major entrance have a door viewer or interview grille?

WINDOWS

- Are windows and wall air conditioners anchored and protected by steel grillwork to prevent removal from the outside?

- Are all non-ventilating windows permanently secured?

- Are all windows accessible from the ground, balconies, trees, ledges, roofs and the like protected by grilles?

- Are all windows kept Closed and locked when not in use?

- Have emergency escape provisions been incorporated into one or more window grilles?

- Are all sliding and hinged glass doors secured with a metal grille gate?

- Are all sliding glass doors and windows secured by a rod (charley bar) in the slide track?

EXTERIOR OF APARTMENT

The following questions should be considered to enhance security:

- Is apartment height within the rescue capabilities (ladder height) of the fire department?

- Is the balcony (or other apartment windows) accessible from another balcony, ledge, roof or window?

- Are the public areas of the building controlled and well lighted?

- Can lobby and elevator be viewed from the street?

- Are secondary entrances to the building and parking controlled?

DOORS

- Can each exterior (regular, sliding, French, etc.) door be adequately secured?

- Does the primary lock on each door work?

- Are all doors kept locked?
- Can any door be opened from the outside by breaking a door glass or sidelight?

- Have all unused exterior doors been permanently secured?

- Are all keys accounted for?

- Have all "hidden" keys (under door mat, etc.)

EXTERIOR OF SINGLE-FAMILY OR DUPLEX DWELLING

- Are gates kept locked?

- Are there handy access routes (poles, trees, etc.) which may be used to get over the barrier?

- Is public or residence lighting sufficient to illuminate all sides of the dwelling?

- Are all lights working at sufficient height to prevent tampering?

- Have hiding places near doors, windows ~ garage or parking area been illuminated or eliminated?

- If garage is available, is it used and kept locked?

SAFE NEIGHBORHOODS

- Is unit in good residential area with a low crime rate?

- Do other employees live nearby?

- Is the police and fire protection adequate and within 10 minute response time?
- Are there a number of alternate routes to and from the dwelling?

EXTERIOR OF SINGLE-FAMILY OR DUPLEX DWELLING

- Is the property well defined with a hedge, fence or wall in good condition?

- Are the gates solid and in good condition?

COMMUNICATION SYSTEMS

Communication Facilities

In considering any suggestions relative to Communication Systems, it should be understood that any system can be compromised and therefore by definition is not completely secure. Unless you are an Intelligence Officer or member of a Special Forces team using microburst technology to transmit coded communications through secure government satellites, you should consider that your communications have already been compromised. The objective of this book is to offer suggestions that you can consider in reducing your risk.

Satellite ground stations, microwave parabolic reflectors, and communications towers and supports should be located on rooftops, with limited access to the public. Where this is not possible, the equipment should be installed with fences and alarms. Closed circuit television (CCTV) with video recording capability should be considered and included where justified.

Systems

Integration

Security systems in new buildings or buildings undergoing renovation should be installed with distributed wiring schemes that use local telecommunication closets as distribution points. This will provide expansion capability, future networking capability, ease of maintenance, and full function implementation of the security system. At a minimum, the communications link and interface between the sensor, output devices, and computers should include conduit, multi-conductor twisted shielded cable and terminal cabinets. However, recent technology such as fiber-optic cables should be considered in planning the wiring distribution scheme.

Data distribution and gathering used for security wiring must be secure. Where possible, integrate security wiring with other systems such as telephone, paging, energy management, etc. In every case, the design of the communications link should allow ready installation and inter-connection of cameras, sensors, and other input-output devices. All life safety equipment and accessories should be Underwriters Laboratory (UL) approved.

Outlying facilities should link security systems to the nearest security control center. Systems should be compatible with existing systems or replace existing systems with the new systems.

Telecommunications

Because they are so easily accessed and intercepted, corporate telecommunications present a highly vulnerable and lucrative target for anyone interested in obtaining trade secrets and competitive information. Increased usage by businesses of these links for bulk computer data transmission and electronic mail including the internet makes telecommunications intercept efforts cost-effective for intelligence collectors worldwide. As an example, prior to the internet, approximately half of all overseas telecommunications were facsimile transmissions which, because they are emanations, may be intercepted by foreign intelligence services since many of the foreign telephone companies are foreign owned. In the case of the internet, any number of unknown providers may have access to transmissions which could include anything from an e-mail to attached data files including audio and video. In addition, many American companies have begun using what is called electronic data interchange, a system of transferring corporate bidding, invoice and pricing data electronically overseas.

This type of information is invaluable to many foreign intelligence services which support their national businesses.

Many corporations are falsely reassured in assuming that because access to their computers is controlled, specific files can be read only by authorized users. It has been demonstrated, however, that an innovative "hacker" connected to computers containing competitive information, can evade the controls and access that information. For example, in a widely publicized case, referred to as the "Hanover Hacker Case", a foreign intelligence service employed computer hackers to access U.S. restricted data bases, obtaining both software and defense-related information. The service was able to do this because, although the computers themselves were secure, the telecommunications network that linked them was vulnerable by virtue of poorly implemented security mechanisms.

A typical economic espionage operation scenario might be as follows:

1. A foreign intelligence service rents an office near the targeted U.S. firm or in another location strategically selected to provide easy access to telecommunications facilities or transmissions used by the U.S. firm.

2. Sophisticated electronic listening posts are set up in the office and manned around the clock.

3. The listening posts eavesdrop on telephone, fax, telex and computer communications.

4. All intercepted communications are fed into computers, which sift through the material for valuable data.

5. Reports and briefs are prepared and passed to the foreign rival of the U.S. firm.

Economic espionage is serious and will certainly continue to increase as international relations become more and more a matter of economic, rather than military competition.

This threat is exacerbated by the increased use of extremely vulnerable electronic communications. You must assume that all overseas telecommunications are intercepted, recorded, organized into reports and reviewed for economic intelligence by everyone interested in the information. To stay ahead of our foreign competitors, we must "button-up" all competitive and proprietary communications.

Most foreign common carriers are government-controlled or owned. Trade secrets/data, marketing strategies, and personnel information which are discussed or sent over host country telephone lines are easily obtained by foreign interests.

Electronic Media Path

Electronic data is recovered easiest when a signal is not multiplexed or mixed with other data signals, i.e. data transmitted from a telephone instrument to a telephone switch. Only a minimal investment is required to retrieve data not masked with other voice or data. For this reason, it is better to use standard dial-up versus dedicated lines. Data/voice that is routed on major transmission paths (such as microwave, satellite transmission) have less likelihood of being monitored by hackers or low cost monitoring operations, because the cost of sifting through such a volume of information to access one target is often cost prohibitive. However, a well-financed intelligence gathering operation may find satellite or microwave transmissions the best intercept opportunity, since they can be monitored at great distances with little or no threat of detection.

Electronic Transmission Threats and Vulnerabilities

A threat is a fact, idea, situation, person, or thing which is perceived to menace, exploit or attack any vulnerability in security safeguards. Anyone involved in international communications should be aware of the following threats and vulnerabilities.

Threats

Many foreign phone systems are either owned or controlled by the host government. This allows the government to easily monitor transmissions of selected U.S. corporations.

Intelligence agencies of third party nations, terrorists, and criminals also monitor electronic transmissions. While monitoring is more difficult for them, than for the host country, the equipment required for such surveillance can be easily obtained by almost anyone.

Business and technical data obtained from U.S. corporations may be, and often is, provided to foreign competitors and potential customers.

Personal information may be used to kidnap executives for financial gain or political purposes.

Electronic equipment, such as facsimile machines, telephones, and desktop computers, may be altered to make electronic monitoring easier. These alterations may be made either to the transmitting/receiving device itself or to the lines leading to and from the devices.

Vulnerabilities

Telecommunications monitoring may be done at a phone company's switching facilities; phone lines may be tapped or bugged; or microwave transmissions may be intercepted anywhere between the two microwave transmitters. In any event, telecommunications monitoring may be virtually undetectable.

Telephones do not necessarily cease transmitting once they are hung-up. Conversations taking place near a phone may be transmitted to the foreign state's phone system switching facility and can be monitored anywhere between the phone and that facility.

Employees of U.S. corporations are often not aware of the threat to their transmissions.

Most international U.S. corporate telecommunications are not encrypted. Some countries do not allow encryption of telecommunications traffic within their borders, but it should be considered where feasible for any transmission of competitive information.

Sophisticated computers are often used to scan communications for "key words" and intercept any communication containing these triggers. Many telecommunications transmissions will contain "key words", used to identify information of interest to a third party. A key word can be the name of a technology, product, project, or anything else which may identify the subject of the transmission.

Encryption should be the first line of defense since it is easier for foreign intelligence services to monitor lines than to place "bugs", however encryption will provide little if any security if a careful examination for audio "bugs" elsewhere in the room is not conducted.

Suggested Counter-Measures

The following suggestions may be considered in order to improve the security of your telecommunications transmissions. These suggestions may be augmented by other measures which may be applicable to your specific situation.

- Computer links, facsimile transmissions, E-mail, and voice transmissions can all be encrypted. Encrypt electronic transmissions whenever possible.

- Neutralize the vulnerability of telephones. A small, company controlled switch installed within the facility can help ensure that conversations are not continued to be transmitted through handsets which are "hung-up", and therefore serve to decrease the threat of covert line access.

- Avoid "key words" or phrases which may be used by intelligence agencies and others to search recorded conversations for subjects of interest. Examples would be project names, product names, the names of persons of interest (e.g. heads of state, CEO's, etc.) and classification labels such as "sensitive" and "company confidential".

- Positively identify all parties participating in phone conversations or receiving the facsimile transmissions. Whenever possible, utilize your corporate transmission facilities instead of those of the host government.

- Corporate offices should be located in facilities totally controlled by the corporation.

- Always keep at least one phone and facsimile machine secured in a container equipped with a combination lock, and restrict access to the combination. This will help maintain the integrity of that equipment.

- Check connecting lines to telecommunication devices (telephones, computers, fax machines, etc.) monthly to ensure that the line has not been replaced or modified by unauthorized personnel.

- Placing stickers on phones warning of hostile monitoring will be helpful to maintain awareness.

Hacking into computers is now a standard tool for those involved in espionage and computer crime. Once an intruder has gained entry, he/she may be able to view, change, or destroy valuable company data and information. Electronic terrorism, placing a corporation's information assets at risk, is a reality.

Effects of Telecommunications on Computer Security

Telecommunications technology provides for electronic "highways" which now enable a person to directly access a computer system on another continent. Many U.S. corporations are dependent for their very survival on data being stored and processed on these computers. It is therefore mandatory that access control security.

The following suggestions should be considered in reducing the risk:

- Apply access control software and procedures to the corporation's networks; keep the intruder off the "highway". Also ensure that the corporation's computer systems are protected.

- Mandate that all users change passwords at least once every 60 days, allow no more than three consecutive invalid passwords before suspending a user ID, and insure that all passwords are at least six characters in length and contain a number and letter. Also, encourage employees to use passwords which do not relate to their lives (names of family, pets, sports teams, etc.). Hackers often gain entry by simply guessing passwords. These precautions will make their job harder.

- Control the phone numbers to the corporation's networks and computer systems as competitive information. Minimize their distribution and notify corporate employees that the numbers should be guarded.

- Test corporate networks for the existence of unauthorized modems which could provide access to eavesdroppers.

- Encrypt computer to computer sensitive transmissions, to include electronic mail.

- Require all personnel to agree in writing before they are granted access to corporate networks and computer systems that they will keep competitive information confidential and will abide by the corporation's information protection standards.

Video Conferencing

The threat to video conferencing is essentially the same as that to other types of telecommunications, in that adversaries can purchase or replicate specific equipment used by an American company and then either tap into the line or use other means to monitor both audio and video.

Although encryption is available for some video conferencing installations, many countries do not allow any type of encryption and others allow only that type which they can break.

Although video conferencing can be monitored, such monitoring requires a greater effort; however, the capability is well within the means of a foreign intelligence agency.

Couriers

Because of the extreme vulnerabilities to telecommunications and the restrictions placed upon the use of data encryption in many foreign countries, it may be best to hand carry information to, from and within overseas areas. The same precautions should be taken for hand carried packages as was described earlier for hand carried personal computers. That is, the package should never be out of the courier's direct control. It should stay with the courier at all times and never be checked in one of the temporary storage lockers often found at airports and in train stations, even for a short time.

Computer Technology

Computers can pose enormous security problems. While they contain great volumes of information, they also concentrate it, and if not protected, they can make the task of the information thief much easier.

The emergence of low-cost technologies, such as small computer systems including the Palm type computers with modems and cameras, can contain a huge amount of data and be carried in a coat pocket. These devices allow everyone to be more productive but this new level of technology comes with an increase in security risk. The radical increase in offices driven by the personal computer has taken computer security out of the hands of a small circle of experts who once focused on securing self-contained computer rooms.

Computers were once stationary objects, secured by placing them behind locked doors. Today, many computers are carried in a briefcase or coat pocket and include a full range of wireless communication features including Global Positioning Systems.

It is now recognized that the information stored in and processed by a computer is often more valuable than the equipment itself. Assuring the confidentiality, integrity and availability of that information has become a common concern for an ever-widening group of managers, information systems professionals and end-users.

Travel with Computers

Business travelers who carry and use personal or laptop computers are at risk—particularly if they are unaware of common sense security measures which should be adopted to protect computers and their contents from theft and unauthorized data access.

Computer Theft

It is obvious to a knowledgeable observer by the distinctive shape of the carrying case and the special care taken by the owner, when a person is carrying a computer. Because of this, the personal computer is a clear target for its intrinsic value. A ready market for stolen equipment and the computer's compact size make the theft a very lucrative, low risk venture for the criminal.

A personal computer should never be checked with other luggage, but should always be part of your carry-on baggage that will stay with you at all times. Likewise it should never be checked in a temporary airport or train station storage locker, even for a short time.

Greater risk is associated with the information stored on the hard disk of the personal computer. There has always been a degree of risk associated with carrying competitive information in a briefcase, although the bulk and weight of documents limit the number. However, it is possible to store thousands of notes, memos, and full documents on a personal computer hard disk drive. Therefore, the loss or theft of a PC poses a significantly greater risk of valuable information loss than ever experienced in the past.

Unauthorized Access

Unauthorized access occurs when someone accidentally or deliberately reads, modifies, or deletes computer files without your specific permission. Because personal computers do not typically impose data access controls, it is your responsibility to protect your data. While using your computer, protect the information from casual, "over-the-shoulder" viewing by others. Log-on and data encryption software can provide additional protection. Obviously, as the size and clarity of portable computer screens continue to increase, so too does the vulnerability to unauthorized observation by people in airport waiting rooms, cafeterias or snack bars, as well as in your plane seat. Positioning oneself so that it is impossible for others to observe the screen can be achieved in a restaurant or snack bar, but is very difficult if not impossible in one's plane seat. One possible strategy is to work on more mundane, non-confidential, non-sensitive work on the plane, and make the presumption that the screen will indeed be observed. Sometimes the aircraft crew will prohibit use of a portable on the aircraft.

Portable Computers & Foreign Customs

It is not necessary to steal your computer to steal the information. It is possible that while traveling in a foreign country, your computer could temporarily be out of your sight for what might appear to be an innocent "security" or "customs" inspection. In these instances, information could be stolen by a variety of methods, leaving your computer intact and you unaware that valuable information about you and or your company has been compromised. The international traveler must bear in mind that a portable computer and information it contains is a valuable asset and even in the United States, some "security" personnel are not U.S. citizens and may have criminal backgrounds. The national requirements for bringing in such a device vary from country to country, e.g., some countries absolutely forbid bringing in a personal computer except one manufactured in that particular country. Therefore, before even starting on the trip, it is important to check with your legal and security offices concerning customs requirements and necessary documentation. Otherwise, long delays, risk of confiscation, and possible frustrating experiences in attempting to communicate in another language may await the traveler at the airport.

Working With Computers From Hotels

Persons traveling in the U.S. expect high quality telephone service. It would not be appropriate to assume that the same will be the case when traveling overseas. In many countries, the telephone service is owned and operated by the national post, telephone and telegraph company. The quality of service, as well as the technical standards and conventions used, will vary dramatically from country to country. For example, in many countries, it is impossible to simply pull the removable jack from the telephone handset in the room, and plug it into the modem in the PC. Types of jacks and connections differ from country to country, and sometimes within the same country.

Your company may be targeted by a foreign intelligence service which is able to monitor your communications. In most foreign countries only a few central "switching points" serve to control all international telephone calls whether voice, fax or data stream. Intelligence agencies can tap into these sources without indicating to you that such activity is underway.

Special Risks When Using Cellular PCs

The cellular portable computer is technology having unique security considerations, which one might easily overlook. The system is essentially a personal computer with an integrated modem which is a device used to change signals understood by telephone technology into signals understood by computers, and vice versa.

There is also a built-in cellular telephone which allows a person with a single action to place a call to a computer system, connect the personal computer to it, and interact with a host computer. Sometimes overlooked with this technology is the fact that cellular telephone communications transmit signals and are, therefore, vulnerable to unauthorized interception, recording, and subsequent analysis. The necessary monitoring equipment is readily available to foreign intelligence services and to the more sophisticated business espionage agent. Therefore, one should consider carefully whether such inter-ception is acceptable.

Virus Contamination And Detection

Special care must always be taken when receiving a computer file or even an e-mail from a trusted source. Even a trusted source could unknowingly forward an infected file to you. Many viruses are intended to destroy files on a person's hard and/or floppy disks, which could have a catastrophic effect on the user of the PC. Some are designed to covertly enter your computer, search for key files and transmit them back without your knowledge. Since much has already been said about computer viruses, it is not necessary to review theory again here. Suffice it to say that whenever someone copies a program from a bulletin board, or receives a floppy disk from someone else, that program or floppy disk should be scanned to identify any known viruses present within the programs in question. Many such virus scanning programs are available at reasonable cost, and their use is highly recommended. In addition, there are some very effective "firewall" programs that should be utilized when available. Most vendors of virus scanning programs are constantly updating their virus libraries and make the new updates available for "automatic" download.

The Computer Systems Manager

There are many security considerations which anyone providing computing services to multiple users must provide, regardless of where the computing facility is located. They include physical access control, magnetic media control, the effective operation of access control sub systems, restricted utility program control, testing for system vulnerabilities, classification of competitive information in the system, printer controls, special controls of the enterprise's most important information, access from terminals not under the enterprise's control, use of supplemental, contractor or vendor personnel within the facility, and finally disaster backup and recovery.

Physical Access To Computing Facility

Because one cannot assume that employment practices are the same from country to country, it is not always possible to dictate what employees can do or where they can go. For example, in certain countries it is not permitted to log the fact that a specific person accessed a specific data set at a certain time on a certain date, because such a log could be misused to inappropriately monitor his/her work habits, speed, productivity, etc. Likewise, in some countries, there are resident fire marshals in the facility who do not work for the enterprise, but are authorized access to each and every part of the physical facility. Factors such as these must be understood and carefully planned for in the security plan.

Telecommunications Lines

U.S. telecommunications carriers are private corporations, subject to stringent government controls in the public interest. Often, in other countries, the public carrier is a governmental agency responsible for post, telephone and telegraph. In some, the distinctions between the interests of private industry and the national economy as a whole are blurred. In those, the telephone agency could monitor the telephone lines and provide the information gathered to its own private industry to the detriment of an American company. Because this possibility could be compounded by the activities of a foreign intelligence service, it would be prudent to carefully evaluate practices for the transmission of important competitive information.

Magnetic Media Control

For some of the same reasons pertaining to telecommunications, the manager must be sensitive to mailing or physically carrying magnetic media from one country to another. While the metal detection devices used at most airports no longer damage the information on magnetic media, other dangers, such as an interaction with the local customs authorities, could be far more damaging to a business. In either mailing or carrying, accountability is lost once the material is turned over to local customs personnel to be "cleared". Often, the time involved as well as the other details of what "cleared" means are not always spelled out to private industry.

Use of Encryption

One method of protecting the secrecy of competitive business information is through the use of encryption technology. Simply stated, encryption is the process whereby information which is normally readable is rendered incomprehensible by either physical devices or programs so that it can be transmitted over public telephone lines with no fear of it being compromised. Once received, the encrypted information is decrypted back to understandable language. Certain data encryption algorithms used to encrypt and decrypt data may not be exported from the United States without special licensing. Likewise, some countries do not permit the importation of such programs without special licensing agreements. Even if the most sophisticated data encryption program can't be used, it would be good to consider using some method of data encryption to preserve the integrity of your data.

Distributed Printer Control

Generally, physical access to printers used within a computing center is well controlled. However, small, powerful, distributed printing facilities, which can be readily hooked-up with printed output routed directly to such devices by any employee, are coming increasingly into use. It is strongly recommended that attention be given to ensuring that printed output may be picked up only by the information owner or his/her representatives. This can be accomplished by placing the printers in a room having a key, cipher lock, or other controlled access system.

International Travel & Computers

The following questions should be considered:

- Does the local power supply match your system's requirements? Are electrical power transformers, filters, surge protectors or uninterrupted power supply (UPS) units available to protect your equipment?

- Does the government impose restrictions on the import of computer hardware and software into the country?

Environment

- Will the computer be used in a low humidity area where damage from static electricity may be sustained? Are carpets treated? Are humidifiers available?

- Will the computer be used in a hot, dusty climate? Are office temperature controls sufficient? Are dust covers available?

Physical Security

- Is the work area kept clear of soft drinks, coffee and other liquids which, when accidentally spilled, may damage equipment?

- Are diskettes physically labeled and handled as directed by the manufacturer?

- Are sensitive diskettes sufficiently write-protected to avoid accidental or malicious damage or destruction?

- Are backup copies stored off-site?

- Is the computer sufficiently protected from acts of sabotage, tampering and theft?

- Are modems (particularly those with an automatic answer feature) disconnected or powered off when not in use?

- Are film printer ribbons, sensitive printouts and diskettes burned, shredded or degaussed as appropriate to prevent inadvertent information disclosure?

System Security

- Are spare, user-serviceable parts available in the event of failure?

- Are backup copies of software and data produced periodically?

- Has a backup system (contingency) been identified to continue critical operations in the event of a failure/disaster? Has it been tested?

- Are system hardware and/or software controls present to authenticate individual system users? Are passwords changed frequently and are they easily guessed?

- Is a security erase or file scrub program present on the system that will over-write sensitive data on the hard disk when a file is deleted? Is it used?

- Are sufficient controls in place to prevent violation of manufacturer's copyright and license agreements?

Virus Protection

- Are software and data diskettes received from reliable, trustworthy sources?

- Is software received from outside sources scanned for computer viruses with current virus detection software?

James R. Doyle

THE ESPIONAGE THREAT

INTRODUCTION

Personnel engaged in foreign travel for business or pleasure and those assigned to field activities in foreign countries should be aware that they are possible targets of espionage. Espionage is a favorite method of intelligence gathering by hostile intelligence services. The prime targets of these agencies include all individuals with knowledge of or access to, sensitive technical data on items such as lasers, missiles, computers, and microelectronics equipment, as well as other classified or unclassified government information.

Any foreign country is a prime area for hostile intelligence services. Many Americans mistakenly believe that just because they are in a country "friendly" to the U.S. that they are immune from intelligence gathering just because they are Americans. The operatives of a foreign intelligence service need not be foreigners, nor does an encounter with a foreign intelligence agent need to be extraordinary in any way. A casual acquaintance, for example, could be an ordinary citizen, a diplomat, or an American who has been recruited as a foreign agent.

Some of the techniques employed by hostile intelligence networks to obtain valuable information include attendance at technical and scientific meetings, personal surveillance, electronic surveillance, mail compromise, and exploitation of human weaknesses. Conventions, seminars, conferences, and symposia are key sources of technical and scientific information for foreign intelligence agents. They are generally open to representatives from all nations, including hostile countries. Foreign agents are extremely proficient in obtaining the information at these meetings without disclosing anything of significant value in return. All participants should exercise great care in preparing formal papers to be presented at international conferences and submit them for security review well in advance of their presentation or publication. If participating in panel discussions, each individual must be especially alert to the possibility of inadvertently disclosing vital defense information during spontaneous discussions or in answering questions.

I recall, on one occasion, attending a "closed" conference of international security professionals. I noted the great care taken to assure that only authorized personnel had access to the building and after entering the building how everyone was registered and screened. I also noted how we were carefully escorted to a "secure" auditorium for the presentations by some of the world's best authorities on international security. It was later noted that all of the presenters had used a "wireless" microphone for the auditorium sound system which meant that anyone in the surrounding community with a readily available radio scanner could monitor and record the conference. Obviously, that didn't happen again, at that conference. The real lesson learned at this conference was, that no matter how secure the environment and how experienced you may be there will always be vulnerabilities to recognize and overcome.

Police-like controls placed on traveler's movements in foreign countries provide an excellent means of maintaining personal surveillance. In fact, a visitor may be "targeted" upon application for a visa. Guides and interpreters are frequently members of, or cooperate with, secret police agencies. Waiters, cab drivers, hotel personnel, and other such inconspicuous individuals are also known to be major contributors to the intelligence effort. A considerable amount of information is divulged when the visa application is completed. This information may easily single a person out for special attention during an entire stay in a foreign country.

Some foreign travel agencies invariably "arrange" for American travelers to stay at the better class hotels. In many cases, Americans of special interest are often assigned to rooms in which listening devices or other special means of surveillance have been permanently installed. Travelers should assume that the hotel room is equipped with devices to overhear or record conversations. Devices also may be installed through which a person can be physically observed, even while the room is dark. In addition to such devices as microphones, telephone taps, and miniature recorders, intelligence operatives today use infrared and night vision cameras, closed-circuit TV, and other highly advanced equipment.

Do not search for such devices, and do not make an issue of it if one is found. The presence of such equipment may not necessarily be personally significant. The device(s) may or may not be monitored during the visit, or they may be monitored only on a random basis. Do not try to neutralize the devices by methods such as running tap water and playing a radio, because some modern devices are so sophisticated they cannot be neutralized. The best defense is to engage only in light, uninformative conversation. Outside the hotel room, other areas such as vehicles, train compartments, restaurants, conference rooms, and other public places, may also be monitored. Miniature microphones with transmitters or recorders can easily be secreted on an individual in a group. It is even technically possible to record conversations in open, outdoor areas; however, these areas are normally more secure than indoor locations.

Another source of information is the personal mail of the traveler. Some foreign countries routinely examine the mail of American travelers for counterintelligence and positive intelligence. When utilizing foreign mail services, avoid revealing personal or family problems of a confidential nature or any information that is self-incriminating, or of a positive value to foreign intelligence gatherers. Be extremely careful of the content and to whom it is directed, as matters discussed can be used as pressure points against the individuals concerned.

Avoid revealing anything that might be of possible value to the foreign intelligence collection agency. Be temperate in the use of alcoholic beverages. Aside from creating embarrassing or even scandalous scenes, overindulgence may place a person in a position of possible compromise.

In some cases, inebriated persons were maneuvered into compromising situations and photographed. Such entrapment was later used as a basis for blackmailing the victim into espionage activities. This technique is one of the oldest and most favored methods of compromising a targeted individual.

When seeking to subvert, compromise, blackmail, or recruit Americans for espionage purposes, foreign intelligence agents fully exploit inherent human frailties. Agents are alert to detect any indiscreet or immoral behavior. They scrutinize personal habits, character, behavioral traits, and mannerisms to determine irregularities in such matters as sex, liquor, smuggling, black market activities, illegal currency exchange, and contacts with dissidents. In addition to arranging situations in which Americans are involved in illicit sex affairs, they have also deliberately planted compromising material in their possession or played on their sympathies in an effort to involve them in illegal or discreditable acts. The American traveler, being a guest in a foreign country as well as a representative of the United States, should maintain personal behavior beyond reproach at all times.

COUNTERING THE ESPIONAGE THREAT

Foreign Travel Precautions

The following suggestions should be considered to avoid potential risk:

- When applying for passports or visas, always list current or past military affiliations. In one instance, a representative of a tour agency was reported to have advised military personnel to list a civilian occupation in place of their true military status on visa applications because visa applications were occasionally turned down if a military affiliation was listed. Such evasion of facts could lead to a charge of espionage.

- Adhere to all conditions of the visa; violations can lead to lengthy detentions.

- Do not make any oral or written reference to your involvement with intelligence, military or other related activities within the United States.

- Do not make drastic or unplanned variations in itinerary. Record the address and telephone number of the U.S. Embassy or Consulate in each host or major city in which a visit is planned. Keep your passport on your person at all times and memorize the identification number.

- Do not engage in black-marketing or other illegal activities.

- Learn the applicable laws and rules of the country.

- Be careful about accepting invitations and do not drink too much or engage in promiscuous acts.

- As a guest in a foreign country and a representative of the United States, maintain a high level of personal behavior.

- Be aware that audio (listening) devices and hidden cameras are sometimes planted in rooms.

- Do not take overt action if the room is "bugged" or under any other type of surveillance. Continue normal conversation or activity, giving no indication that the surveillance has been detected. Report the details to the U.S. Embassy or Consulate, and to the company security officer upon return.

- Avoid irregularities in personal behavior because they constitute the most profitable area of exploitation by intelligence agencies.

- Do not accept letters, personal messages, photographs, packages, or other material to be carried openly or smuggled in or out of the country for any reason.

- Make an accurate and complete declaration of money (including traveler's checks) and all valuables (including cameras and jewelry whether worn or carried). Retain a copy of this declaration until departure.

- Never pick up discarded souvenirs, statues, or artifacts under any circumstances. Purchase such items in approved shops only, making certain that a receipt is provided for each purchase. Do not sign any receipts for money or services unless assured of, and furnished, an on-the-spot copy that clearly identifies and itemizes the nature of the transaction.

- Do not make any oral or written statements that might be exploited for propaganda purposes.

The Corporate Executive Survival Guide

- Do not sign petitions while traveling or attending conferences, however innocent they may appear.

- Do not photograph military personnel, equipment, installations, defense plants, or other military or restricted areas.

- Refrain from photographing slum areas, ghettos, or underprivileged persons in the host country.

- It is good policy to refrain from photographing airports and train yards. Taking photographs in some countries always involves potential problems. Formal permission should be obtained well in advance as to "where and when" a camera can be used.

- Be aware that clothing can be tagged with invisible dyes and/or radioactive materials. This can be done at a dry cleaning establishment or in the room. If a letter were placed in the tagged pocket and later mailed, it could be retrieved and traced. Be careful about what you write and to whom.

- Use personal stationery and not that from a local hotel when writing letters. Also, purchase stamps at a post office or Embassy outlet. Stationary and stamps obtained at a hotel or other source can be tagged with invisible inks or radioactive tracers. Assume that letters will be opened and read.

- Do not reveal personal opinions in correspondence, or write about controversial issues that might prove embarrassing to the United States government, the writer, or the addressee.

- Be alert to overly friendly tourist guides, interpreters, maids, and other foreign nationals who show an undue interest in your welfare. Be particularly wary of guide personnel who "Just happen" to know your specialty field or weakness. Do not trust interpreters with matters of confidence.

- Obtain medical or dental service only from a U.S. Government facility or from persons or institutions approved by U.S. Consular officials.

- Report to the nearest U.S. Embassy if an approach has been made, or if involved or entrapped in a conspiracy to commit espionage. If indiscreet or otherwise compromised, discuss the situation in confidence with any of these U.S. officials. Above all, do not attempt to get out of an embarrassing situation alone or assume the role of a self-appointed counteragent.

- Report any incident involving detention, harassment, and or provocation to the company security officer within 24 hours after returning from travel.

- Report any dealings with representatives from hostile countries or other designated countries as soon as possible to the company security officer. This action allows the security officer to effect proper reporting, protect the employee's record, allow the proper authority to monitor the contacts, and detect recruitment operations as they develop.

- Recognize when an association evolves from one of strictly business to one of a more personal nature.

- Be aware that a key first step taken in recruitment scenarios by intelligence officers is the cultivation of a personal rapport and social relationship with targeted individuals.

- Avoid meetings away from the office.

- Do not solicit or accept gifts or special favors.

- Avoid one-on-one meetings.

- In dealings with foreign nationals, remember that when someone begins to aggressively solicit classified or sensitive information, consider whether the inquiry is normal or innocent curiosity. It may be an attempt to exploit you. Such inquiries should be immediately reported to the U.S. Embassy or company security officer.

- Do not take any classified documents or information out of the United States. In fact, do not take anything along on your trip unless absolutely needed. Do not take your company identification badge when traveling in foreign countries. A passport and drivers license are sufficient identification for foreign travel.

THE TERRORIST THREAT

Introduction

Terrorist activities are a worldwide ongoing threat and since 11 September 2001, U.S. citizens are aware that they can become a target of an attack almost anywhere at any time. Terrorism is the unlawful or threatened use of force or violence by a revolutionary organization against individuals or property, with the intention of coercing or intimidating governments or societies, often for political or ideological purposes. Political terrorism is calculated and rational, not "mindless". Terrorists usually seek to create a credible threat or political leverage, rather than mass destruction. Their immediate objectives are primarily psychological (as opposed to territorial) to instill fear among the populace, disrupt the government, induce a general loss of confidence in the existing social order or governmental policies, and provoke legal authority to adopt repressive measures. The more common types of violence committed by terrorists include bombing, hijacking, kidnapping, and assassination. Robbery committed to finance operations or acquire weapons also plays an important role in furthering terrorist objectives.

Most terrorists seem to lack respect for life, gender, age, race, creed, color, or national origin. They seem intent primarily on disruption, destruction, and publicity. Incidents throughout the world have tended to reinforce this assessment of their intent. Their targets have been located primarily in the free world or their actions have been aimed at free-world countries. Prime targets in the past have included embassies and consulates, airline terminals, and aircraft. Random acts have run the gamut and have involved kidnappings and assaults, destruction of utilities such as power stations, and isolated rocket attacks. Designed to counter the terrorist threat, the protective measures contained in the following "Countering The Terrorist Threat" section will help the traveler have a safer and more secure journey.

The likelihood of terrorist incidents is increasing and varies according to country or area of the world, generally depending on the stability of the local government and the degree of frustration felt by indigenous groups or individuals. In the past, government institutions and facilities were the primary targets with a relatively small number of attacks directed at American foreign business operations and civilians. Since 11 September 2001 the public has become more aware that innocent civilians, including civilians in the U.S., are at a much greater risk.

When an act of terrorism does occur, it often has dire consequences: murder, hostage taking, property destruction. Much has been learned about the mentality of terrorists, their methods of operation, and the behavior patterns of both victims and perpetrators.

Alert individuals, prepared for possible terrorist acts, can minimize the likelihood that these acts will be successfully carried out against them. While there is no absolute protection against terrorism, there are a number of reasonable precautions that can provide some degree of individual protection.

COUNTERING THE TERRORIST THREAT

While total protection from acts of terrorism is impossible, understanding the following basic protective measures will significantly reduce your risk:

- Be aware that individual precautions can substantially reduce the probability of a successful terrorist act.

- As a foreigner, maintain a "low profile" by avoiding, to the extent possible, local news coverage, ostentatious dress and activities, and large social events.

- Know what to do in emergencies.

- Know and avoid high-risk areas and be cautious when mingling with crowds.

- Vary travel routes and patterns and avoid predictable personal routines.

- Keep office personnel and families informed of itinerary and whereabouts.

- Be alert for surveillance, be cautious with strangers, and avoid casually giving personal data such as address and telephone numbers.

- Know enough of the host country language to master emergency phrases and be able to use the telephone.

The following suggestions should be considered in dealing with a hostage situation:

- Recognize the possibility of becoming a hostage and be aware that the U.S. Government will work to obtain your release.

- Know that chances of survival are high and that personal conduct can influence treatment in captivity.

- Have family affairs in order, including an up-to-date will, appropriate powers of attorney, and measures taken to ensure family financial security. Issues of continuing the children's education, family relocation, and disposition of property should be discussed with family members.

- Provide assurance of cooperation to the terrorists, especially during the abduction phase.

- Stay alert after seizure, note sounds, direction of movement, passage of time, conversations of terrorists, and other information that might be useful.

- Understand the emotional impact of being kidnapped to help in the recovery from the initial shock and fear.

- Anticipate isolation and possible attempts at disorientation.

- Attempt to develop rapport with the terrorists. Seek areas of mutual interest without displaying sympathy with the captors' cause or ideology.

- During interrogations, Take a simple, tenable position and stick to it, be polite and remain calm.

- Give short answers, talk freely about non-essential matter, but be guarded when conversations turn to matters of substance.

- Do not be lulled by a friendly approach.

- Briefly affirm belief in basic democratic principles, and if forced to present written or taped terrorist demands to authorities, state clearly that the demands are from the captors, and avoid making pleas that appear to support the terrorists.

- Maintain your dignity and respect by actions not demands.

- During rescue operations, avoid sudden moves. The safest action is to drop to the floor and remain there until rescued.

U.S. Terrorist Policy

U.S. policy is firmly committed to resisting terrorist blackmail. The U.S. Government will not pay ransom for the release of hostages. It will not support the freeing of prisoners from incarceration in response to terrorist demands. Concessions to terrorist blackmail would merely invite further demands. The U.S. Government actively encourages other governments to adopt a similar position. While the U.S. Government will not negotiate with terrorists on the substance of their demands, it does not rule out contact and dialogue with hostage takers if such action will promote the safe release of hostages.

In terrorist incidents abroad, the U.S. Government looks to the host government to exercise its responsibility under international law to protect all persons within its territories and to bring about the safe release of hostages. However, it is clear that some foreign governments do support some terrorist groups. In some cases, the U.S. Government may be able to provide foreign governments the services of terrorism experts and other specialized assistance, including military equipment, and personnel to fight terrorist activities.

Specific U.S. Policy Guidance

In the event U.S. citizens are taken hostage abroad, the U.S. Embassy will convey U.S. policy to the host government. The embassy will encourage the host government to resolve any terrorist incident in a manner that, while safeguarding the lives of the hostages, does not permit the terrorists to achieve their objectives. The host government will be reminded of its obligation to bring the terrorists to justice.

International cooperation to combat terrorism is essential because all governments, regardless of philosophy, are vulnerable.

Use of Force

If the host government asks for advice from the U.S. Government regarding the use of force to resolve an incident, a response will probably be as follows: (1) The ultimate decision regarding a strategy for dealing with terrorists and the successful termination of an incident must remain with the host government, and (2) the U.S. Government believes it is inappropriate to provide advice because it would not be party to the negotiations or negotiating process.

In the past, experience has shown that most hostage situations, including hijackings, result in a peaceful solution when using a strategy designed to buy time and wear down the terrorists however; the events of 11 September 2001 have demonstrated, at least in the case of hijackings, a more pro-active and direct approach may be the only survival option left for the victim.

Humanitarian Appeals

Although there is only a limited chance of successfully appealing to the terrorists' humanitarian instincts, indirect appeals may have a positive influence and may cause terrorists to be concerned about alienating key support groups, sympathetic governments, or world opinion.

Appeals to the following groups or individuals may prove to be valuable:

- The United Nations Secretary General.

- Third World countries considered friendly to the terrorists.

- The dean of the local diplomatic corps.

- Spouses and children of hostages asking for the return of their family members.

- The terrorists' leaders or supporters, who may profess innocence to involvement with the specific incident.

- Religious leaders.

- The counterproductive aspects of reporting on any operational activities of the police, military, or their counter-terrorism forces should be emphasized.

Caution with press interviews of unknown or amateur "experts" on terrorists' motivation or background should be urged.

Kidnapping Survival Guidelines

Kidnapping is a terrifying experience, but you possess more personal resources than you may be aware of to cope with the situation. Remember, if they had wanted to kill you they would not have taken you alive so you are only of value to them alive, and they want to keep you that way.

The common hostage responses of fear, denial, and withdrawal are all experienced in varying degrees. You may be blindfolded, drugged, handled roughly, or even stuffed in the trunk of a car. If drugs are administered, don't resist. Their purpose will be to sedate you and make you more manageable; these same drugs may actually help you to get control of your emotions, which should be your immediate goal. If conscious, follow your captors' instructions.

Kidnapping can take place in public areas where someone may quietly force you, by gunpoint, into a vehicle. They can also take place at a hotel or residence, again by using a weapon to force your cooperation in leaving the premises and entering a vehicle. The initial phase of kidnapping is a critical one because it provides one of the best opportunities to escape.

The following suggestions should be considered if in an abduction situation:

- If you are in a public area at the time of abduction, make as much commotion as possible to draw attention to the situation.

- If the abduction takes place at your hotel room, make noise, attempt to arouse the suspicion or concern of hotel employees or of those in neighboring rooms. The fact that an abduction has taken place will be brought to the attention of authorities and the process of notification and search can begin. Otherwise, it could be hours or days before your absence is reported.

- Once you have been forced into a vehicle, you may be blindfolded, physically attacked (to cause unconsciousness), drugged, or forced to lie face down on the floor of the vehicle. In some instances, hostages have been forced into trunks or specially built compartments for transporting contraband.

- Do not struggle in your confined state; calm yourself mentally, concentrate on surviving.

- Employ your mind by attempting to visualize the route being taken, take note of turns, street noise, smells, etc. Try to keep track of the amount of time spent between points.

- Once you have arrived at your destination, you may be placed in a temporary holding area before being moved again to a more permanent detention site. If you are interrogated retain a sense of pride but be cooperative.

- Only divulge information that cannot be used against you.

- Do not antagonize your interrogator with obstinate behavior.

- Concentrate on surviving; if you are to be used as a bargaining tool or to obtain ransom, you will be kept alive.

- After reaching what you may presume to be your permanent detention site (you may be moved several more times), quickly settle into the situation.

- Be observant—Notice the details of the room, the sounds of activity in the building and determine the layout of the building by studying what is visible to you. Listen for sounds through walls, windows or out in the streets, and try to distinguish between smells.

- Stay mentally active by memorizing as many details as possible. Exercise your memory and practice retention.

The Corporate Executive Survival Guide

- Keep track of time. Devise a way to track the day, date and the time, and use it to devise a daily schedule of activities for yourself.

- Know your captors. Memorize their schedule, look for patterns of behavior to be used to your advantage, and identify weaknesses or vulnerabilities as an opportunity escape.

- Remain cooperative. Attempt to establish rapport with your captors or guards. Once a level of communication is achieved, try asking for items which will increase your personal comfort. Make them aware of your needs.

- Stay physically active, even if your movement is extremely limited. Use isometric and flexing exercises to keep your muscles toned.

- If you detect the presence of other hostages in the same building, devise ways to communicate.

- <u>Do not</u> be uncooperative, antagonistic, or hostile towards your captors. It is a fact that hostages who display this type of behavior are kept captive longer or are singled out for torture or punishment.

- Watch for signs of *Stockholm Syndrome* which occurs when the captive, due to the close proximity and the constant pressures involved, begins to relate to, and empathize with, the captors. In some cases, this relationship has resulted in the hostage become empathetic to the point that he/she actively participates in the activities of the group. You should attempt to establish a friendly rapport with your captors, but maintain your personal dignity and do not compromise your integrity.

- If you are able to escape, attempt to get first to a U.S. Embassy or Consulate to seek protection. If you cannot reach either, go to a host government or friendly government entity.

Hostage Survival

Any traveler could become a hostage. The odds of that happening are extremely low when the number of travelers is compared to the number of people that have actually become a hostage. However, there is always a chance that a traveler could end up being in the wrong place at the wrong time. With this in mind, the traveler should make sure that his/her affairs are in order before they travel abroad. Items of particular importance to an individual in a hostage situation are an up-to-date will, insurance policy and a power of attorney for the spouse. If these items have been taken care of before departure, the employee will not have to worry about the family's welfare and the hostage can focus all of his/her efforts on the one thing of paramount importance and that is **SURVIVAL!**

To survive, travelers should realize that there are certain dynamics involved in a hijacking or a kidnapping, and, to increase their ability to survive, they must understand how these interacting forces affect the end result. Each individual involved in an incident of this type will have an impact on the eventual outcome. One wrong move by either a victim or a perpetrator could easily result in a disaster rather than a peaceful conclusion to the incident.

The first thing that a traveler should remember is that he or she is not the only one that is scared and nervous. Everyone involved is in the same emotional state, including the perpetrators. Fear can trigger a disaster, and it does not take much for some individuals to set off a defensive spate of violence. Whether it is a demonstration of violence to reinforce a demand or to incite fear in the minds of the hostages, the violence will be motivated by fanaticism and/or fear and that violence will be directed at the person(s) who are perceived to be a threat or a nuisance to the hijackers.

Hijacking Survival

In the past, hijackers were not motivated to use a hijacked aircraft as a tactical weapon. Since 11 September 2001 the rules changed and we learned how effective this type of attack could be. In the past if you remained compliant with the demands of the hijackers there was a good chance the aircraft would land (somewhere) and you could survive. Now, in some situations, the only hope of survival may be in attacking the hijackers and recovering control of the aircraft.

The physical takeover of the aircraft by the hijackers may be characterized by noise, commotion, and possibly shooting and yelling, or it may be quiet and methodical with little more than an announcement by a crew member. These first few minutes of the hijacking are crucial.
The following suggestions should be considered if you are in a hi-jacking situation:

- Assess the situation carefully and try to determine the "true" objective of the hijackers.

- Stay calm, and encourage others around you to do the same.

- Remember that the hijackers are extremely nervous and are possibly scared.

- Comply with your captor(s) directions if you feel this will produce a peaceful outcome.

- If shooting occurs, keep your head down or drop to the floor.

- Remain alert and look for an opportunity to your advantage.

Once the takeover of the aircraft has occurred, you may be separated by citizenship, sex, race, etc. Your passport may be confiscated and your carry-on luggage ransacked. The aircraft may be diverted to another country or as in the case of 11 September 2001 may be used as a greater terror weapon. The hijackers may enter into a negotiation phase which could last indefinitely and/or the crew may be forced to fly the aircraft to yet another destination. During this phase passengers may be used as a bargaining tool in negotiations, lives may be threatened, or a number of passengers may be released in exchange for fuel, landing/departure rights, food, etc. This will be the longest phase of the hijacking.

The following suggestions should be considered during this phase of the hijacking:

- If you are told to keep your head down or maintain another body position, talk yourself into relaxing into the position; you may need to stay that way for some time.

- Prepare yourself mentally and emotionally for a long ordeal.

- Do not attempt to hide your passport or belongings.

- If addressed by the hijackers, respond in a regulated tone of voice.

- Use your time wisely by observing the characteristics and behavior of the hijackers, mentally attach nicknames to each one and notice their dress, facial features and temperaments.

- If you or a nearby passenger is in need of assistance due to illness or discomfort, solicit the assistance of a crew member first. Do not attempt to approach a hijacker unless similar assistance has been rendered by them for other passengers.

- If you are singled out by the hijackers, be responsive but do not volunteer information.

The last phase of the hijacking is resolution, be it by use of a hostage rescue team or resolution through negotiation. In the latter instance, the hijackers may simply surrender to authorities or abandon the aircraft, crew and passengers.

The experience of others will be helpful to you if you are the victim of a hijacking. Blend in with the other airline passengers. Avoid eye contact with your captors. Remember there may be other hijackers covertly mixed among the regular passengers.

Although captors may appear calm, they cannot be trusted to behave reasonably or rationally at all times. Stay alert, but do not challenge them physically or verbally if possible. Comply with their instructions.

If interrogated, keep answers short and limited to nonpolitical topics. Carry a family photo; at some point you may be able to appeal to captors' family feelings.

Minimize the importance of your job. Give innocuous reasons for traveling. Never admit to any accusations.

Armed Assault on the Ground

Hostages taken by ground assault are in a situation similar to hijacking except that it occurs within buildings. Business offices, banks, embassies, and trains have been targets. The same advice for dealing with hijackers applies to ground assaults. Should shooting occur, seek cover or lie flat on the floor.

Terrorist Demands

U.S. Government policy is to make no concessions to terrorist demands. However, such a decision on the part of private individuals or companies is a personal one and in some special circumstances may be made by the family or company of the victim. Whatever the decision, it should conform to local law.

Terrorist Surveillance

Terrorists may shadow an intended victim at length and with infinite patience before an actual abduction or assassination is attempted. Initial surveillance efforts may be clumsy and could be spotted by an alert target.

In most cases, more than one individual is a likely candidate for the terrorist act. Usually the choice is based on the probability of success. In one documented instance, both an American and another country's representative were under surveillance. Though the American was the first choice of the terrorists, their surveillance showed that it would be more difficult to kidnap him. Consequently, the other individual was abducted and spent a long period in captivity.

Precise risks of surveillance and popular local tactics can be explained by your company's security representative. However, you must also learn to cultivate a "sixth sense" about your surroundings.

Know what is normal in your neighborhood and along your commute routes, especially at choke points. If you know what is ordinary, you will notice anything extraordinary such as people who are in the wrong place or dressed inappropriately, or cars parked in strange locations.

Be particularly observant whenever you leave your home or office. Look up and down the street for suspicious vehicles, motorcycles, mopeds, etc. Note people near your home who appear to be repair personnel, utility crew teams, even peddlers. Ask yourself if they appear genuine.

Become familiar with vehicle makes and models; learn to memorize license numbers. Determine if a pattern is developing with specific vehicles. See if cars suddenly pull out of parking places or side streets when you pass. Cars with extra mirrors or large mirrors are suspicious.

Be aware of the types of surveillance: stationary (at residence, along route, at work); following (on foot, by car); monitoring (of telephone, mail); searching (of luggage, personal effects, even trash); and eavesdropping (electronic and personal). An elaborate system involving several people and cars might be used.

Make their job tougher by not being predictable. Eat at different times and places. Stagger professional and social activities; don't play tennis "every Wednesday at three," for example.

Know the choke points on your routes and be aware of other vehicles, vans, or motorcycles as you enter those bottleneck areas. Search out safe havens that you can pull into along the route.

Drive with windows rolled up to within 2 inches of the top and lock all doors. Report any suspicious activity promptly to law enforcement.

Avoid using unlicensed cabs or cabs that appear out of nowhere. Do not permit taxi drivers to deviate from desired route.

Be circumspect with members of the press, as terrorists often pose as journalists. Do not submit to interviews or allow photographs to be made in or of your home.

Always speak guardedly and caution children to do the same. Never discuss travel or business plans within hearing of servants. Surveillants consider children and servants to be a prime source of information. Always assume that your telephone is tapped.

In elevators, watch for anyone who waits for you to select your floor, then pushes a button for the one just above or below yours.

If you become aware of surveillance, don't let those watching you know you are onto them. And certainly never confront them. Immediately notify your appropriate company representative.

Memorize emergency numbers, and carry change for phone calls.

Captivity

A hostage-taking situation is at its worst at the onset. The terrorists are nervous and unsure, easily irritated, often irrational. It is a psychologically traumatic moment for the hostage. Violence may be used even if the hostage remains passive, but resistance could result in death.

If taken hostage, your best defense is passive cooperation. You may be terrified, but try to regain your composure as soon as possible and to organize your thoughts. Being able to behave rationally increases your chances for survival. The more time that passes, the better your chances of being released alive.

Behavior During Captivity

The following suggestions should be considered while in captivity:

- As in the case of hijackings, try to establish some kind of rapport with your captors. Family is a universal subject. Avoid political dialogues, but listen attentively to their point of view. If you know their language, listen and observe; and if addressed, use it.

- Plan on a lengthy stay, and determine to keep track of the passage of time. Captors may attempt to confuse your sense of time by taking your watch, keeping you in a windowless cell, or serving meals at odd hours. However, you can approximate time by noting, for example, changes in temperatures between night and day; the frequency and intensity of outside noises—traffic, whistles, birds; and by observing the alertness of guards.

- Maintain your dignity and self respect at all times.

- Manage your time by setting up schedules for simple tasks, exercises, daydreaming, and housekeeping.

- Build relations with fellow captives and with the terrorists. If hostages are held apart, devise ways to communicate with one another. Where hostages are moved back and forth, to bathrooms for example, messages can be written and left. However, do not jeopardize your safety or the safety or treatment of others if attempting to communicate with fellow captives seems too risky.

- Maintain your physical and mental health; it is critical to exercise body and mind. Eat food provided without complaint; keep up your strength. Request medical treatment or special medicines if required.

- Establish exercise and relaxation programs. Exercise produces a healthy tiredness and gives you a sense of accomplishment. If space is confined, do isometrics. Relaxation reduces stress. Techniques include meditation, prayer, daydreaming.

- Keep your mind active; read anything available. Write, even if you are not allowed to retain your writings. If materials are not available, mentally compose poetry or fiction, try to recall Scripture, or design a house.

- Take note of the characteristics of your captors and surroundings: their habits, speech, contacts; exterior noises (typical of city or country); and other distinctive sounds. This information could prove very valuable later.

- If selected for early release, consider it an opportunity to help remaining hostages. Details you have observed on the terrorists and the general situation can assist authorities with a rescue.

- You can expect to be accused of working for the government's intelligence service, to be interrogated extensively, and to lose weight. You may be put in isolation; your captives may try to disorient you. It is important that you mentally maintain control.

Avoidance of Capture or Escape

Efforts to avoid capture or to attempt escape have in most cases been futile. The decision, however, is a personal one, although it could affect fellow hostages by placing them in jeopardy. Several other considerations should be weighed.

To have any chance of success, you should be in excellent physical condition and mentally prepared to react before the terrorists have consolidated their position. This, also, is the riskiest psychological time. You would need to have a plan in mind, and possibly have been trained in special driving tactics or other survival skills.

If you are held in a country in which you would stand out because of race or other physical characteristics, if you know nothing of the language or your location, or if you are held in a country where anti American or anti-Western attitudes prevail, you should consider the consequences of your escape before attempting it.

If you conclude that an escape attempt is worthwhile, take terrorists by surprise and you may make it. If their organization has a poor track record of hostage safety, it may be worth the risk.

Rescue

The termination of any terrorist incident is extremely tense. If an assault force attempts a rescue, it is imperative that you remain calm and out of the way. Make no sudden moves or take any action by which you could be mistaken for a terrorist and risk being injured or killed.

Even in a voluntary release or surrender by the terrorists, tensions are charged and tempers volatile. Very precise instructions will be given to the hostages, either by the captors or the police. Follow instructions precisely. You may be asked to exit with hands in the air, and you may be searched by the rescue team. You may experience rough treatment until you are identified and the situation has stabilized.

Finally, it's worth keeping in mind the following facts about terrorism:

- The overwhelming majority of victims have been abducted from their vehicles on the way to or from work.

- A large number of people taken hostage ignored the most basic security precautions.

- Terrorist tactics are not static. As precautions prove effective, they change their methods.

- There is a brief "window of vulnerability" while we learn to counter their new styles.

COUNTER-TERRORIST TECHNIQUES

- Do not settle into a routine.

- Vary times and routes to and from work or social engagements.

- Remember, there is safety in numbers. Avoid going out alone.

- When traveling long distances by automobile, go in a convoy. Avoid back country roads and dangerous areas of the city.

- A privately owned car generally offers the best security but avoid ostentatious cars.

- Keep your automobile in good repair and the gas tank at least half full.

- Driving in the center lane of a multiple lane highway makes it difficult for the car to be forced off the road.

CRISIS MANAGEMENT

Introduction

Since the beginning of time, people have encountered diverse catastrophic events that have resulted in great pain and suffering, and enormous loss of lives, and hundreds of billions of dollars in property damage. An analysis of these catastrophes discloses certain generic characteristics. Some, such as war, insurrection, and acts of terrorism, as in the case of the *11 September 2001* attack, are rooted in differences of political philosophies. Others, such as criminal acts and industrial accidents, are the result of behavioral/societal problems or human error. Still others, such as earthquakes and violent storms and resulting floods, originate from natural phenomena over which people have no control.

Catastrophic events frequently spawn conditions that may be even more insidious than the catastrophes themselves. Among these conditions are serious health hazards, such as polluted water and food supplies and disrupted sanitation systems, which may cause the spread of diseases of epidemic proportions. Effective emergency planning for such problems will greatly reduce their impact on the community where the disaster strikes.

People have only a limited ability to control or to prevent some of these events and will never have the ability to prevent others, such as earthquakes, violent storms, and volcanic eruptions. Although we are unable to prevent such catastrophic events, we have learned and continue to learn a great deal about them. The most valuable lesson learned about natural phenomena is that the implementation of effective contingency measures for emergencies will substantially lessen the loss of life, serious injury, and property damage.

Preparing for emergencies is the focus of this book. It is essential to prepare for both those emergencies over which we have limited control and those over which we have no control. Application of preventive measures is also important to survival from catastrophic events. Contingency planning for emergencies should include the periods before, during, and after the incident.

Human beings are inclined to react to events as they occur rather than to try to anticipate or plan for them. This inclination could prove costly because many disasters, such as lightning strikes, earthquakes, and acts of terrorism, including the *11 September 2001* attack, are not preceded by a warning and an inappropriate spontaneous reaction could be fatal.

The guidelines presented here were initially designed to assist representatives of U.S. corporations abroad to prepare judiciously for emergencies however the events of *11 September 2001* clearly dictate that a domestic Crisis Management Plan is required. Planning and forethought are important, but so is flexibility in execution. A static, inflexible emergency plan will almost certainly result in a lack of preparedness and a poorly rated crisis response.

You are reminded to supplement the guidelines with knowledge of the contingency plans in place and available through the government of the country of residence and to be sure that the emergency plans adopted are not in violation of local laws.

On the front of the National Archives Building in Washington, D.C., an adage is inscribed—"The Past Is Prologue." In the context of the subject of this book, this adage should be regarded as axiomatic. In the interest of safety for all concerns, family, employees and property, you should never yield to the temptation to ignore contingency planning for emergencies because of "a feeling that it won't happen to me" or" it can't happen here." Such an attitude may be costly.

CRISIS MANAGEMENT GENERAL

The Crisis Management guidelines provide in this book, are intended to provide information on how to plan for and respond to a variety of emergency situations in a foreign country. The objective is to provide you with a framework of contingency planning tools. As you read, you will recognize that this framework of planning tools can also be applied in the United States.

CRISIS MANAGEMENT ORGANIZATION

CRISIS MANAGEMENT TEAM

A Crisis Management Team should be established at the corporate headquarters level and at all principal business or country sites, depending on the corporate structure. The Crisis Management Team should be composed of managers from such departments as legal, security (assets protection and risk management), finance, human resources, personnel, and public/government relations. In large corporations, local or country Crisis Management Teams should be structured to report to the corporate Crisis Management Team regarding any crisis and/or response. The local manager should appoint a senior executive as the team's coordinator prior to the development of a local Crisis Management Plan; a company official should contact the nearest Embassy or Consulate for assistance and coordination. Each embassy or consulate can provide advice to private American organizations regarding emergency planning.

The Crisis Management Team must operate within the guidelines of general authority set forth by the corporation board of directors or Executive Committee. The plan must resolve fixed issues in advance and deal only with variable elements during the crisis.

The organizational structure of the local Crisis Management Team will depend on the corporate resources available. The organization should be chaired by a senior company official who will be the Crisis Management Coordinator. The local or country Crisis Management Team should also include representation from such departments or functions as administration, legal, security, finance, personnel, communications, and public relations.

Crisis Management Planning Guide

It is recommended that each corporate headquarters develop a Crisis Management Plan and a Crisis Management Team to coordinate corporate crisis activities and decisions on which local or country plans are based. This coordination will create consistency and offer corporate security officers and other senior management officials an opportunity to address matters in the country plans that are specific to the country.

When the corporate Crisis Management Team and/or headquarters approve the local Crisis Management Plan, the Crisis Management Coordinator should conduct drills of the various elements of the plan to ensure that they are realistic and can be implemented in real-life conditions.

The Crisis Management Plan, or portions thereof, should be both in English and in the local language so that all employees can contribute fully in implementing it in an emergency.

Crisis Management Plans will differ from country to country. In some countries certain elements of the Crisis Management Plan may be unnecessary and/or inappropriate.

Sensitive elements of the Crisis Management Plan that cannot be shared with all employees should be appropriately marked with a company classification stating the level of sensitivity of the document and the distribution controls.

CRISIS MANAGEMENT TEAM FUNCTIONS

Functions of the Corporate Crisis Management Team

The corporate Crisis Management Team will manage any incidents directly affecting corporate Headquarters (management, employees, and assets) and designated subsidiary companies. It will also act as the decision-making authority for the management of the incident by subsidiary local Crisis Management Teams.

To ensure a consistent corporate response, the corporate Crisis Management Team should consider the utility of dispatching a Crisis Management Team representative to the location involved; that representative will thereafter assist in the activities of the local Crisis Management Team. These representatives should be briefed on their terms of reference toward local officials and U.S. Government representatives.

The corporate Crisis Management Team, under the direction of the Crisis Management Coordinator, should be responsible for developing and communicating to company business units and local Crisis Management Teams the applicable procedures and practices to be used.

Functions of the Local Crisis Management Team

- The local Crisis Management Team will appoint the Crisis Management Team members to develop the information needed and resources available. In making functional assignments, some responsibilities may require 24-hour coverage in certain situations. Alternates should be identified for each function. Neither members of the Crisis Management Team nor their alternates should be personally involved in the incident being managed.

- The team will formulate and develop detailed plans and procedures for handling emergency situations.

- A crisis management center should be located within the company facility. It should have the necessary equipment available for rapid activation during an emergency. The equipment could include as a minimum, communications equipment, tape recorders, emergency plans and procedures, a log to record all actions taken during the crisis, necessary office equipment and supplies, and appropriate maps and building plans, as deemed necessary. Support personnel should be identified.

- An assessment of the nature, degree, and likelihood of threats to corporate interests (personnel, facilities, information, and other assets) should be conducted to determine the vulnerability of company personnel, facilities, or assets to those threats.

- The team will communicate the contents of the Crisis Management Plan to the appropriate employees.

- The team will test the Crisis Management Plan on a regular basis to ensure that it is feasible and realistic. Whenever the plan is found deficient, immediate corrections should be made. The plan should contain the names and telephone numbers of key government and embassy personnel and private organizations and individuals that the Crisis Management Team should consider briefing or consulting with before, during, or directly after an emergency situation.

Responsibilities of the Corporate Crisis Management Team

- The corporate Crisis Management Team will develop corporate strategies and policies.

- The corporate Crisis Management Team should be responsible for, and oversee, all actions of the local Crisis Management Team.

- To facilitate company communications, the corporate Crisis Management Team may need to dispatch a representative to the location involved.

Responsibilities of the Local Crisis Management Team

The members and alternates of the Crisis Management Team should be assigned the responsibilities that follow:

1. The Crisis Management Coordinator is the person responsible for preparing and implementing the Crisis Management Plan. This person should speak English, receive proper training, possess the appropriate psychological makeup, and be known at the U.S. Embassy or consulate. The Crisis Management Coordinator directs and supervises the members of the local Crisis Management Team and is responsible for the following tasks:

    a. Preparing the Crisis Management Plan.

    b. Forwarding the Crisis Management Plan to the corporate Crisis Management Coordinator for review by the corporate Crisis Management Team representing specific functional areas.

    c. Coordinating the Crisis Management Plan with the responsible regional security officer or the most appropriate official at the U.S. Embassy or consulate.

    d. Reviewing the Crisis Management Plan on a semiannual basis to ensure that it is current.

    e. Training personnel who have Crisis Management Plan responsibilities.

    f. Practicing the Crisis Management Plan and evaluating Crisis Management Team responses.

    g. Ensuring that all appropriate corporate company employees are aware of the Crisis Management Plan and its functions.

    h. Preparing a written report for senior management regarding the Crisis Management Team's training and its subsequent evaluation.

i. Coordinating the Crisis Management Plan with responsible officials of all in-country facilities or sites.

j. Establishing liaison with the U.S. Embassy or consulate security officer, local law enforcement, public emergency officials, and other corporate Crisis Management Teams, if appropriate.

k. Implementing the plan when directed by the senior company official or authorized designee.

SECURITY INCIDENT COORDINATOR

Security/Incident Coordinator: The Security/ Incident Coordinator is responsible for briefing the Crisis Management Team on the nature and degree of threat to company interests (personnel, facilities, information, and assets). This coordinator initiates investigations to validate threats and is authorized to convene the Crisis Management Team when appropriate. He or she also provides security and is prepared to brief the Crisis Management Team on physical protection of all assets during times of crisis; coordinates warden activities; and maintains law enforcement liaison.

Administration-Personnel-Medical-Coordinator: This coordinator should make available personnel and medical records as well as essential services. He or she should also ensure that the embassy consular officer has a list of all U.S. citizens (including information on dependents), employed by the firm in advance of any crisis.

Legal Advisor: The Legal Advisor is responsible for assessing the corporate liabilities and risks (criminal and civil) as well as personal liability of Crisis Management Team members for Crisis Management Plan actions.

Financial Coordinator: The Financial Coordinator should establish bank sources for funds in the country involved and be familiar with currency requirements and how funds can be provided on short notice.

Public Relations Coordinator: This coordinator should develop and maintain conventional media relationships for crisis-situations, including contact with host government press agencies, as well as the Public Affairs Officer at the U.S. Foreign Service post. He or she is responsible for employee communications during crisis periods and for assistance to an affected employee and/or his or her family, if appropriate.

Business Unit Manager: This individual represents the operating component or business unit that is the victim of the incident.

ACTIONS DURING A CRISIS

When a crisis situation or local condition that may have an adverse impact on the safety or security of the company's personnel or assets develops, consideration should be given to the following actions:

- Convene the Crisis Management Team.

- Verify the threat.

- Advise the corporate Crisis Management Team of the crisis and anticipated actions of the local Crisis Management Team.

- Assess the crisis, including possible outcomes. In civil unrest situations, for example, the crisis may threaten many company assets. As one asset is protected, another may become vulnerable. A desired goal of crisis management is to develop and plan responses so that the asset under attack is protected yet other assets are not placed in jeopardy.

- Obtain executive profile information files, if appropriate.

- In kidnap or hostage situations, activate and dispatch to crisis location the local negotiating team; be prepared to implement a negotiated agreement.

- Determine company options and goals in responding to the crisis.

- Delegate duties not in the Crisis Management Plan to be performed by Crisis Management Team members.

- Maintain liaison with the corporate security structure, advising them of the problem and action to be taken.

- Advise the U.S. Embassy of the actions being taken.

- Report local Crisis Management Team actions to corporate Crisis Management Team organization and update those reports as necessary.

- Notify host government and law enforcement agency at the appropriate level.

- Establish liaison locally as deemed appropriate (other American or friendly company, chamber of commerce, etc.).

- Schedule further Crisis Management Team meetings to handle or monitor crisis as deemed necessary.

- Provide the location and telephone number of the Crisis Management Team crisis management center and the alternative off-site location to appropriate personnel.

- In the event of hostage release be prepared for evacuation, debriefing, and rehabilitation.

CRISIS MANAGEMENT TEAM RESPONSE TO ACTS OF TERRORISM

Key Local Contacts

The local Crisis Management Team should maintain a list of all Crisis Management Team members and 24-hour telephone numbers. In addition, the Crisis Management Plan should list all U.S. Embassy and host government agencies and security contacts (names, titles, addresses, and 24-hour telephone numbers) who would respond to acts of terrorism such as bombings, seizures of owned facilities, assassinations or attempted assassinations, assaults on personnel and/or dependents, Kidnappings or attempted Kidnappings, and hostage taking. The following are suggested contacts at the U.S. Embassy:

- Ambassador.

- Deputy Chief of Mission.

- Economic Officer.

- Administrative Officer.

- Commercial Officer.

- Regional Security Officer.

- Consular Officer.

Suggested contacts with the host government, depending on circumstances, might be the following:

- Head of State.

- Minister of Interior.

- Government intelligence agency.

- Chief of Police.

- Senior police official responsible for area in which company facilities and residences are situated.

- Senior official responsible for airport security.

- Senior official responsible for investigations.

- Senior official responsible for responding to acts of terrorism.

Upon receipt of a terrorist threat, action against company personnel, dependents, or facilities, the following action should be taken:

- The local Security/Incident Coordinator should notify the corporate security department by telephone, telex, computer or telegram.

- The local company senior executive should immediately notify the respective corporate management of an emergency situation who, along with corporate security, will notify the corporate Crisis Management Team of the emergency.

- The local Crisis Management Team should immediately begin efforts to confirm the incident and evaluate the emergency.

Crisis Reports

The immediate passing of information about an emergency event is vital to allow the correct functioning of the corporate Crisis Management Team and to permit the corporation to respond to its responsibilities. The report should include:

- Nature and circumstances of threat or incident, including date, time, and location.

- Nature of threat or attack and injuries and damages sustained.

- Full data concerning affected employees, including names and addresses of next of kin in the order that they or other interested parties should be notified.

- Report on contacts and assistance offers to next of kin including their specific location.

- If kidnapping and/or hostage taking occurs, provide:

a. Location, number, and identity of victims.

　　b. Number and identity of terrorists involved, organization(s), weapons used, or other descriptive information.

　　c. Terrorist demands or claims.

　　d. Local assessment of the situation, including effect on business operations.

　　e. Report injuries, if any.

- Initial actions taken by host government to respond to terrorist threat.

- If company personnel, dependents, and facilities are threatened or are subjects of a terrorist attack; describe the local company's preliminary effort in arranging enhanced security, medical assistance, etc., with host country officials (police, foreign ministry, etc.).

- Precautionary measures taken for other employees at the location of the incident and elsewhere in the host country.

- Telephone number and the name of the U.S. Embassy (consulate) officer monitoring the incident.

- Statement on whether police are involved or whether media coverage has occurred.

- Name of person sending message along with complete address, telephone number, and telex number for future contacts.

CRISIS MANAGEMENT TEAM ASSESSMENT OF A HOSTAGE SITUATION

As the terrorist act unfolds, the Crisis Management Team, in conjunction with the host country and embassy officials should continue to review the following:

- Threats by terrorists.

- Need for extra security measures, security arrangements for the hostage family, special communications arrangements, and supplemental personnel and equipment.

Terrorists

What is known about the terrorists?

What are their goals, philosophies, and tactics?

What pressure points affect the terrorists i.e., local political parties, state supporters, religious groups, other sympathizers, or international organizations?

Host Government

What is host government policy regarding terrorist demands?

What are host government capabilities to negotiate with terrorists?

What are host country laws regarding negotiating and paying ransom to terrorists?

Hostages and Other Victims

What is their significance to the terrorists?

Are health and personnel records available on hostages?

Do hostages have any capability to assist in achieving their own release?

Is psychiatric expertise available?

Are aircraft available for negotiators, psychiatrists, medical staff, security, etc.?

What on-site intelligence resources are available?

If there are victims, what arrangements should be made for treatment of the injured or disposition of remains and personal property?

Action Options

Should senior U.S. Government officials or corporate senior executives be encouraged to intervene with the host government?

Consider the most senior level at which contact with the host government should be established.

Critical negotiating issues with the hostages include:

    a. The potential crucial threat to the life of the hostage.

    b. The corporation has the authority to negotiate release.

    c. The company will cooperate with law enforcement officials.

    d. It must be recognized that negotiating is an extremely sensitive issue and corporations should consider, in advance, responses to possible hostage negotiations.

What company resources should be deployed to the scene of the incident?

If no Crisis Management Team exists locally in that country, should a negotiating team be deployed?

What immediate assistance should the company provide to the families of the hostages and other victims?

What security measures need to be taken to protect other senior employees of the company or its assets?

James R. Doyle

Hostage Negotiations

In the event of a hostage taking, some type of communication can be anticipated in the form of a letter, a telephone call, an audio tape or videotape, or possibly a hand-delivered message or tape to the office or home of the hostage. If legal, and/or appropriate to do so, place a recorder on the appropriate telephones at home and office of the hostage and monitor them around the clock in the early stages of the incident. Also assign someone, if the police do not, to establish effective liaison with the appropriate post office to ensure that all mail directed to the hostage's home is immediately delivered, regardless of the time of day or night. Handle the contents of such mail with great care to ensure that it is not unduly handled, to protect latent fingerprints and other evidence.

Telephones in many foreign countries are monitored regularly by the authorities, especially in crisis situations. It is necessary, therefore, not to expect privacy of such telephone conversations. If sensitive calls must be made, go to a public telephone or use an encryption device on your telephone.

In any crisis situation requiring negotiations or dialogue with terrorists or hostage takers, it is imperative that the Crisis Management Team member responsible for conducting the dialogue not have ultimate decision-making authority and should make that fact clearly understood to the terrorists or hostage takers. This strategy provides negotiators with a credible delaying tactic because they can explain that they will do the best that they can but that they must take up the problem with their boss, etc. The top-ranking executive, either at the local or headquarters site, should never be the Crisis Management Team member cast in the role of the negotiator.

CRISIS MANAGEMENT TEAM AND CATASTROPHES AND NATURAL DISASTERS

As soon as possible after a catastrophe and/or disaster occur, corporate headquarters should be notified. The corporate Crisis Management Team should consider the following:

- Confirm that the appropriate officials at corporate headquarters have been informed in accordance with the Crisis Management Plan.

- Designate telephone numbers to be used for the crisis period (equipped with recording equipment) and then make arrangements for 24-hour manning of the telephone. Establish communication with appropriate U.S. and host government entities.

The initial report should provide as much of the following information as possible to Corporate Headquarters:

- Caller's name (spelled out) and job title.

- Facility location (city and country).

- Date, time, severity, and location of crisis.

- Nature of crisis.

- Number of people affected (killed, injured, and evacuated).

- Extent of damage to company facilities.

- Effect on business operations.

- Host government involvement.

- Telephone, computer, FAX, and telex number for future contacts.

- Alternative communications channel.

- Nature and extent of assistance requested from corporate headquarters.

Initiate those portions of Crisis Management Plan associated with disasters and/or catastrophes.

James R. Doyle

COMMUNICATIONS IN A CRISIS SITUATION

Reliable communication is a key factor in the successful management of any crisis. To ensure that adequate communications are available in emergency circumstances, the following basic capabilities should be considered:

- A local communications net with employees and authorities to include an employee warden system.

- A national link to locations in the country where other facilities are located and national authorities are headquartered.

- An international link to the company's corporate headquarters.

CRISIS MANAGEMENT TEAM AND PUBLIC AFFAIRS INFORMATION

Coordination between the company spokesperson at the scene, the local Crisis Management Team, and the corporate Crisis Management Team is essential. Guidance from the corporate Crisis Management Team should be requested on any policy consideration or interpretation. All releases to the media should pass through and be cleared by the Corporate Crisis Management Team. Clear communications and coordination for media releases are vital during a crisis. Misinformation or failure to consider all factors before commenting to the media can jeopardize security and the objectives of the corporation.

Responsibilities of the Spokesperson

The spokesperson should consider the following:

- The spokesperson will require a direct line of communication with the local and corporate Crisis Management Teams to assure access to the latest information.
- If the crisis is extended in duration, an alternate spokesperson should also be considered.
- The spokesperson should have a designated work location to facilitate receipt and dissemination of updated information.
- The spokesperson should consider having available a briefing room equipped with telephone jacks and telephones that can be made available to the media at briefings.
- The spokesperson should deal only with accredited media representatives.
- The spokesperson should have access to officials and experts who can provide background information on all aspects of the specific event.
- The spokesperson should issue factual information at periodic briefings.
- All press inquiries should be referred to the authorized spokesperson. No comment should be made unless it is authorized by the Crisis Management Team.

Handling Media Interests

- It is essential to establish a regular coordination with corporate headquarters and the corporate Crisis Management Team concerning statements to be made to the press.
- The spokesperson should not act as the terrorist's "messenger" to the public.
- Live interviews with participants and the use of mini-cameras at or near the site of the incident should be discouraged.

- Prudence by the press regarding actions that might frighten the terrorists or promote their cause should be urged.

- The counterproductive aspects of reporting on any operational activities of the police, military, or their counter-terrorism forces should be emphasized.

- Interviews with unknown or amateur "experts" on terrorists' motivation or background should be carefully reviewed and considered.

CRISIS MANAGEMENT EVALUATION

Following any crisis incident, a critical review or evaluation of the crisis management actions taken should be conducted. A review should be conducted of the Crisis Management Plan and the Crisis Management Team planning and assessment procedures and how Crisis Management Team responded to the crisis.

Methods used for evaluation could include:

- A written critique of the entire event by all Crisis Management Team members.

- Interviews with the victim(s) and/or family.

- Final evaluation report, with recommendations for any required changes in the current Crisis Management Plan.

- Local Crisis Management Team report to the corporate Crisis Management Team of final details of the incident and analysis of the team's operation.

BUSINESS RECOVERY

An integral part of a corporate Crisis Management Plan is the organized recovery phase. The following elements should be considered in the recovery phase:

- A report detailing the loss of all key personnel due to a crisis incident.

- Assignment of temporary replacements for affected management personnel.

- Development of a damage assessment report.

- Provide assistance or time off for personnel so that their personal losses (family members injured), homes or vehicles can be properly handled.

- Replacement of critical materials and equipment.

- Establish the availability of business records. (Prior planning is required so that the appropriate records have been copied and/ or stored at a secure or other location.)

- Implement computer disaster recovery plans to include company minicomputers and personal computers.

- Prepare a final management report including a recovery financial analysis.

EMERGENCY MANAGEMENT EXERCISES GENERAL

A comprehensive crisis management plan should include a simulation exercise. The exercise should include potential crisis events and other emergency situations.

Previous sections in this book have dealt with several aspects of crisis management. This section offers some suggestions on how to develop an exercise that will enable both corporate officials and crisis team members in developing a critical analysis of how to effectively use any and all available resources. As with the Crisis Management Plan in general, the suggestions presented here could also be used by other groups including public service, volunteer etc, in developing their own emergency management exercises.

EXERCISE GUIDELINES

We should first define the organizational system that is the subject of an exercise. This may not always be the entire organization. It may be an operating entity in a specific geographical location or locations. In defining the organizational system, a good first step is to analyze the organization's mission and its capabilities to accomplish that mission. Such specific factors, such as studies of markets for products and services, could play a key role in defining the organizational system, particularly when the organization has a vital link to the indigenous economy, some public policy issue, or a unique program.

The next task is to identify those forces that impact the organizational system. In an era of low intensity conflict, critical forces could include food, energy, strategic materials, financial services, drugs, population growth, economic development, manufacturing and trade, technology transfer, environmental pollution, space travel, law of the sea, terrorism, business fraud, and the theft of information.

Next, we need to assemble enough information to analyze the trends and major relationships associated with each force. This type of analysis can be used to set the theoretical framework for various emergency management exercises. Sources of information in developing the framework may include interviews with area experts; market analysis; politico-military analysis; chamber of commerce and private sector contacts; liaison with government departments; and indigenous contacts in business, industry, and public organizations. The information can be used to develop a baseline scenario or normative scenario for the exercise.

Depending on the nature of your business and the potential threat, you may want to consider participation in an established emergency exercise system that has already been developed by either the local, state or federal government agency. Any of these agencies can tell you about scheduled events and how you may qualify for inclusion.

DEVELOPING AN EXERCISE SCENARIO

The scenario is the heart of the emergency management exercise because it has the potential to describe, in detail, probable, possible, impossible, or unfavorable events in the future. Events in the scenario may occur simultaneously or in sequence. They tell a story about the real world or the logical outcome of a series of future events.

To write scenarios, an organization pulls together an ad hoc team representing multiple disciplines related to the core business and the usual support functions of personnel, information systems, finance, security, legal, public relations, program managers, marketing and strategic planning, and sales. There may be other functions unique to a particular organization. The team should be given a time frame for envisioning the emergency situation and some guidance on certain assumptions for problems and change. The team should validate those assumptions and determine whether certain events could realistically occur now or in the future. A full description of those events could present a complete picture of likely emergencies the organization may have to face. Each event should relate to one of the validated assumptions. Each event in the emergency situation must be clearly defined and documented. If it is challenged during exercise play, it may become the basis for an alternative scenario.

The concept of alternative scenarios permits the group to play several possible emergency events simultaneously. This complexity will enable management to look at the effect of multiple possibilities on the total organizational system. The use of alternative scenarios should help management envision the best courses of action in real emergencies.

The scenario technique is particularly suited for emergency management exercises to be used by business, government, or industry in politico-military, politico-economic, and other international issues.

Results from those scenario exercises can be used as a lead-in to other analyses.

Some advantages of the scenario technique include:

- It can call attention, dramatically and persuasively, to a large range of possibilities that must be considered when analyzing emergency actions and alternatives.

- It can serve as a realistic case study when there is a shortage of actual examples.

- It makes it possible to envision possible alternative outcomes of present events.

- It enables key management players to visualize the influence of certain government and industry leaders on social, economic, cultural, political, economic, and military factors.

- It prevents reliance on pure abstract considerations and forces an analysis of real details.

The exercise team, in its role as control element for the exercise, should perform the following tasks:

- Assemble a wide variety of credible materials.

- Assure the relevancy of scenario information to the organizational system.
- Develop and write the various scenarios.

- Develop and write the combined exercise plan.

- Schedule and regulate the pace of the exercise.

- Supervise the physical layout, which includes communications, use of references, sources, and meeting facilities.

- Develop a method to facilitate a working liaison with top management.

- Evaluate the exercise and the players.

Control element's feedback session: In this session, the control element gives the management team its interpretation and observations. The management team can compare the results of this feedback with its self-evaluation.

Joint planning and future dialogue: Generally, the control element members will agree to informal networking after the exercise. This permits future dialogue and insight into the response and content of the baseline and alternative future scenarios.

EMERGENCY EXERCISE SUMMARY

Following is a summary of the plan requirements in developing an Emergency Management Team Exercise:

Top Management

- Define the organizational system.

- Identify the emergency situations impacting the system.

- Review those trends impacting each situation.

Exercise Control Team

- Develop a baseline scenario.

- Develop a variety of alternative scenarios.

- Create an exercise layout.

- Conduct a comprehensive exercise evaluation.

  a. Self-evaluation.

  b. Control element feedback session.

  c. Joint planning and future dialogue.

Administrative supplies and support for the exercise may include the following:

- Telecommunication support for telephones and other equipment as required.
- Two rooms (not more than 60 feet apart) and a neutral meeting room.
- A secure storage container for confidential information.
- Flip pads.
- Felt tip markers.
- Masking tape.
- Scotch tape.
- Writing pads.
- Paper clips.
- Word Processing support.
- Binder clips.
- Two-hole paper punch.
- Roll correction tape.

- Burn bags for destroying papers.

- Scissors.

- Area maps (as required).

- Portable clock.

- Refreshments and comfort items.

- List of ad hoc team members including:

   a. Names.

   b. Telephone numbers.

   c. Titles.

   d. Specialty areas.

CIVIL UNREST

The objective of this section is to provide suggestions for managing a crisis situation such as criminal acts, civil unrest, coupe etc. Although it is not possible to plan for every eventuality, it is only prudent to make certain contingency plans outlining how company employees should react in emergency situations.

Emergency management is to prepare for response to and recovery from emergencies of any kind. In developing a plan for emergency preparedness, the first step is to assess the current level of vulnerability. For example, businesses located in a country that has experienced a history of anti-American demonstrations should determine the probability of its facility or employees becoming involved in a demonstration or other more serious action and devise ways to protect against such incidents. Alternatively, businesses located in countries with a history of coups or a high crime rate should place a high priority in developing plans to deal with these emergencies. However, regardless of the location of a company or the history of security problems in the region, all areas of emergency planning should be included in each plan. Often, a relatively benign political situation can change quickly.

The first step in developing any plan for emergency preparedness is to obtain significant management commitment to preparedness. To ensure an effective security plan, every company should appoint an on-site security manager and develop a Crisis Management Plan. This person should be the point of contact for the company regarding security matters; his or her responsibilities should include:

- Ensuring that an organized method of disseminating information exists.

- Guaranteeing that lines of communication between the nearest U.S. Embassy, Consulate and Civil Authorities exist.

- Developing a "safe area" to retreat to in the event of an emergency.

American companies located overseas should make immediate contact with the nearest U.S. Embassy to receive information on the criminal, law enforcement, political, and terrorist situation in the host country. The U.S. Embassy can provide information regarding what you can expect in the way of assistance from your government and the host government.

The designated security manager should make a point to establish contact with other American companies and organizations in the area to determine their experience with the law enforcement and the criminal elements in the area. If no other American companies or organizations are represented, the manager should try to locate companies or organizations with which the U.S. Government has close ties.

It is recommended that periodic contact be made with representatives of these other firms or organizations to exchange information on criminal activities, threats, and the reaction of the responsible law enforcement agencies.

The U.S. Embassy should be provided with a list of key company personnel and telephone numbers for contact in an emergency. Each company or organization should develop an emergency notification system to be used to contact employees or their families.

If a company does not have a medical staff, it is recommended that a list of English-speaking doctors be developed for use in an emergency situation involving mass casualties. This information can also be obtained from the nearest U.S. Embassy or consulate.

CRIMINAL ACTS

In many countries, local or national law enforcement officials cannot be depended on for even basic services, because of substandard or nonexistent training and low pay. Therefore, employees should be trained to accept responsibility for their own security, through security awareness seminars, books, and other information. Training should take place on a frequent basis to reinforce individual awareness and responsibility.

Residential Safety

The following suggestions should be considered in planning for residential security:

- Housing for employees should be in relatively safe, stable neighborhoods. The U.S. Embassy, local police, and other Americans in the area can provide information regarding neighborhoods.

- The on-site security manager should be responsible for approving a residence. Particular attention should be given to the surrounding neighborhood, that is, the condition of streets, density of vehicular and pedestrian traffic, access into and out of the neighborhood, and the location and nationality of owners of surrounding residences. Additionally, the location and types of trees and shrubs should be noted, as well as the presence of parking and the quality of lighting at night.

- Another important factor to be considered in residential selection is the type of residence. An apartment located above the ground or first floor is usually considered more secure than a single family dwelling. However, if an apartment is chosen, care should be taken to ensure that there are no exterior balconies or footholds that would enable would-be thieves to climb up to the apartment from the ground. In addition, apartments should not be selected on floors above the fire fighting and rescue capabilities of the local fire department.

- Once a residence is approved, adequate technical (alarm systems) and physical (solid exterior doors and fences and/or walls) security should be provided.

Personal Safety

Personal safety is largely the responsibility of each individual. Regardless of the local threat, you should take the same safety precautions that you take when in a large urban area of the United States. The following suggestions should be considered when planning for personal safety:

- Keep a low profile. Do not dress provocatively or wear flashy or obviously expensive jewelry.

- Learn about the city as soon as you arrive. Most large cities have areas considered generally unsafe after dark or even during the day. Additionally, there may be some areas where Americans are at greater risk.

- Do not walk alone after dark.

- Keep alert. If you are walking and believe someone is following, go to a public or well lighted area.

- Women should keep a firm grasp on purses to avoid being an easy target for a snatch-and-run attack. Keep the amount of money and credit cards you carry at a minimum.

- Learn at least a few phrases in the local language so you can ask for help, if needed. In some situations a cry for "help" will go unanswered but a cry of "fire" may attract attention.

- Keep your vehicle in good repair with an adequate amount of fuel at all times. Keep the doors locked, and do not pick up hitchhikers. If possible, avoid parking on the street or in unattended parking lots.

CIVIL UNREST

In many countries, coups are not an uncommon occurrence, and all Americans residing in those areas should make special efforts to keep abreast of the local political situation, because it can sometimes change almost overnight. It is particularly important to use local employees' contacts and knowledge.

The following suggestions should be considered when preparing for civil unrest:

- Keep lines of communication between businesses and the U.S. Embassy or consulate open during times of unrest.

- Assume a high level of responsibility for your personal protection. Don't rely totally on the U.S. government for direction. Company management may want to respond more quickly in accordance with corporate requirements.

- Monitor local news media television, radio, and newspapers—for political developments or increasing anti-American rhetoric.

- Maintain adequate (2-3 weeks) stockpiles of nonperishable food and drinking water.

- Keep vehicles fueled for an immediate evacuation.

- In the event an evacuation, employees will have the option of sending their dependents to a safe country.

- In times of unrest, have a bag packed for each member of the family for evacuation on short notice.

- For emergencies, keep on hand an appropriate amount of money and/or traveler's checks.

- If the threat warrants, consider having available an open airline ticket available for each family member to a "safe haven" country. You should check with the appropriate airlines in advance for their specific rules and conditions covering refunds etc.

- Consolidate important personal records and documents for easy access and transportation. Keep passports and necessary visas up to date.

- Have a pre-planned telephone contact system to ensure that all employees are aware of what is happening.

If a coup is attempted, the following suggestions should be considered:

- Remain at present location if possible until further instructions are received from the company security manager or U.S. Embassy or consulate. Remember that you have to assume a high level of personal responsibility and make decisions that are in your best interest which might include moving to another location to avoid death or injury.

- Under no circumstances should individuals go to the troubled area(s) to find out what is occurring.

- Stay away from windows to avoid sniper fire. If possible, relocate to a room that offers the greatest degree of safety from outside gunfire. When necessary, seek added protection by lying on the floor behind a durable piece of furniture.

- Stay aware of locations of emergency egress in the event of a forced evacuation, and keep an emergency bag with important documents nearby.

- If you are in the open or on the street, seek cover and remain close to the ground.

- If possible remain in contact with the U.S. Embassy or consulate or the company security manager.

- Monitor local media stations for news updates.

WAR OR ACTS OF WAR

In some areas of the world such as the Middle East, there have been almost constant wars in progress over a period of many years. For example, since the end of World War II, few of the countries that make up the Middle East have been without war or internal unrest for extensive periods.

In limited or local wars, life goes on and so does business. In any case, the political situations can change rapidly and should be monitored continuously. Since a war can have the same effect on personnel, resources, and physical plant as a violent coup, the actions just described for safety during a coup also apply to the war situation. One obvious difference between a war and a coup is that in a war situation you will definitely know the belligerents and their attitude toward Americans. In the event of a coup, that information may not be readily available.

If your business is associated with or even perceived to be associated with or contributing to the war effort of either party, it may become a target. In this case, your survival will depend on the host government or the attacker if you are in captured territory.

In the event of any act of war, the first consideration will be the possible impact on American expatriate employees and whether they and their families should be evacuated. In any event, this section will provide some suggestions that may be helpful in the decision making process.

SABOTAGE

Acts of sabotage against your business may be initiated for a number of reasons and may come in many forms. The nature of the specific acts committed will, to a great extent, determine how they should be handled. For example, the prevention and control of internal sabotage is frequently the primary responsibility of the organization's security manager. Prevention and control of external sabotage will normally require the assistance of the local police, although in some instances, depending on location, targets, and severity, the host country's defense forces may become involved.

In the event of sabotage directed at equipment or personnel located outside your facilities you may consider the following suggestions to reduce your vulnerability:

- Immediately report all suspicious incidents to the company security manager or police.

- Consider assigning guards to protect fixed assets or to escort personnel, equipment and supply shipments while en route.

- Provide two-way radios for personnel and equipment operators and train them to properly use the radios.

- Vary routes and times of movement of personnel and equipment to avoid routines.

Depending on the nature of the threat, the first priority may be to gather all personnel in one location (on company premises) or to evacuate the premises and have all employees return to their living quarters and remain there with their families to await further instructions.

NATURAL DISASTERS

People have been unable to prevent natural phenomena, which often result in natural disasters, such as cyclones, hurricanes, typhoons, earthquakes, tornadoes, floods, lightning strikes, volcanic eruptions, and the like.

The objective of this section is to provide the individual or American company working abroad with a set of suggestions for surviving and minimizing property damage from natural disasters often referred to as "acts of god". The suggestions in this section may also be applicable in the U.S.

Information provided here must also be supplemented with information available from the government of your country of residence. For example, warning signals for approaching storms may differ from one country to the next, or evacuation from low-lying terrain before an imminent flood may be mandatory rather than optional in some countries. It is your responsibility and the responsibility of your loved ones to learn and abide by local laws, customs, and caveats dealing with natural disasters in your host country. It is not likely that all members of a family unit will be together at home when a natural disaster strikes, therefore, you should ensure that all members of the family are sufficiently conversant with the necessary precautionary guidelines in advance. This advance planning and awareness will ensure peace of mind for all members of the family.

CYCLONES/HURRICANES/TYPHOONS

Tropical cyclones, hurricanes, and typhoons are regional names for what is essentially the same phenomenon. Depressions in the tropics that develop into storms are called tropical cyclones in some parts of the world, hurricanes in other areas, and typhoons in still other areas. For the purposes of this discussion, these storms will be referred to as cyclones. Winds in tropical cyclones reach constant speeds of 74 miles per hour or more and blow in a large spiral around a relatively calm center know as the "eye." In the Northern Hemisphere, the circulation is counterclockwise, and in the Southern Hemisphere, it is clockwise. Stated simply, cyclones are giant whirlwinds in which air moves in a large tightening spiral around the eye. Near the center of the cyclone, winds may gust to more than 200 miles per hour. The entire storm can dominate an ocean surface and lower atmosphere over tens of thousands of square miles.

The eye of the cyclone is deceptively insidious. If the storm is moving at its average speed of 20-30 miles an hour and the eye passes directly through a location, the winds may subside to relative calm and torrential rains may yield to a partly cloudy or even a clear sky. Many people have been killed or injured when the calm eye lured them out of shelter, only to be caught in the maximum winds at the far side of the eye, where the wind blows from a direction opposite that of the leading half of the storm.

Tropical cyclones are frequently described as the most devastating of all natural phenomena because of their tremendous size, relatively slow movement, and at times absence of movement, as well as their highly erratic path or direction.

Clearly, the tornado is a much more violent storm (with wind speeds approaching 300 miles per hour), but its time on Earth is short and its devastating destructive path is infinitesimal by comparison to the cyclone. The average path width of a tornado is 425 yards and the average path length only 25 miles. Consider the worst cyclone on record, which struck Bangladesh in 1970, killing more than 200,000 people with damage in the billions of dollars. No tornado has ever even closely approached such unprecedented proportions of death, human suffering, and property damage.

Recommended Action to Lessen the Effect of Cyclones

Over the years, much research and experimentation have been undertaken by meteorological scientists, governments, and emergency planners throughout the world on the subject of tropical cyclones. These efforts indicate that the effect of cyclones can be substantially reduced, especially personal injury and loss of life, by effective emergency preparedness. The objective of the following suggestions is to stimulate awareness in planning for such and event. Do not adopt an attitude that nothing can be done about natural disasters. A good understanding of storm phenomena, effective planning, and adequate preparation will lessen the impact on you, your loved ones, and your property.

Safety Rules—Before the Storm

The following suggestions should be considered in preparing for the storm:

- Most developed nations have cyclone/hurricane/ typhoon warning or alerting systems in place. Learn and abide by them.

- Listen to television and radio reports concerning progress of the storm.

- Enter each storm season prepared. June through November is the hurricane season in the United States, but seasons vary in other parts of the world. Learn the months and duration of the season where you reside.

- Establish an emergency supply of boards, tools, batteries, first- aid supplies, nonperishable foods, and other equipment that you will need in the event a cyclone strikes.

- When a cyclone becomes imminent in your area, plan your time before the storm arrives and avoid the last minute rush, which might leave you marooned or unprepared.

- Remain calm until the emergency ends.

- Leave low-lying areas that may be swept by high tides or storm waves.

- Leave mobile homes for more substantial shelter. Mobile homes are particularly vulnerable to overturning during strong winds. Damage can be minimized by securing the homes with heavy cables anchored in concrete footings.

- Moor your boat securely before the storm arrives or evacuate it to a designated safe area. When your boat is moored, leave it and do not return until the wind and waves subside.

- Board up windows or protect them with storm shutters or tape. Danger to small windows is mainly from wind-driven debris. Larger windows may be broken by wind pressure.

- Secure outdoor objects that might be blown away or uprooted. Garbage cans, garden tools, toys, signs, porch furniture, and a number of other harmless items become missiles in cyclone winds. Anchor them or store them inside before the storm strikes.

- If possible, remove coconuts and other heavy fruits such as mangos from trees before the storm strikes and secure them so they do not become flying missiles.

- Store drinking water in clean bathtubs, jugs, bottles, and cooking utensils; the water supply may be contaminated by flooding.

- Monitor the storm's position through radio broadcasts on a battery-powered radio. Utilities will almost certainly be interrupted.

- Keep your car fueled. Service stations may be inoperable for several days after the storm strikes because of flooding or interrupted electrical power.

- If your home is sturdy and on high ground remain there; if it is not, move to a designated shelter and stay there until the storm is over.

- Remain indoors during the cyclone. Travel is extremely dangerous.

- Know where emergency medical assistance can be obtained and where Red Cross disaster stations will be set up before the storm hits. Learn the safe routes to those locations.

- Beware of the eye of the cyclone. If the calm storm center passes directly overhead, there will be a lull in the wind lasting from a few minutes to half an hour or more. Stay in a safe place unless emergency repairs are absolutely necessary. Remember, at the other side of the eye, the winds rise very rapidly to cyclone force and come from the opposite direction.

When the Cyclone Has Passed

The following suggestions should be considered when the storm has passed:

- Stay out of disaster areas. Unless you are qualified to help, your presence might hamper first-aid and rescue work.

- Drive carefully along debris-filled streets. Roads may be undermined and may collapse under the weight of a car. Landslides along roadways are also a hazard.

- Avoid loose or dangling wires, and report them immediately to the power company or the nearest law enforcement officer.

- Report broken sewer or water mains to the water department.

- Prevent fires. Lowered water pressure may make fire-fighting difficult.

- If power has been off during the storm, check refrigerated food for spoilage.

- Remember that cyclones moving inland can cause severe flooding. Stay away from river banks and streams.

Tornadoes spawned by cyclones are among the worst killers in terms of all storms. The following suggestions should be considered in the instance of a cyclone-spawned tornado:

- If you are alerted to a tornado through the radio or if you sight such a storm, seek inside shelter immediately, preferably below ground level.

- If the tornado catches you outside and there is not time to escape, lie flat in the nearest depression such as a ditch or ravine.

- Remain indoors during the storm, preferably in an interior room without windows.

- When electric power is disrupted, turn off appliances and light switches so that electric circuits will not be overloaded when electricity is restored.

- Keep refrigerator and freezer doors shut. Food will stay cold for hours if you keep the cold air inside.

- Use the most perishable foods first.

- Have coloring books and crayons to keep young minds busy to prevent boredom. Keep other appropriate games for your children where they are immediately accessible.

Unfortunately, many people do not prepare in advance for severe storms and they rapidly exhaust their survival supplies. Every home should have a survival kit which is immediately available in the event of a natural disaster. The following suggestions should be considered in preparing a survival kit:

- Flashlight
- Fresh batteries
- Portable radio
- First-aid kit
- Bottled water

- Sterno
- Candles
- Matches
- Canned and nonperishable foods
- Manual can opener
- Hammer
- Nails
- Duct tape
- Plywood sheets
- Rope
- Canvas tarpaulin
- Inflatable raft
- Life preservers
- Cooking and eating utensils
- Plastic bags for storage of waste and trash

TORNADOES

A tornado is a violently swirling column of air in contact with the ground. Tornadoes usually develop from strong or severe thunderstorms. Their time on Earth is short, and their destructive paths are rather small. Yet, when one of these short-lived, local storms marches through populated areas, it leaves a path of almost total destruction. In seconds, a tornado can reduce neighborhoods into rubble.

Although most tornadoes strike during the spring and summer, it is important to realize that they can occur anywhere, at any time. The winds of the tornado can reach speeds of 100 to 300 miles per hour, and the tornado travels at an average speed of 30 miles per hour. Tornadoes can topple buildings, roll mobile homes, uproot trees, hurl people and animals through the air for hundreds of yards, and fill the air with lethal, windborne debris. Since the direction tornadoes travel can be erratic and may change suddenly, get to shelter immediately!

If You Are in a House or Apartment

The following suggestions should be considered in a tornado:

- The safest place is in the basement in a corner against an outside wall or underneath the basement stairway.

- For added protection, get under something strong, such as a workbench or heavy table. If possible, cover your body with a blanket or sleeping bag. Protect your head with anything that is available.

- Avoid windows! Flying debris does most of the killing, and the worst kind of flying debris is broken glass.

- Avoid taking shelter underneath a floor that supports the refrigerator, washing machine, piano, or other heavy objects.

- Avoid rock or brick walls and chimneys. They have a tendency to collapse straight down.

- If the house has no basement or if there is not enough time to get to the basement, move to an interior closet, an interior bath-room, or the innermost hallway on the lowest floor. Because the walls are closely tied together, they will hold together better in the high winds.

If You Are in a Mobile Home

The following suggestions should be considered in a tornado:

- Seek other shelter immediately.

- Do not get under a mobile home.

- Make arrangements with friends or neighbors who have basements. When the weather looks threatening, go there.

Encourage your mobile home community to develop its own shelter.

If You Are in a Motor Vehicle

The following suggestions should be considered in a tornado:

- Do not stay in a motor vehicle during a tornado as it is the least desirable place. Cars, buses, and trucks easily become flying missiles as a result of tornados winds.

- Never try to outrun a tornado in your car.

- Stop your vehicle and get out. Seek shelter someplace else. Try to get into a basement. Do not get under or next to your vehicle; it may roll over on you.

If You Are Outdoors

The following suggestions should be considered in a tornado:

- If you are outdoors and there is no basement or building to get into, get as far underground as possible. Remember, your best chance for survival is to get away from the killing winds.

- Do not stand up and watch the tornado.

- Seek shelter in a ditch, gully, ravine, or culvert. Even just a low spot in the ground is going to give you some protection.

- Do not get into a grove of trees. Remember to protect your head.

If You Are in a Long-Span Building

The following suggestions should be considered in a tornado:

- Grocery stores, theaters, civic centers, shopping centers, gymnasiums, and swimming pools are especially dangerous because the entire roof structure is usually supported solely by the outside walls. The tornado winds knock out the supporting walls and the roof collapses.

- If there is not enough time to get to another building, go to the restroom, the next best place to be. The concrete block walls, metal partitions, and plumbing help hold things together as well as to help support any falling debris.

- If the building is coming apart and there is no time to go anywhere, seek shelter right where you are. Try to get up against something that will support or deflect the falling debris. In a department store, get up against heavy shelving or counters. In a theater, get under the seats. Remember to protect your head.

- If there is time to get out of long-span buildings, try to get to a building that has a basement. If no building is available, remember to get out of the winds and into a ditch, gully, or ravine.

In a School, Hospital, Nursing Home, or Office Building

The following suggestions should be considered in a tornado:

- Get into the innermost portion of the building with the shortest span.

- Avoid windows and glass doorways.

- Get into the basement if possible.

- Do not use elevators; the power may go off and you could become stuck on the upper floors.

- Do not open windows; time is too valuable and flying glass is dangerous.

- Students and patients should be moved from the upper floors first.

- Get into the inside hallways and close the doors to the outside rooms. This action will keep flying glass and debris to a minimum. Get everyone against the hallway walls, facing the wall.

- Protect your head, and make yourself as small a target as possible by crouching.

- Keep away from the ends of the hallways.

Be Prepared

No matter where your shelter is, have a few basic supplies there. Have spare clothing, blankets or sleeping bags, a portable radio and/ or weather radio, and a flashlight. Fresh drinking water and some food are helpful, as well as a few tools to help you dig out in case of collapse.

Since tornadoes usually take out power lines, practice getting to your shelter under blackout conditions at least once before the tornado season begins and occasionally throughout the season.

EARTHQUAKES

The devastation caused by an earthquake is not confined to those areas of the world on or near fault lines. Earthquakes can cause severe damage hundreds of miles away from a fault line.

During an earthquake, the "solid" Earth moves like the deck of a ship. The actual movement of the ground, however, is seldom the direct cause of death or injury. Most casualties result from falling objects and debris because the shocks can shake, damage, or demolish buildings.

Earthquakes may also trigger landslides, cause fires, and generate huge ocean waves called tsunamis.

This section offers suggestions to assist you in preparing for an Earthquake. Other suggestions may also be available from local, state and federal agencies and organizations such as the Red Cross.

Home Checklist

The following suggestions should be considered as part of your home checklist:

- The water heater is attached to the wall studs with galvanized plumber's tape to prevent tipping. Galvanized plumber's tape can be found at your local hardware store.
- There are no cracks in your home's foundation. Cracks wider than one-eighth inch indicate potential weakness.
- Your house is attached to the foundation with bolts through the sill.
- The exterior foundation cripple walls (the walls that enclose the crawl space under your home) are properly braced.
- Children's play areas are located away from earthquake hazards. Walls of brick, adobe or concrete block without steel reinforcement, and masonry veneers or chimneys often collapse in earthquakes.
- Household chemicals are stored so that containers will not easily tip over and spill their contents.
- Contact an architect, engineer or local building official for advice on needed repairs or strengthening. If you live in an apartment, ask the building owner to do these repairs.
- Know the locations of emergency exits, fire alarms, and fire extinguishers.

Emergency Supplies

The following suggestions should be considered in preparing your basic supplies for home and office:

- Portable radio (extra batteries).

- Flashlights. Any two-battery cell lights are excellent. Lights using more than two "D" battery cells or any lights requiring higher voltage batteries should be of the sealed "safety" type. Batteries last longer if stored in the freezer.

- First-aid kit and handbook.

- Enough water for each family member for at least one week and also keep a canteen of water in the car.

- Canned food, non-electric can opener, required medications, and powdered milk for at least one week.

- Pipe or crescent wrenches to turn off gas and water supplies.

- Alternate means of cooking such as a barbecue or camp stove that can be used outdoors. Be sure to store fuel out of children's reach.

- Small bottle of chlorine bleach to purify drinking water.

The safest places in your home should be away from heavy furniture or appliances which might shift in an earthquake, masonry veneers (e.g. fireplace) which might fall, and large panes of glass that might break.

Check the location of your gas, electric, and water main shutoffs. Know how to turn them off. If in doubt, ask your gas, power, and water companies.

You should have a place where your family can reunite after the earthquake. You may be at work when the earthquake occurs, or the children may be in school. Know the earthquake plan developed by your children's school. You may have to stay at your workplace for a day or two following a major earthquake. Transportation and communication may be disrupted. Make sure your family has a plan for what to do wherever they are when the earthquake occurs.

You should know the locations of your nearest fire and police stations and local emergency medical facilities.

Organizing Your Neighborhood

It may take up to 72 hours or longer for emergency assistance to reach you after a major earthquake. You and your neighbors will have to depend on one another to cope with the damage and injuries until help arrives. Just like your family, your neighbors will be better able to cope with the aftermath of an earthquake or any disaster if everyone is prepared.

Some communities with an existing program to watch out for the property and welfare of other residents, such as "Neighborhood Watch," may include earthquake preparedness as part of their program.

Community Preparedness

This section offers suggestions for developing a Community Preparedness Plan.

Schedule a meeting of your neighbors to discuss earthquake preparedness. Your local, state and federal agencies may be able to assist you with suggestions and materials. In addition, community organizations such as the Red Cross may be able to assist you with speakers, films, and printed materials.

Develop and distribute a questionnaire in person well in advance of the scheduled meeting. There may be an initial lack of enthusiasm in the community for such an activity so you may want to consider including copies of newspaper clippings from earlier crisis events to support your suggestions.

The following suggestions should be considered in developing the questionnaire:

- Number of residents per household.
- Home telephone number.
- Work address and telephone number.
- Name, address and telephone number of school(s).
- Telephone number of relatives.
- Special skills, such as nursing or radio operation that could be helpful in an emergency.

At the meeting, assign emergency tasks to each person. Assign enough work to maintain interest, but not enough to discourage volunteers. Try matching assignments with special skills. Selected individuals should have professional skills or first-aid training. Individuals with radio experience could handle communications. Plumbers and electricians could help restore utility service.

During an Earthquake

The following suggestions should be considered during an Earthquake:

- If you are indoors, get under a desk or table and hang onto it. Stay clear of windows, fireplaces, and heavy furniture or appliances. If you rush outside, you may be injured by falling glass or falling debris. Do not try using the stairs or elevators while the building is shaking or while there is danger of being hit by falling glass or debris.

- If you are outside, get into an open area, away from buildings and power lines.

- If you are driving, stop but stay inside your vehicle. Do not stop under trees, light post, electrical power lines or signs.

- If you are in a mountainous area, be alert for falling rock and other debris that could be loosened by the quake.

After an Earthquake

The following suggestions should be considered in the aftermath of an Earthquake:

- Check for injuries, use proper first aid, and seek out and treat the most seriously injured first.
- If a person is not breathing—use mouth-to mouth resuscitation to revive them.
- If a person is bleeding—put pressure over the wound. Use clean gauze or cloth, if available.
- Do not attempt to move seriously injured persons unless they are in immediate danger of further injury.
- Cover injured persons with blankets to prevent shock.
- Wear shoes to avoid injury from broken glass and debris.

The following suggestions should be considered as potential risk:

- Fire or fire hazards.

- Gas leaks. If a leak is suspected or identified by the odor of natural gas, shut off the main gas valve or wait for the gas company to check it and they will turn it back on.

- Damaged electrical wiring. If there is any damage to your house wiring, shut off power at the control box.

- Downed or damaged utility lines. Do not touch downed power lines or objects in contact with them.

- Downed or damaged chimneys. Approach chimneys with caution. They may be weakened and could topple during an aftershock. Don't use a damaged chimney; it could start a fire.

- Fallen items in closets and cupboards. Beware of items tumbling off shelves when you open the door.

- Immediately clean up any spilled medicines, drugs, or other potentially harmful materials such as bleach, lye or gasoline or other petroleum products.

- Check your food and water supplies.

- Do not eat or drink anything from open containers near shattered glass.

- If power is off, plan meals to use up frozen food or food that spoils quickly.

- Use barbecues or camp stoves outdoors for emergency cooking.

- If water is off, you can use supplies from water heaters, toilet tanks, melted ice cubes, canned vegetables.

- Do not search for a gas leak with a match, or lit smoking material.

- Let the gas company turn on the gas.

- Do not use lighters or open-flame appliances until you are sure there are no gas leaks.

- Do not operate electrical switches/appliances, including telephones, if you suspect a gas leak. The appliance may create a spark that could ignite the leaking gas.

- Only use telephones in an emergency. You could tie up lines needed for emergency services.

How to Shut Off a Gas Supply

Typically, the main shut-off valve is located next to your meter on the inlet pipe. You can use a crescent or pipe wrench and give the valve a quarter turn in either direction. The valve should run crosswise on the pipe and this should close the line. You should know how to turn off the gas supply in an emergency. If in doubt, you should contact your service provider.

How to Shut Off Electricity

Locate the ON/OFF switch on the circuit breaker box or fuse box. The main fuse nearest the heavy cable coming into the building can also be shut off. You should know how to turn off the electricity in an emergency. If in doubt, you should contact your service provider.

Disinfecting of Water

There are several effective and well tested water purification kits available through most camping and hunting outdoor retailers. We recommend that you obtain one of these kits and store it with your emergency supplies. In an extreme emergency situation you may want to consider the following:

Before attempting disinfecting, first strain water through a clean cloth or handkerchief to remove any sediment, floating matter or glass.

Water may be disinfected with 5.25% sodium hypochlorite solution (household chlorine bleach.) DO NOT use solutions in which there are active ingredients other than hypochlorite. Use the following proportions:

Clear Water

Water	Solution
1 quart	2 drops
1 gallon	8 drops
5 gallons	1 teaspoon

Cloudy Water

Water	Solution
1 quart	4 drops
1 gallon	16 drops
5 gallons	1 teaspoon

Mix water and hypochlorite thoroughly by stirring or shaking in a container. Let stand for 30 minutes before using. A slight chlorine odor should be detectable in the water. If not, repeat the dosage and let stand for an additional 15 minutes. Water may also be purified by boiling rapidly for at least 3 minutes.

Cooperate With Public Safety Efforts

The following suggestions should be considered in order to assist public safety efforts:

- Do not use your telephone except to report medical, fire or violent crime emergencies.

- Turn on your portable radio for emergency information and damage reports.

- Do not go sightseeing afterwards, especially in beach and waterfront areas where seismic waves could strike. Stay away from heavily damaged areas.

- Keep streets clear for emergency vehicles.

- Be prepared for aftershocks. Most of these are smaller than the main quake, but some may be large enough to do additional damage.

THUNDERSTORMS AND LIGHTNING

Lightning always accompanies thunderstorms. One strike of lightning can carry 100 million volts and a heat so intense that it can boil and evaporate the sap in a tree. Lightning travels 200 miles per second; it can take less than 1 second for lightning to fatally strike a person. Usually, people are not directly struck. The strike may hit a tree, and the person near the tree receives a small charge, only 1-2 seconds of that small charge can cause death. Lightning causes many thousands of building and forest fires each year, and it kills more people than either hurricanes or tornadoes combined. Of those people struck, two-thirds survive. Probably more people would survive if those at the scene knew how to react.

When someone is struck by lightning, all cells in the body stop functioning. The sudden voltage can place the victim in suspended animation for 5-20 minutes. This causes a halt to respiration, heartbeat, and metabolism. An observer could easily assume that the victim is dead, and many people probably die because of this faulty assumption. This is not true. The lightning enters and exits the body in a second.

First Aid for Victims of Lightning Strikes

The following suggestions should be considered when providing first aid to the lightning victim:

- Check the breathing of the person who seems to be unconscious or even dead. If the person is not breathing, begin mouth-to-mouth resuscitation and try to find a pulse. If there is no pulse, begin cardiovascular resuscitation and continue until the body takes over and resumes normal function. This may take a long time, but with your efforts you are sustaining life. When the heartbeat does return, it often begins with a very slow beat and gradually returns to normal. It is also possible that the heart and breathing may stop and start many times. Therefore, victims must be watched continuously until professional help arrives. Even after recovery, the person may appear cyanotic (blue) or complain of numbness and even paralysis. Others will suffer from headache or amnesia. You should be alert to these symptoms and mention them to the medical professionals when they arrive; however, a first-responders primary concern is to sustain breathing and heartbeat.

- Many victims also have burns, ranging from minor redness to third-degree charring, after being struck by lightning. The skin may appear charred in two areas: the point where flow of electricity entered the body and the point where it exited—usually the feet. Treat these burns by covering them with sterile gauze. The depth of injury may be greater than it appears.

- Lightning may create debris and also cause people to be thrown about, resulting in wounds and broken bones. These are treated the same way as any wounds or fractures. First try to control bleeding and then cover and splint possible breaks. To be sure, keep a close watch on breathing and heartbeat and, if they stop, begin emergency procedures.

Precautions To Take During Thunderstorms

The following suggestions should be considered during a thunderstorm:

- Go inside when a thunderstorm develops. While inside, do not use the telephone or stand between a door and a window.

- If you are in an all-metal vehicle, stay there. In a car, do not lean against the doors or play a citizen band radio. If you are in a convertible car, get indoors.

- It may be advisable to unplug the television set and other appliances, e.g., air conditioners, etc. If lightning strikes a power line, the electrical surge could burn out your set. Do not, however, unplug the set during a storm—an electrical surge at that moment could cause severe injury.

- If you cannot get indoors, do not stand under a natural lightning rod, such as a single tree in an open area. Avoid small sheds or barns standing alone in open spaces.

- Try not to be the tallest object in an area. Do not stand on a hilltop or an open beach. Look for a cave, an overhang, a gully, or a ditch that is lower than ground level, but not one that is filling with water.
- Stay away from wire fences, metal pipes, railroad rails, or any other metal path that could conduct lightning and carry it to you.

- If you are on a vehicle such as a motorcycle, golf cart, or bike, get off and find safe shelter.

- Do not carry anything made of metal, such as golf clubs, an umbrella, or a metal tennis racket. Put it down and come back for it after the storm.

- Get away from and out of water. Do not stay out in a small open boat. In a boat, go below deck or get as low as possible. Stay as far away as you can from the mast of a sailboat.

- If you are in the woods, find a low area under a thick growth of small trees, but be alert for flash floods. A camp tent in the woods is probably safe if the tent is not pitched near a tall, isolated tree or in an open space.

- As the storm descends, resist running out to take clothes off the line.

- If you feel your hair stand on end, suggesting that lightning is about to strike, drop to your knees and bend forward, putting your hands on your knees. Do not lie flat. You want as small an area as possible touching the ground to minimize the danger of your body acting as a conductor.

OTHER NATURAL DISASTERS

The natural phenomena described in this section do not normally receive the amounts of publicity that the previously described storms do, but they can be equally dangerous.

Winter Storms

Blizzards are the most dramatic and perilous of all winter storms, characterized by strong winds bearing large amounts of snow. Most of the snow accompanying a blizzard is in the form of fine, powdery particles, whipped in such great quantities that at times visibility is only a few yards.

The following suggestions should be considered if you are trapped in a blizzard:

- Avoid overexertion and exposure. Exertion from attempting to push your car, shoveling heavy drifts, and performing other difficult chores during the strong winds, blinding snow, and bitter cold of a blizzard may cause a heart attack—even for people in apparently good physical condition.

- Stay in your vehicle. Do not attempt to walk out of a blizzard. Disorientation comes quickly in blowing and drifting snow. Being lost in open country during a blizzard is almost certain death. You are more likely to be found and more likely to be sheltered in your car.

- Keep fresh air in the car. Freezing wet snow and wind-driven snow can completely seal the passenger compartment.

- Beware of carbon monoxide and oxygen starvation. Run the motor and heater sparingly and only with the downwind window open for ventilation.

- Exercise by clapping hands and moving arms and legs vigorously from time to time, and do not stay in one position for too long.

- Turn on dome light at night to make the vehicle visible to work crews.

- Keep watch. Do not permit all occupants of the car to sleep at once.

Winter Storms Checklist

Keep ahead of the winter storm by listening to the latest weather warnings and bulletins on radio and television. The following suggestions should be considered as part of your winter storms checklist:

- Check battery-powered equipment before the storm arrives. A portable radio or television set may be your only contact with the world outside the winter storm. Also, check emergency cooking facilities and flashlights.

- Check your supply of heating fuel. Fuel carriers may not be able to service you if winter storm buries your area in snow.

- Keep an extra food supply. Your supply should include food that requires no cooking or refrigeration in case of a power failure.

- Prevent fire hazards due to overheated coal or oil burning stoves, fireplaces, heaters, or furnaces.

- Stay indoors during storms and cold snaps unless you are in peak physical condition. If you must go out, avoid over-exertion.

- Shoveling snow can be extremely hard work for anyone in less than prime physical condition and has been known to bring on a heart attack, a major cause of death during and after winter storms.

- If you live in a rural area, make necessary trips for supplies before the storm develops or not at all; arrange for emergency heat supply in case of power failure, and be sure camp stoves and lanterns are filled.

Your automobile can be your best friend—or your worst enemy—during winter storms, depending on your preparations. Have your car winterized before the storm season begins. The following suggestions should be considered in preparing your vehicle checklist before the storm season:

- Ignition system
- Battery
- Radio
- Lights
- Tire tread
- Fuel system
- Lubrication
- Exhaust system
- Window scraper
- Heater
- Brakes adjusted
- Wiper blades
- Defroster
- Snow tires installed
- Chains
- Antifreeze
- Winter-grade oil

During the winter storm season you should be prepared for the worst case scenario. Carry a winter storm survival kit in your car, especially if cross-country travel is anticipated.

The following suggestions should be considered in preparing a winter storm survival kit:

- Blankets
- Sleeping bags
- Matches
- Candles
- Empty 3-pound coffee can with plastic cover
- Facial tissue
- Paper towels
- Extra clothing
- High-calorie nonperishable food
- Compass and road maps
- Knife
- First-aid kit
- Shovel
- Sack of sand
- Flashlight or signal light
- Windshield scraper
- Battery booster cables
- Tow chains
- Fire extinguisher
- Catalytic heater
- Ax
- Handheld Global Positioning System (GPS) with integrated map.

Winter travel by automobile is serious business. Take your travel seriously. If you are fortunate enough to have a Global Positioning System installed in your vehicle this will greatly aid in your navigation when visibility is poor. In addition to directing you to your destination, it will notify you in advance of upcoming turns which will greatly reduce last minute turns and reduce accidents.

If the storm exceeds or even tests your limitations, seek available refuge immediately. Plan your travel and select primary and alternate routes. Check latest weather information on your radio. Try not to travel alone; two or three people are preferable. Travel in convoy with another vehicle, if possible. Always fill gasoline tank before entering open country, even for a short distance. Drive carefully and drive defensively.

Dress to fit the season. If you spend much time outdoors, wear loose-fitting, lightweight, warm clothing in several layers; layers can be removed to prevent perspiring and subsequent chill. Outer garments should be tightly woven, water repellent, and hooded. The hood should protect much of the face; cover the mouth to ensure warm breathing and to protect the lungs from the extremely cold air. Remember that entrapped, insulating air, warmed by body heat, is the best protection against cold. Several layers of thinner protective clothing are more effective and efficient than single layers of thick clothing; and mittens, snug at the wrists, are better protection than fingered gloves.

Flash Floods

Flash floods are a fact of life, and death frequently occurs along the rivers and streams of the world. These deaths result from heavy rains filling natural and manufactured drainage systems, to overflowing, with raging water.

Flash flood waves, moving at incredible speeds, can roll boulders, tear out trees, destroy buildings and bridges, and scour out new channels. Killing walls of water can reach heights of 10-20 feet. You will not always have warning that these deadly, sudden floods are coming.

The moment you first realize that a flash flood is imminent, act quickly to save yourself. You may have only seconds and should consider the following suggestions:

- Get out of areas subject to flooding, including dips, low spots, canyons, washes, etc.

- Avoid already flooded and high velocity flow areas. Do not attempt to cross a flowing stream on foot where water is above your knees.

- If driving, know the depth of water in a dip before crossing. The roadbed may not be intact under the water.

- If the vehicle stalls, abandon it immediately and seek higher ground; rapidly rising water may engulf the vehicle and its occupants and sweep them away.

- Be especially cautious at night when it is harder to recognize flood dangers.

- Do not camp or park your vehicle along streams and washes, particularly during threatening conditions.

General Floods

A general flood usually provides ample warning time to those in its path. It is much slower to develop than the flash flood. Flooding occurs when sufficient rain has fallen to cause rivers to overflow their banks and when melting snow combines with rainfall to produce similar effects.

Flood Safety Rules

Before the flood:

The following suggestions should be considered before the flood:

- Keep materials on hand such as sandbags, plywood, plastic sheeting, and lumber.

- Install check valves in building sewer traps to prevent flood water from backing up in sewer drains.

- Arrange for auxiliary electrical supplies for hospitals and other operations that are critically affected by power failure.

- Keep first-aid supplies at hand.

- Keep your automobile fueled; if electric power is cut off, service stations may not be able to operate pumps for several days.

- Keep a stock of food that requires little or no cooking and no refrigeration; electrical power may be interrupted.

- Keep a portable radio, emergency cooking equipment, lights, and flashlights in working order.

- Know your elevation above flood state.

- Know your evacuation route.

After a flood warning:

The following suggestions should be considered:

- Store drinking water in clean bathtubs and in various containers. Water service may be interrupted.

- If you are forced to leave your home and time permits, move essential items to safe ground; fill fuel tanks to keep them from floating away, and grease immovable machinery.

- Move to a safe area before access is cut off by flood water.

During the flood:

The following suggestions should be considered:

- Avoid areas subject to flooding.

- Do not attempt to cross a flowing stream where water is above your knees.

- Do not attempt to drive over a flooded road; you can be stranded or trapped. The depth of water is not always obvious.

After the flood:

The following suggestions should be considered:

- Do not use fresh food that has come in contact with flood waters.

- Boil drinking water before using. Wells should be pumped out, and the water tested for purity before drinking.

- Seek necessary medical care at nearest hospital. Food, clothing, shelter, and first aid may also be available at Red Cross shelters.

- Do not visit disaster areas; your presence might hamper rescue and other emergency operations.

- Do not handle live electrical equipment in wet areas; electrical equipment should be checked and dried before being resumed to service.

- Use flashlights, not lanterns or torches, to examine buildings, because flammable may be inside.

- Report broken utility lines to appropriate authorities.

Heat Wave

Heat kills by taxing the human body beyond its abilities. U.S. Government statistics, from the U.S. Chamber of Commerce, indicate that in the United States more direct casualties result annually from heat and solar radiation than from other natural hazards, such as lightning strikes, hurricanes, tornadoes, floods, or earthquakes.

Problems for Special Populations

Elderly people, small children, chronic invalids, those on certain medications or drugs, and people with weight and alcohol problems are particularly susceptible to heat reactions, especially during heat waves in areas where a moderate climate usually prevails.

Heat Wave Safety Tips

The following suggestions should be considered during a heat wave:

- Slow down. Strenuous activities should be reduced, eliminated, or rescheduled to the coolest time of the day.

- Individuals at risk should stay in the coolest available place, which may not necessarily be indoors.

- Dress for summer. Lightweight, light-colored clothing reflects heat and sunlight and helps the body maintain normal temperatures.

- Put less fuel on your inner fires. Foods (like proteins) that increase metabolic heat production also increase water loss.

- Drink plenty of water or other nonalcoholic fluids. Your body needs water to keep cool. Drink plenty of fluids even if you do not feel thirsty. People who: (1) have epilepsy, kidney, or liver disease, (2) are on fluid-restrictive diets, or (3) have a problem with fluid retention should consult a physician before increasing their consumption of fluids.

- Do not drink alcoholic beverages.

- Do not take salt tablets or increase salt intake unless specified by a physician.

- Spend more time in air conditioned places. If you cannot afford an air conditioner, spend some time each day (during hot weather) in an air conditioned environment if possible, because it affords some protection.

- Do not get too much sun. Sunburn makes the job of heat dissipation much more difficult.

EPIDEMICS AND EMERGENCY CARE

INTRODUCTION

A significant challenge to any health care system is the occurrence of a sudden disaster such as a flood, earthquake, or hurricane. Such events create a period in which decisions made can alter the balance between life and death. The word disaster implies that the established systems of medical care are overwhelmed or destroyed. With this in mind, we will examine the question of epidemic and emergency care concerns during a crisis.

Even under normal conditions, health risks exist everywhere, and for this reason, international travelers are advised to contact their local health department, physician, or private or public health agency at least four weeks prior to departure to obtain current health information on countries that they plan to visit. It is very important to be aware of health problems associated with your scheduled destination. This focus on education, prior to departure, can assist you in overcoming a spontaneous situation arising from some emergency after your arrival.

EPIDEMICS

We can examine the role you can play in protecting yourself from an epidemic situation. From the educational approach, you can review the medical history of an area. Wherever you might travel, medical statistics have been collected, analyzed, and summarized evaluating diseases past and present. Although most authorities agree that significant reporting problems exist, they still feel that the information gathered is very useful in monitoring and reflecting an area's current state of health. Although executives who travel cannot personally do all of the research involved, they can assign it to someone on their staffs. Without this slight advance preparation, you could be placing yourself at risk.

Most industrialized countries have virtually eliminated the problem of epidemics as primary disasters, but outbreaks can result in connection with some other disaster *or as an isolated terrorist event.* Although poorer developing countries also rarely experience outbreaks of communicable diseases, when it happens after a disaster, it usually involves encampment of populations where meticulous attention to sanitation is not a priority. The most prevalent diseases in populations stricken by disaster are food intoxication because of bacterial toxins or water contamination resulting from the breakdown of sanitation systems.

Because disease can erupt in the aftermath of a disaster, health authorities monitor epidemiological factors that determine the potential for transmitting communicable diseases. Some of these factors may include:

- Changes in preexisting levels of disease.
- Population displacement.
- Population density.
- Disruption of public utilities.
- Interruption of basic public health services.

All diseases have specific preventive recommendations. Generally these recommendations are routine public health measures that apply to everyday life. Although some guidelines may seem obvious, we need to think in terms of the factors listed.

The following concerns should be considered after a disaster:

- *Safe water for drinking and washing:* If the local water system becomes contaminated, do you have treatment capability or stored emergency water for drinking and personal hygiene? Would the local authorities be able to communicate a contamination problem to you, or could you identify a problem immediately?

- *Sanitation:* When normal sanitation systems stop working, a temporary system must be established immediately to prevent further health complications. Adequate water supplies are necessary to clean hands to prevent further spread of disease while executing routine duties such as food preparation or care of the sick and injured.
- *Food preparation:* You should have access to adequate food and the means to prepare it properly and eat only well cooked foods while they are hot.

- *Insect and animal control:* The concerns noted above, water contamination, sanitation, and food preparation, will determine the impact of animals and insects in a disaster area. They can become carriers in some situations if attention is not given to vector control. In areas where insect and animal diseases are endemic, use screening and insect repellent and avoid contact with animals as much as possible.

- *Crowding:* As the population density increases, all emergency services will feel the effects. When any system is overwhelmed, it creates additional problems that need quick solutions. If an epidemic potential exists, departure from the general area will remove you from the danger, but often this is not feasible. Remember, epidemics can occur after a disaster when encampments become necessary.

- *Disease surveillance, identification, immunization, isolation, and treatment:* Authorities will investigate rumors and reports of diseases, test for factual results, report to decision makers, and provide continuous monitoring through the recovery phase after an epidemic.

EMERGENCY CARE

After any disaster, emergency care becomes a main part of the recovery. When we think of emergency care, many things come to mind, such as ambulance technicians at an accident scene or the hospital emergency room. These two situations are far removed from the types of scenes found in the aftermath of a disaster. It is possible that local authorities could be completely overwhelmed and committed for several days, depending on the size of the disaster. The importance of knowing life safety procedures and first-aid techniques cannot be overstressed during this initial period of a disaster.

The first 24 hours are critical in saving the lives of injured victims. A medical assessment should be done immediately, or as soon as possible, following the disaster. Some injured people will not be able to survive the ordeal, and your limited response should be used where it can do the most good. Those who have training in first aid need to organize the others and use them in assisting and treating the injured, thus starting to care for the injured and keeping the others busy to reduce the risk of panic. A morgue must be established to separate the deceased people from the survivors. Separation is as much for psychological as for physical purposes.

In a disaster setting, survival could depend on an ability to care for yourself, your family, or your group for several days, independent of any local, regional, or national assistance. Survival studies have suggested that it is dangerous to be passive and to wait for help. You should be ready to assume a high level of personal responsibility and take charge, assess, plan, and act, using the resources at hand to maximize your chances to bring yourself and your group through the ordeal.

In most industrialized urban work settings, health care systems are organized so that the vast majority of health problems are handled quickly, effectively, and with a minimal loss of life. As you travel, the responsibility for knowing emergency care techniques and health related information increases proportionately with the distance that separates you from a health care system or program on which you can depend. Health organizations recommend a working knowledge of first aid, health profile research for all destinations, and on arrival, familiarization with health care resources available locally. Advance planning and research is always recommended before a trip.

James R. Doyle

Types of Disasters Common to an Area

Natural

- Storms in both hot and cold climates.

- Topological disasters such as avalanches and floods.

- Telluric and tectonic events such as earthquakes and volcanic eruptions.

- Biological problems such as insects and all forms of epidemics.

Man-made

- Terrorist Attacks

- Civil disobedience.

- Warfare.

- Refugee influx.

- Accidents.

The information provided here should give you some idea of the magnitude of past disasters and their impact on the local population and effects on health. This information should assist you in determining the types of supplies that you will need, the training needed to use the supplies, and finally the kinds of drills or exercises needed to prepare the population for that type of emergency.

The following suggestions should be considered as part of any basic earthquake disaster plan:

- Mitigate the occurrence of structural disasters. Significant efforts have been made to refine construction specifications to enable buildings to withstand the destructive effects of earthquakes.

- Minimize the number of casualties through controlling nonstructural danger. Nonstructural mitigation is the method by which you can earthquake-proof your environment. This can be done at work and at home to prevent injury from flying debris, falling furniture or fixtures, fire explosion, and other types of threats to life.

- Prevent further casualties. After the first earthquake, you should prepare for aftershocks. Extreme care should be given to detecting possible gas leaks, ignition points, damaged water reservoirs, etc., to prevent additional injuries. Seeking a safe place and remaining there while you make a damage assessment is important.

- Develop search and rescue skills utilizing appropriate equipment to locate and assist victims. Without the means to extricate victims, you will be unable to treat them for injuries.

- Maintain first-aid supplies in several locations to protect them from total loss. A system of several self-contained medical kits will increase chances of their availability after the event. Trained rescue groups should administer first aid to people who have been extricated. Com-munication will be necessary to coordinate the emergency care effort and to evacuate the injured to hospital facilities where available.

- Evacuate the injured. Mobilization of transport will be accomplished through a communication link. If you are in a foreign country, it will be beneficial to predetermine the location of English-speaking medical personnel and facilities. Communications at any level will be impossible without bilingual capabilities.

Preparation is the key to emergency response in most cases, including emergency care.

The following suggestions should be considered as a summary to emergency care planning:

- Know your health status. Be aware of health conditions pertaining to you, your family, or your group. Conditions such as epilepsy, diabetes, or heart disease will need special response and planning.

- Know the potential disaster conditions of your area. Check into previous disasters to understand the implications for you, your family, and your group.

- Prepare for the possibilities by keeping stored food and water, locating areas for temporary shelter, keeping on hand a radio, flashlights, extra batteries, blankets, search and rescue plans, simple tools, etc.

- Learn first aid. Become current in first-aid techniques not only for your protection and your loved ones but also so that you can assist in the emergency care phase of a disaster.

- Have a plan. Maintain and practice a short and simple plan of action.

The following actions should be considered as part of an additional casualty care plan:

- Field rescue and first aid.

- Emergency field surgical stabilization.

- Casualty clearing where casualties are concentrated at a collect-ion point for evacuation.

- Medical evacuation to definitive care facilities.

Any type of disaster may involve large mass casualties that can substantially exceed the capacity of locally available emergency medical resources. This type of incident may require summoning outside aid and a shift to nonstandard ways of treating patients. In a disaster situation, it is understood that there will be overwhelming numbers of patients needing treatment simultaneously.

When treating people who have been involved in a disaster, you must care for patients efficiently and do the greatest good for those who can benefit most. This austere approach to field medical resources, along with the unfavorable environment surrounding a disaster, creates a real challenge to those who must become involved with providing medical assistance during an emergency situation.

Disaster teams must be organized to function effectively. These teams cannot be set up at the time of the incident, so units must be created before the disaster. They must be trained, skilled, equipped, and ready for mobilization, deployment, and action. Disaster responses are serious business and there is a real need for the individual to be prepared and ready to meet the challenge.

INDUSTRIAL ACCIDENTS

Planning

Planning and preparation are critical for coping with industrial accidents and for controlling losses under emergency conditions. Emergency plans tailored to a specific industry, location, or anticipated catastrophic event could be the basis for rational responses to particular emergency conditions. The industrial emergency plan that is properly focused should include guidelines that enable the manager and response team members to make well-balanced decisions during an emergency.

The following general objectives should be the basis for any industrial accident plan:

- Protect the people.

- Protect the property.

- Continue operations.

In keeping these general objectives in mind as a framework, this section will focus on three emergency conditions that may occur on industrial sites: *chemical accidents, fires, and nuclear and radiological incidents*. Each condition has its own unique requirements for emergency planning. In the sections that follow, you will find practical suggestions that will serve as the basis for formulating an effective emergency plan that satisfies response team requirements at a specific site for each of the three conditions.

EVACUATION PLANNING

GENERAL

An evacuation plan is designed to cope with those situations that could require an evacuation of private sector expatriate employees and/or their dependents, which removes them from the specific and/or general source of risk or threat, to an out-of-country location. It outlines procedures to ensure an orderly, safe, and expeditious evacuation of expatriate employees and their dependents.

There are circumstances in which it is obvious that a U.S. corporation operating abroad must consider sending employees and dependents out, such as times of serious terrorist threat, insurrection, or other civil disorder or when a natural disaster or other event poses serious hazard to their safety or so overburdens the country's ability to protect, feed, and house its citizens that departure is the best course of action.

Occasionally, there are other signs of hazard, such as gradual, almost imperceptible decline in services, shortages in goods or services, capital flight, increased government travel restrictions, decreased internal security, and declines in the attitudes of established contacts. Country managers should be alert to these changes and continuously evaluate the local conditions for signs of deterioration so that they can consider a gradual and orderly evacuation.

If the U.S. Government were to sponsor an evacuation of Americans from a given country, it would be coordinated and controlled by the U.S. Department of State. It is noted that the U.S. Embassy cannot order private American citizens to depart, but must inform them of impending danger and may offer evacuation assistance from the U.S. Government when necessary. However, it is also considered prudent for companies operating overseas to develop evacuation plans. Evacuation should only occur when authorized by the company senior manager in country, or appropriate headquarters manager. Any evacuation ordered by a company senior manager should be coordinated with the U.S. Embassy. Past experience indicates that both companies and employees in foreign locations show a reluctance to develop, maintain, or implement evacuation plans. This reluctance stems from a false sense of security developed through the absence of personal threats and the lack of access to uncensored news reports.

The fundamental factors in conducting a safe and efficient evacuation in a destabilized overseas environment are thorough prior planning, continuous and comprehensive analysis of potential security threats, and timely decision making concerning the evacuation itself. Effective management of these factors should facilitate the evacuation process of expatriates in a timely and orderly fashion.

ORGANIZATION

An evacuation organization is comprised of in-country management that is responsible for making evacuation decisions on the scene and communicating them to the remainder of the employees. The senior manager is usually assisted by an Expatriate Evacuation Committee.

The purpose of the Expatriate Evacuation Committee is to refine, tailor, and coordinate the evacuation plan to ensure that it is functional. The Expatriate Evacuation Committee coordinates imple-mentation of the plan. Liaison and coordination between the Expatriate Evacuation Committee and the local or corporate Crisis Management Team should be required. If a local Crisis Management Team exists, the Expatriate Evacuation Committee should function within the overall framework or the Crisis Management Team.

The Expatriate Evacuation Committee should meet on a semiannual basis or sooner if conditions dictate, to review current events and trends and to assess future periods. The evacuation plan should be reviewed at these intervals, and minutes of the meetings should be prepared and maintained on file. A deteriorating political climate would indicate more frequent meetings.

EVACUATION PREPLANNING

The following suggestions should be considered in developing an evacuation plan:

- Employees and their families should register with the U.S. Embassy or, if one is not present in the host country, with the embassy's local representative.

- The Expatriate Evacuation Committee should maintain liaison with the U.S. Embassy or, if one is not present in the host country, with the embassy's local representative.

- Evacuation plans should be communicated to employees, and a test of the employee notification system should be conducted periodically.

- The Expatriate Evacuation Committee should determine that adequate information and personnel files are available.

- If appropriate, local staging areas and embarkation points for assembly of personnel and their families should be identified. Preliminary security plans for the sites should be developed. As a general rule, it is preferable to assemble evacuees at a secure staging location other than the embarkation point and then to move them to embarkation points in groups, sized to the transport capacity and on a schedule calculated to minimize the exposure of evacuees and the means of transport at the embarkation point.

- The Expatriate Evacuation Committee should be in contact with representatives of other companies so that rumors of evacuations can be verified.

- Primary and alternate modes of travel should be identified. Contacts and commitments from carriers and agents should be maintained. Preliminary arrangements should be made to have local nationals available to drive to and translate at airports, roadblocks, checkpoints, etc.

- The Expatriate Evacuation Committee should consider an agreement with other multinational companies in the area to assist one another in evacuation and should also consolidate the use of transportation equipment.

- The Expatriate Evacuation Committee should distribute applicable sections of the evacuation plan to employees on a need to know basis.

- The Expatriate Evacuation Committee should designate authorized persons to issue return-to-work instructions.

- In the event of any emergency, personnel should be directed to stay away from the area of trouble or potential trouble and to advise all other personnel accordingly. During major disturbances, all personnel should be advised to return to their living quarters and to remain there until they receive further advice.

- No personnel should be allowed unilaterally to attempt either to travel internally or to leave the country without authorization and direction.

- The success of evacuating personnel is enhanced greatly by having advance warning so that most personnel can be withdrawn by commercial airline. The time required and the procedures necessary to obtain exit visas should be determined.

- Local laws should be observed at all times unless the situation results in a total breakdown of authority.

- An evacuation of personnel under hostile conditions from local authorities and/or the general public is usually not advisable. The risk of harm to personnel is greater when trying to move about the country than when maintaining a low profile and staying indoors. Waiting for the situation to stabilize generally is far less risky than traveling about.

- The decision to evacuate personnel under hostile conditions should be taken only when the risk of staying put becomes greater than the risk of being exposed. These conditions could arise during a period of civil disorder, a military uprising, or outside military intervention. If a hostile evacuation is necessary, it is hoped that all dependents and nonessential personnel will already have been withdrawn by commercial airline. This action presumes that some advance warning of worsening conditions within the country or of military action from outside the country will have been received and acted upon. Should an emergency arise suddenly without advance warning to withdraw nonessential personnel, and if the circumstances dictate an evacuation under hostile conditions, companies will have to rely on support from outside sources. The safety of all personnel and dependents is of the utmost importance. In no case should any action be taken if that action puts the personnel and dependents in more jeopardy than they are in already.

EVACUATION PROCEDURER STAGES

The objective of the evacuation procedures is to establish a set of contingency plans for the withdrawal or evacuation of staff and dependents from the host country.

The evacuation process usually evolves in phases. The following suggestions should be considered when developing a phased evacuation plan:

Phase I - Alert Stage - A warning to companies and individuals of host country instability.

Phase II - Limited Action - An increased preparation for evacuation includes those preparations made under conditions of increased tension or instability that could lead to partial or complete evacuation of expatriate employees and their dependents.

Phase III - Evacuation Phase - The final preparation and/or evacuation includes those preparations made under conditions in which the decision to evacuate is imminent or has already been made. Withdrawal and cessation of business is imminent or underway.

In the event an evacuation is not considered prudent due to changing conditions, a "Stand Fast" order could be implemented in which employees and their dependents would remain in their quarters or other designated location for an extended period of time until conditions improve.

EVACUATION GUIDELINES

Phase I—Alert Stage

- This is a period during which routine collection and assessment of information about local and international events are in progress.

- Documents should be identified or set aside for possible future destruction.

- Potential staging areas for assembling employees and their dependents should be reviewed and/or selected.

- The senior manager should consider meeting periodically with the expatriate employees to review current events and trends. It is important to develop a procedure to deal with rumors that have a tendency to emerge with the onset of any crisis situation. The best countermeasures are to have an open line of communication designed to address rumors and a set of clear evacuation instructions.

- Evacuation priorities should be established and individually assigned. The following categories should be considered:

  a. First priority-dependents.

  b. Second priority-individuals other than key expatriate employees.

  c. Third priority-key expatriate employees.

- Alternate routes to the international airports, seaports, or land borders should be established and checked for travelers' ability under emergency conditions.

Phase II—Limited Action, Increased Preparation for Evacuation

- This phase should be initiated when, in the judgment of the senior manager, a situation has reached a level of tension or instability that could lead to partial or complete evacuation of expatriate employees and their dependents. The earlier an evacuation decision can be made, the more likely it can be affected in a calm, secure, and less politically sensitive atmosphere.

- The contents of departure kits (described in the next section) should be examined and reviewed.

- An inventory of household effects should be prepared in duplicate. One copy should be with the employee and his or her dependents and one copy should left behind with an appropriate corporate representative. The possibility of having to secure or abandon personal property prior to evacuations should be addressed.

- Normal work routines should continue; however, certain preparatory actions, such as obtaining required clearances, conducting programmed document destruction to begin on the order of the senior manager, etc., should be undertaken, if appropriate.

Phase III—Evacuation Phase, Final Preparation and/or Evacuation

This phase should be initiated when, in the judgment of the senior manager, the situation has deteriorated to the point that the decision to evacuate is imminent or has already been made. At this point, the company home office should arrange for the services of other companies and outside commercial resources necessary to support and coordinate the evacuation process. It is assumed that total withdrawal of personnel will not meet active resistance from the authorities.

The senior manager should determine whether it would be prudent and desirable to relocate evacuees from their quarters to pre-selected primary or alternate staging area(s), prior to proceeding to the international airport or other departure site(s), for final coordination of the evacuation.

A special "Stand Fast" phase should be implemented in the event that evacuation is not considered prudent under certain circumstances, for example, if a coup has occurred. This concept is one in which operations may slow down or even temporarily be suspended. Employees and their dependents would remain in their compound or quarters for an undetermined period of time, awaiting further instructions. Liquids, canned foods, medicines, and staples to support the family for an extended period, should be kept on hand to support such an eventuality, depending on the local situation. Instructions to and between families should be transmitted by whatever means available, depending on the circumstances.

EVACUATION DEPARTURE KIT

The Evacuation Departure Kit referred to earlier in "Phase II" is a collection of items that should always be available for use in an emergency situation. The kit should be in two parts: Part 1 consisting of sustenance items and equipment and Part 2 of a secure waterproof packet of vital personal papers and documents and an Evacuation Departure Kit checklist. The kit should be checked periodically for completeness and timeliness. It should be properly tagged for identification and in a state of complete readiness at the outset of "Phase II".

Supplies & Equipment

The following suggestions should be considered when preparing for an evacuation:

- Without hoarding, maintain a reasonable supply (5-7 days) of food, water, and fuel. If you have a personal or company automobile, be sure it is ready for immediate use. Maintain a full fuel tank and a reasonable supply of spares and other extras as may be necessary. Also, periodically check oil, water, and tires.

- Maintain a family-size first-aid kit and an adequate supply of necessary prescription medicines.

- Have a flashlight with fresh batteries and/or candles.

- Keep a lighter and supply of matches, preferably waterproof and windproof.

- Keep a small battery-operated short-wave radio with fresh batteries. Monitor the local news media, Voice of America, and the British Broadcasting Company closely, if available, for relevant announcements from the local government or the U.S. Embassy. The embassies will be closely monitoring any situation and will provide further information to the liaison contact person.

- Have one blanket and/or sleeping bag for each family member.

- Do not carry excess baggage. Confirm in advance the amount of baggage that will be permitted on a U.S. Government sponsored evacuation aircraft. You may be permitted as much as 66 pounds of clothing and personal effects per individual however this is subject to change and as such, should be confirmed in advance. Carry the most essential items such as documents, money and other valuables in a small handbag or carry-on bag in case it becomes necessary to restrict baggage further.

- Pets most likely will not be allowed in the emergency evacuation process. Consequently, owners need to be sure that they make appropriate custody arrangements.

- Do not include any alcohol, firearms or any other weapons in the evacuation kit.

- Keep a supply of street and road maps of the metropolitan and rural areas.

Evacuation Documents & Checklist — Vital Personal Papers and a Checklist

Evacuation documents should include a current passport with appropriate visas for all members of the family. In addition, any personal papers and documents including driver's license, medical records, vaccination records, insurance records etc. should be included as vital personal papers.

If passports are retained in the custody of the company, they should be returned at the time of evacuation. The company should have obtained the necessary exit documentation. In addition, sufficient cash in U.S. dollars and traveler's checks should be a part of your kit to cover family incidental expenses while en-route to a safe haven.

Warden Systems - General Considerations

Experience has proven that during times of increased threat or actual emergency, a warden network consisting of responsible employees who will not be heavily engaged during an emergency, is an especially effective way to communicate with employees residing in a specific area.

A pyramid configuration of individuals having access to private telephones and residing centrally in areas of concentrated employee population is recommended for establishing a warden network. This configuration should also permit the designation of alternate wardens in the event that a primary warden is unavailable for any reason.

The Expatriate Evacuation Committee should establish a periodic review and schedule of meetings with the wardens to assure the following items are current and available:

- Up-to-date International Certificates of Vaccination.

- Current inventory of household effects.

- All host country identification papers.

- Essential personal papers including birth certificates, marriage license, etc.

- Copies of your U.S. Federal income tax return, if it has not already been sent to a safe place of record.

- A blank company expense statement to keep track of expenses.

- A contact lists showing names, addresses, telephone numbers, and number of dependents

EVACUATION ACTION RESPONSIBILITIES

Warden Coordinator

- Prepares lists of wardens and other contacts to cover the employee population.

- Meets periodically with wardens and alternates to review responsibilities and update requirements.

- Activates the warden system on direction from the Expatriate Evacuation Committee, passing information to the employee group and receiving it, as appropriate.

Wardens

- Prepare, update, and maintain a list of telephone numbers and addresses of employees and dependents residing in the warden's area.

- Appoint at least one sub-warden or alternate who can substitute for the primary warden in his or her absence. Provide alternate warden with copies of the lists of employees within the area of responsibility.

- Along with the warden coordinator, be familiar with assembly or staging areas and movement routes.

- Keep employees in the warden area informed about the location of the designated assembly areas and movement routes.

- Develop a "pyramid method" or "cascade" approach for contacting the individuals within the area of the Expatriate Evacuation Committee responsibility. This can be accomplished by having individuals with telephones contact each other and having those without telephones be contacted by an individual who has a telephone and lives nearby.

- Arrange for periodic tests of the network's ability to communicate with employees.

- Maintain a current checklist of documents required as part of the evacuation process and provide a copy to the employee for inclusion in his or her evacuation kit.

James R. Doyle

EVACUATION TRANSPORTATION

Introduction

As a general rule, the U.S. Government does not provide funds for the transportation and movement of persons other than U.S. Government employees from a foreign country. In the event U.S. citizens are evacuated by U.S. Government funded transportation, the U.S. citizen may be ask to pay for the transportation at the time of departure or sign an agreement to reimburse the U.S. government for such transportation.

The U.S. Department of State does have a responsibility to advise U.S. citizens of potential conflicts and threats which could compromise their safety; however as a rule, it does not have the authority to order an evacuation. They may however; offer assistance with an emergency evacuation when necessary.

American companies and their employees should not totally rely on the U.S. Department of State for information on the necessity or timing of an employee evacuation in the event of an emergency situation, however; they should give serious consideration to any security notices provided by the U.S. Department of State concerning the evacuation of U.S. citizens.

During this early warning period, the use of commercially scheduled airlines or chartered aircraft should still be available to facilitate the withdrawal of U.S. citizens. If the company delays evacuation until the U.S. Department of State closes its embassy or post and recommends that all American citizens leave the country immediately, undoubtedly, obtaining transportation and evacuating under these adverse circumstances will be extremely difficult.

In the event of such a notice, the following suggestions should be considered:

- Ensure that the information contained in the notice is made available to all personnel with responsibility for implementing the evacuation process.

- Be prepared to provide the warden coordinator with the names and status's of those individuals contacted and not contacted within specific areas of responsibility.

- If the primary warden expects to be unavailable, ensure that the alternate is available to carry out the warden's responsibilities.

- Advise employees to remain at home or at the office and near a telephone or emergency radio network, if available, to receive instructions from the company and to answer questions from those individuals in areas of responsibility for the evacuation process.

Assessing Travel Options

To determine the feasibility of transportation by common carrier, investigate departure schedules and normal capacity of commercial flights, trains, and ships leaving the area.

Identify the most logical options for assembly and movement of evacuees to the departure or embarkation location while maintaining the best security possible. As a general rule, it is preferable to assemble evacuees at a secure location and then move them to the embarkation point. This can best be accomplished by moving groups appropriate to the means of transportation. This will reduce the tendency to overcrowd and increase the chances of accidental injury and at the same time maintain a reduced profile which could compromise overall security. While this phased approach will improve safety and security, a situation may suddenly develop that requires another approach.

Determine the most appropriate sites at which to assemble potential evacuees in anticipation of moving them to points of embarkation. If a lengthy evacuation is anticipated, special consideration should be given to transit shelter, food, water, and sanitation needs.

The Expatriate Evacuation Committee should appoint a responsible manager to document and list evacuees and to control movement to the embarkation point. The security risks of assembling in one place versus those of remaining in individual homes until departure or the risk of having employees making their way independently to embarkation points should be considered.

In selecting assembly points and routes, be aware of potential choke points, bridges, and areas that could be congested and identify alternate routes if possible. Maps should be developed for each route.

If overland movement out of the country is a possibility, define the circumstances under which overland transportation would be considered and special security precautions that might be necessary.

The Expatriate Evacuation Committee should attempt to anticipate the degree of support or problems that might be offered by the host government in an evacuation situation. Identify contacts and develop procedures that could be helpful with exit formalities. Investigate any departure problems for employees in connection with in-country taxes and any other business-related departure requirements. Consider what assistance should be asked of the host government for security of assembly areas, convoy routes, and embarkation points if appropriate. Assign liaison responsibilities to appropriate company representatives who may have already established a good relationship with the host government and therefore increase the level of cooperation and credibility.

Security protection commensurate with the risk and resources available should be arranged for the various evacuation assembly areas, routes, and embarkation points. Details such as assembly, timing of movements, aircraft schedules, etc., should be protected from unauthorized disclosure.

Any inquiries received from the media regarding a planned evacuation or one in progress should be referred to the Expatriate Evacuation Committee and/or to the designated media relations person. Speculative reasons for the evacuation could be harmful to the evacuation and the company's relationship with the host government.

As evacuees depart the embarkation point by aircraft, vehicle, or ship, the Expatriate Evacuation Committee or designated manager should inform the corporate headquarters of the following:

- Flight data including date, time, destination, ETA, and arrival port or city, if appropriate.

- Detail list of evacuees.

- Number wanting assistance with onward transportation to the United States.

- Number who will stay at point of arrival and need arrangements for lodging, etc.

- Medical assistance needed.

METHODS OF TRANSPORTATION

Scheduled Airlines

- Carriers that serve the area, both foreign and domestic.

- Appropriate people to contact for arrangements.

- Capabilities of scheduled airlines to respond to evacuation requirements, that is, routes, capacity, ticketing requirements, payment, etc.

Nonscheduled "Chartered" Airlines

- Selection of a reliable carrier, foreign and/or domestic.
- Suitability of equipment available.

- Response time in obtaining necessary over-flight and landing authority, fuel, etc.

- Identify, through the U.S. Department of State, names of U.S. carriers that have existing contracts to perform evacuations during periods of emergencies or civil unrest.

Sea Transportation

- Identify shipping companies or shipping agents that serve the area.

- Select shipping agent or charter agent.

- Describe ship to include response time, capacity, and time required reaching safe haven.

- Consider charter of ocean-going yachts and cabin cruisers as a possible method of evacuating small numbers of essential personnel who may have remained in country after evacuation of nonessential personnel and families when it appears that airport embarkation points have been closed, but seaports or shoreline use is still available.

Land Transportation

Transportation by land methods should be examined closely as it is not recommended during sensitive times. Road transportation out of a country should be considered only as a last resort.

The following suggestions should be considered in developing a road transportation plan:

- Identify by name, location, and means of contact any other sources of vehicles that could be used in an emergency, either by rental, loan, or pooling by cooperating companies.

The Corporate Executive Survival Guide

- Have a checklist for road convoy leaders.

- Designate primary and alternate convoy leaders.

- Select routes, primary and alternate, that avoid choke points.

- Plan for rest stops in secure areas.

- Determine availability of vehicles to meet convoy requirements.

- Ensure adequate supplies of personal medical or other special needs. Inventory and have available spare fuel, food, water, tools, first aid, comfort supplies, maps, and compasses with each convoy.

- If the convoy will cross an international boundary, have appropriate documentation for each vehicle.

- Arrange security for the convoy from local authorities, if possible. If the environment is hostile, contact the U.S. Embassy for security assistance.

- Reconnoiter the route in advance by sending an advance vehicle approximately 30 minutes or more in advance of convoy.

- Provide communications capabilities for lead and rear convoy vehicles.

- Make preliminary arrangements to have trusted local nationals available to drive and translate at roadblocks, checkpoints, etc.

- Where possible, overland evacuation in convoy should be coordinated with other entities, particularly UN agencies and diplomatic groups.

James R. Doyle

INDUSTRIAL CHEMICAL ACCIDENTS

Many large corporations with major industrial chemical operations in overseas locations have developed highly sophisticated and effective emergency plans. Small companies, in many cases, need assistance from the larger corporate entities and from the host government. Although assistance from both will take time to develop, each small chemical company must initiate its own efforts to plan for emergencies.

The first considerations in developing an effective emergency plan for accidents at an industrial chemical site are its location and potential effect on surrounding communities. Other factors that may influence emergency planning are the chemical processes, materials handling, product storage, and transportation. The goals, objectives, and general purpose of the chemical unit should be reviewed in conjunction with the study of various potential emergencies that may affect the business and create serious public safety problems in surrounding communities. Some of these problem areas could be toxic releases, fires, explosions, chemical spills, drinking water contamination, or product contamination. When addressing these problem areas, public safety is of paramount importance because past experience shows that numerous chemical accidents have adversely affected local populations and the environment and have caused business interruptions that had a negative effect on the local economy.

A very critical action to be taken in developing preventive measures is the completion of a detailed inventory of all hazardous materials stored at each operating chemical unit. The complete inventory should be made and converted into a simple readable chart form showing the same chemicals in horizontal and vertical columns.

This chart sets up a grid structure that permits members of management, security, safety, and other response team elements to see the potential chemical reactions that could occur at a particular industrial site. The "reactivity grid", as this structure is called by many loss prevention planners, is an excellent aid in emergency planning.

This reactivity grid enables the emergency planner to make an organized and systematic analysis of the effect each chemical in the inventory could have on the other chemicals. The analysis requires each grid to be filled out in the simplest form of technical details.

The second key document needed in emergency planning for an industrial chemical operation is the "material safety data sheet". It may also be known as the "material safety data bulletin," or there may be other designations used to show specific technical data for each chemical.

Copies of these "Material Safety Data Sheets" or technical publications should be kept with all parties, including the emergency response team, or community agencies that have a vital interest in the emergency planning procedures at a particular chemical operation.

Chemical spills or releases usually have priority interest in emergency planning. The inventory, grids, and "Material Safety Data Sheets" provide key information for handling practically any emergency condition. The spill or release event requires rapid and thorough response. A hazardous chemical data sheet could be devised to facilitate quick reference, diagnosis, and action.

Organizing and recording the chemical inventory is a significant preliminary step to emergency planning. The actual plan must be written to cover all emergencies that can occur. It is the basis for an orderly approach to preventing an accident, or it can be used to control accidents that do happen. The emergency plan should be constructed in a format that enables emergency managers to concentrate on solutions to the major problem and still provide a framework for others to solve the small aspects of the emergency. The basic structure to operate in this manner is the "emergency management team", which consists of the general manager, the facility manager; and representatives from the safety, maintenance, engineering, research, finance, security, marketing, sales, medical, industrial hygiene, legal, environmental, and public relations departments. The general manager should appoint a single team member to coordinate all emergency activities; these activities should include plans, rehearsals, and actual implementation. Another staff member should be designated to handle all media events.

The emergency management team must focus on preventing and controlling emergencies in the chemical facility and in the surrounding communities. That is achieved only by exercising a "right to know" philosophy for all company employees and the community. "Material Safety Data Sheets," chemical inventory information, copies of the actual plan, and emergency equipment resources should be shared with the appropriate emergency planning agencies in the local communities.

The unique skills of members of the emergency management team should be highlighted within the team and with community agencies. For example, those team members with highly technical skills in chemical processes could be very valuable to hospitals, other medical authorities, and community responders to various emergencies.

A typical emergency plan for a chemical operation may consist of the following sections, which were researched by the Chemical Manufacturers' Association.

Plant emergency organization

- Designated person in charge and alternates.

- Functions of each key individual and group.

- Telephone numbers, office and home, for key people and alternates.

Plant risk evaluation

- Quantity of hazardous materials.

- Location of hazardous materials.

- Properties of each per "Material Safety Data Sheets ".

- Location of isolation valves.

- Special fire-fighting procedures.

- Special handling requirements.

Area risk evaluation

- Properties of hazardous materials at nearby plants.

- Contacts (names and telephone numbers) at other sites.

- Established procedures for notification of chemical releases at other sites in area.

Notification procedures and communication systems

- Alarm systems.

- Communication equipment i.e. radios, hot lines, etc.

- Emergency organization

    a. Plant management
    b. Local officials and response agencies
    c. Neighboring industry
    d. Nearby residents
    e. Names and telephone numbers including alternates.

- Designated person for media contacts.

- Procedure for notifying families of injured employees.

- Central reporting office.

Emergency equipment and facilities

- Firefighting equipment.

- Emergency medical supplies.

- Toxic gas detectors.

- Wind direction and speed indicators.
- Self-contained breathing apparatus.
- Protective clothing.

Training and drills

- Knowledge of chemicals, properties, toxicity, etc.
- Procedures for reporting emergencies.
- Knowledge of alarm systems.
- Location of fire fighting equipment.
- Use of fire fighting equipment.
- Use of protective equipment, respiration, breathing air, clothing, etc.
- Decontamination procedures for protective clothing and equipment.
- Evacuation procedures.
- Frequent, documented simulated emergencies.

Regular tests of emergency organization and procedures

- Simulated emergencies.
- Documented, frequent alarm system checks.
- Frequent tests of fire-fighting equipment.

- Evacuation practice.
- On-going emergency preparedness committee.

Plan updates

- Annual or more frequent if needed.
- Reflect results of drills and tests.

Emergency response procedures

- Communications.
- Evacuation.
- Medical.
- Special procedures for toxic gas releases i.e. chlorine, etc.
- Hurricane procedures in coastal areas.
- Utility failure procedures.
- Individual unit emergency procedures.
- Bomb-threat procedure.

Detailed operating manuals for each process unit and utility system

- Startup and shutdown emergency procedures.
- Analysis of potential incidents.

- Emergency response and action to be taken for each incident.

Liaison with local medical facilities

- Provide copies of "Material Safety Data Sheets"

- Provide a list of personnel with technical skills to assist in identifying the effects of various chemical agents and mixtures.

Emergency response information is available for all chemical emergencies from the Chemical Transportation Emergency Center (CHEMTREC) in Washington, D.C. CHEMTREC will accept international calls from chemical sites anywhere in the world on telephone number (202) 483-7616. In the United States, they have a toll free number at 1-800-424-9300. In addition, they have a Customer Service number that can assist with registration information at (703) 741-5523 CHEMTREC maintains technical information on approximately 4,000 chemicals, and it will have 300,000 "Material Safety Data Sheets" available for immediate consultation on emergency responses for chemical fires, evacuation distances, and general hazard communication. Industrial chemical sites overseas should consider establishing periodic communication checks with CHEMTREC through their internet website located at:

http://www.chemtrec.org.

Managers of emergency response teams should conduct communication and training exercises with local community agencies. The community agencies and the chemical units should exchange lists of resources to develop a strong mutual relationship. This effort should include a common listing of emergency planning and response resources in nearby industrial sites.

Evacuation and alarm procedures must be prepared in detail for each industrial chemical facility. This portion of an emergency plan must be flexible and applied as emergency situations dictate.

The following suggestions should be considered in developing evacuation procedures:

- Use public address media when appropriate to announce an emergency condition.

- Use prearranged alarm signals for operating personnel who have detailed instructions on various safety steps for emergencies and shutdown.

- Prepare detailed but simple evacuation routes out of buildings and away from the total facility, if necessary.

- Emergency organizations like the fire brigades, fire departments, police, hospitals, and auxiliary volunteer organizations should receive and rehearse, in detail, chemical facility evacuation plans.

A detailed evacuation plan should have, at the minimum, the following emergency information:

- "Material Safety Data Sheets".
- Facility layouts and plots that are up to date.
- Critical storage areas.
- All areas that have protective systems conforming to the required codes.
- Areas to store hazardous material.
- Key personnel and their telephone numbers.
- Location of public facilities that may assist in evacuation.

INDUSTRIAL FIRES

The subject of fire at an industrial chemical site is covered in this section. Fire is a premier emergency of devastating proportions and is often a by-product of some of the other catastrophic events discussed in this book. Firefighting, fire safety, and fire prevention are highly complex subjects. Many excellent and comprehensive works have been published and should be used for additional comprehensive reading.

The management teams operating an industrial chemical site have two options in planning the fire safety portion of a loss prevention plan. The first option is to establish and implement a written policy on fire safety that requires immediate and total evacuation of employees from the workplace on sounding a prearranged fire alarm signal. An effectively developed plan must take into consideration the fire protection needs of a particular chemical facility. The plan must also satisfy the requirements of applicable fire codes, fire standards, laws, and local ordinances.

The following suggestions should be considered in developing a fire prevention plan:

- A list of major workplace fire hazards.

- Proper storage and handling procedures of fuel source hazards.

- Potential ignition sources.

- Existence of a fire brigade.

- Types of fire protection equipment and systems protecting against hazards and ignition sources.

- Names of personnel responsible for maintaining fire protection equipment and systems.

- Procedures for controlling accumulations of flammable and combustible waste and maintaining good housekeeping procedures.

- Maintenance procedures for process safety devices used on heat-producing equipment that prevents the accidental ignition of combustible materials.

- Names, addresses, telephone numbers, and language capabilities of various local community contacts for fire-fighting, arson investigations, and security protection.

- A brief statement on each of the local agencies and surrounding businesses relative to their capability in response time, training, equipment, leadership, experience, and willingness to act on direct orders or from higher authority.

- Actions to be taken in recovering from a severely damaging fire.

- Local management must also provide training in recognizing the fire hazard from materials and processes to which employees may be exposed.

- The fire emergency plan should be reviewed with each employee when he or she is hired and at least once a year.

- The plan must also be kept in the workplace and made available for all employees to review as they desire.

Another management option could involve establishing a fire brigade at an industrial site.
The basic elements considered in developing an organizational policy would include:

- Basic organizational structure of the fire brigade.

- Type, amount, and frequency of training.

- Functions to be performed by the brigade.

There are two basic definitions in fire planning that are necessary for establishing readiness of the fire brigade. One definition deals with "incipient stage fires." An incipient stage fire is one in which the critical or beginning stage can be controlled by portable fire extinguishers, Class II standpipe, or small hose systems, without the need for protective clothing or breathing apparatus. The other definition deals with interior structural fires. Interior structural firefighting requires the physical activity of fire suppression or rescue, or both, inside buildings or enclosed structures that have a fire beyond the incipient stage.

The following suggestions should be considered in developing a plan to establish a fire brigade:

- Assure that employees expected to fight interior structural fires are physically capable.

- Provide training and education for all fire brigade members commensurate with the duties and functions that they are expected to perform.

- Provide the fire brigade leaders with training and education including organization and control that is more comprehensive than that provided to the general membership of the fire brigade.

- Provide fire brigade members with annual training and education when they are expected to fight incipient stage fires and quarterly training and education when they are expected to fight interior structural fires. The quality of the training and education must be similar to that provided by institutions that are widely recognized for the quality and thoroughness of their fire training.

- Inform fire brigade members about special hazards, such as the storage and use of flammable liquids and gases, toxic chemicals, radioactive sources, and water-reactive substances to which they may be exposed during fire and other emergencies and also any changes that occur in relation to the special hazards.

- Prepare and make available for inspection by fire brigade members written procedures for handling special hazards, and include these written procedures in training and education programs.

- Maintain and inspect, on a regular basis, fire-fighting equipment to ensure its safe operational condition.

- Perform monthly inspections on portable fire extinguishers and respirators.

- Provide at no cost to the employee and ensure the use of personal protective equipment.

- Provide, at no cost to the employee, and ensure the use of quality respiratory protection devices.

Pre-fire planning is critical for the effectiveness of a fire brigade. The following suggestions for a pre-fire plan should be considered as a guide in familiarizing brigade members:

- Familiarize the members with structural components that could fail during a fire.

  a. Materials that loses its strength when exposed to fire such as steel and lime mortar.

  b. Unsupported partitions or walls.

- Understand conditions in the building that can become dangerous during a fire

  a. Stacked or high-piled storage.

  b. Hazardous materials.

  c. Utility equipment on the roof that can cause roof collapse.

  d. Manufacturing equipment above the ground floor.

- Know the physical features of the building that might confuse or trap the firefighter during the fire.

  a. Large open areas.

  b. Dead-end corridors or hallways.

  c. Open pits or holes.

  d. Openings into underground utility shafts or tunnels.

- Information gathered during the survey should also include hazards that may be contained within a building, such as:

    a. Flammable and combustible liquids.

    b. Toxic chemicals.

    c. Explosives.

    d. Reactive metals.

    e. Radioactive materials.

    f. Processes performed in the buildings that are inherently dangerous.

- Information on life safety that needs to be collected to plan for occupant protection includes:

    a. Location and size of entrances and exits.

    b. Location of windows suitable for rescue access.

    c. Special rescue problems such as handicapped occupants and large numbers.

Plant management, and in particular the fire brigade, must maintain close liaison with their local fire department. A municipal fire department's main responsibility is to protect the general community, and they will be reluctant to do much more than prevent the spread of fire to adjacent property unless they are familiar with the risks and hazards involved in a particular plant. For this reason, each plant must meet with the local fire department at least once a year to familiarize the department with the plant layout, fire protection systems, special hazards, and any changes that have occurred since its last visit. Such visits are also a good time to work out details for attacking potential fires and defining how the plant brigade can best work with the fire department under fire conditions.

Most fire departments are more than happy to assist in maintaining programs to help prevent and handle industrial fires and to participate in occasional drills. It is also advantageous to have the fire department hydro-statically test the plant fire hose at regular intervals so that the fire brigade is confident about its safety and readiness if it must be used in an emergency.

As soon as a fire has been extinguished, the brigade must begin to restore automatic sprinkler systems, onsite water supplies, fire hoses, and extinguishers to a ready condition. During this process, one brigade member must stand by the control valve for the sprinkler/monitor so that it may be reopened immediately if rekindling occurs. If the fire was large or in a hazardous area, a 24-hour security and fire watch should be established with extinguishers and hose lines in readiness.

Every attempt should be made to determine the cause of the fire, because corrective action may be required to prevent a recurrence. If the fire was of suspicious origin, care must be taken to leave all possible evidence undisturbed, and the proper investigative authorities must be notified. Once everything is under control, the fire brigade should assist with any salvage and clean-up activities that may be required.

Potential explosive mixtures found in most facilities include dust, flammable and combustible liquids, and gases in confined spaces. Since explosions generally occur without warning, it is likely that firefighting activities will have to be supplemented by rescue operations for persons who were working in the area. In performing these firefighting and rescue operations, emergency personnel must be aware of the additional hazards of secondary explosions and possible structural damage to the building.

NUCLEAR AND RADIOLOGICAL INCIDENTS

Industrial facilities using radioactive and nuclear materials or those facilities located near other operations with such materials should develop emergency plans to deal with nuclear and radiological emergencies. In developing a plan in this critical industrial area, the management team should focus on several major responses:

- Ensure a safe and orderly shutdown of operations as required by emergency conditions.

- Remove vital records, files, plant equipment, and vehicles to a safe emergency relocation site.

- Prepare an emergency site that includes accommodations for employees and family members.

- Implement an ongoing vulnerability analysis to reduce the exposure of plant property, equipment, and personnel.

These responses are developed and refined through management actions that are based on crisis relocation planning. Assuming that advance warning of a radiological or nuclear incident is possible, with enough lead time to allow the movement of nonessential personnel and everything critical to rapid business recovery out of designated high-risk areas and the dispersal into surrounding low-risk areas during a radiological or nuclear emergency.

To enhance plant survival during a nuclear emergency, the Federal Emergency Management Agency (FEMA) offers an effective management checklist to assist managers at an industrial site in crisis relocation planning. A partial list of the FEMA work is outlined in the next section.

Control of Human Resources

This section offers key points for systematic assessment and relocation of employees and their families during a nuclear incident. Each industrial facility should appoint a representative of management to coordinate the following actions:

- Develop and maintain a-list of all personnel; names, according to addresses and cities, or districts, in a large city.

- Consult your local Civil Defense office for information on evacuation, and obtain pamphlets, maps, etc., that will be used for your evacuation plan. Provide the Civil Defense authority with the total number of employees and dependents who will need shelter so that he or she can arrange an evacuation site.

- Recruit and assign a volunteer leader by city, district, or districts, so there are 10-20 employees per leader grouped in moderate-sized neighborhoods.

- Instruct volunteer leaders with the information gathered from the Civil Defense office.

- Provide a list of employees in each assigned district to the appropriate leader and the name of leader to employees in his or her district.

- Notify the volunteer leader when an employee moves into or out of his or her district.

- Set up communication links with leaders.

- Notify leaders to hold group meetings to confirm plans.

- Notify leaders when to put evacuation plans into effect.

- Assign a volunteer leader to develop records of the following information for each employee in his or her district:

    a. Number of dependents needing transportation.

    b. Capacity of transportation available at each employee's home.

    c. Special skills of dependents; for example, nursing, construction, etc.

    d. Personnel who are classified as dependents of employees in other industries.

e. Number and kinds of medical problems requiring special diets, medicines, etc.

- Use the records developed to organize and assign transportation. Assign volunteer drivers and use the largest capacity vehicles available.

- Confirm assignments of riders and drivers so that all employees and families, plus supplies for 2 weeks of camping out, are assured of being evacuated. Establish a rendezvous point for all drivers in your group to ensure that everybody in your district is accounted for before leaving for the safe area.

- Prepare a backup plan in case of vehicle breakdown, and fix routes so missing members can be found quickly by tracing routes.

- Notify members in your district of any assignment changes as they occur or periodically.

- Stress the importance of establishing and maintaining a schedule. Otherwise, a person who missed his pick-up may take his own vehicle, create confusion, and add to traffic problems.

- Distribute Civil Defense booklets including lists of what supplies to bring from home, how to shut down a household when an evacuation order is given by authorities, and what routes to take to get to the assigned safe area.

- Conduct group meetings when the coordinator requires, to confirm assignments and to ensure understanding by members.

If you start to plan after the evacuation warning is given, you will need a place large enough to assemble all company personnel. If the company has more than several hundred employees, it may be necessary to divide into groups of 100-200, organized by city or district of residence. Then subdivide into groups of 10-20, by neighborhood, with a volunteer leader to carry out subsequent tasks

Area Shelter

This section offers suggestions for establishing shelter space for employees and their families during a nuclear emergency. A representative of management should be appointed to coordinate the following actions:

- Determine number of employees and family members evacuating, including age and sex.

- Define shelter space requirements needed to accommodate those in shelters.

- Establish shelter stocking requirements.

- Establish host area liaison, obtain and survey assigned space, and assess upgrading requirements.

- Estimate materials, equipment, labor, and time required to prepare shelter space.

- Complete logistics preparation and upgrading sequence for post-warning completion, beginning on warning day.
- Protective housekeeping.

- Industrial resource inventory.

- Equipment inventory and equipment protection.

- Vulnerability rating and analysis of facilities and equipment.

- Protective measures and hardening activities.

- Management of hazardous material incidents.

James R. Doyle

CRISIS MANAGEMENT CONCLUSION

Many American businesses abroad and domestically have experienced first hand the devastation wrought by the types of catastrophes or crises described in this book. Perhaps some of us have felt the pain and loss of a loved one in such tragedies or the impact of substantial property damage. All of us have been exposed through television and the news media to the horrible events such as the 11 September 2001 terrorist attacks. Natural disasters, accidents and terrorist events are going to happen. The best we can do is be prepared so as to reduce our risk and control the damage. We have to prepare and plan for these events as though out life depends on it, because it may. It has been well established that people who prepare themselves by developing contingency plans for emergencies significantly lessen their vulnerability and greatly enhance their opportunity for survival.

Each American business must assume a high level of responsibility for the safety of their employees and corporate assets through emergency planning. Emergency planning cannot be solely delegated to others, such as fire departments, medical personnel, or the government. However, cooperation and coordination with government emergency personnel is, of course useful, even though the degree of assistance will vary, depending on available resources etc. We must recognize that widespread chaos prevails following any major catastrophe, and we should not expect high-quality emergency service from usual providers. Emergency crews of all types are overwhelmed following a disaster. Utility services, such as telephones, electric power, and water and sewer facilities, will most often be disrupted.

Finally, it is imperative that we adopt an attitude of continuous vigilance, especially in those situations where "warning signs" of imminent trouble are apparent. Examples of such events are political or military coupe, civil unrest, terrorist events, and violent storms or floods that might indicate the need to evacuate. Hurricanes, tornadoes, and violent electrical storms are usually preceded by warnings. Hurried, last minute emergency planning is usually inadequate. Above all, avoid the attitude that "it won't happen to me."

Always be prepared, especially in the unfamiliar environment of far away places. Planning for emergencies pays very high dividends. All of us must take this possibility seriously.

U.S. DEPARTMENT OF STATE SERVICES

The U.S. Department of State provides a wide variety of valuable support services to American citizens and companies working in foreign countries. Some of these services include protecting and assisting U.S. citizens living and traveling abroad which includes issuing *Travel Warnings* some areas of the world. They may also assist in determining the welfare of citizens through their *Overseas Citizens Services* office. In addition, they assist U.S. companies in the international marketplace through their *Office of Commercial and Business Affairs*. The U.S. maintains diplomatic relations with over 180 countries and also maintains relations with many international organizations and operates in more than 250 posts around the world. In addition, they keep the public informed about U.S. foreign relations and maintain a 24 hour a day *Operations Center* which is responsible for communications and crisis management. Additional information about the U.S. Department of State can be found on their internet website at:

http://www.state.gov/

Legal Limitations

Consular officers must operate within the laws of the foreign country involved, as well as those of the United States. In legal matters, such as arrests, child custody disputes, and deaths, it is important to keep in mind that the laws of the foreign country apply to persons or property within its territory.

Practical Limitations

In many cases, consular officers cannot personally provide the U.S. citizen with the assistance needed but must seek the cooperation of government officials or qualified professionals in the host country in order to provide it. With few exceptions, no official funds are allocated to pay for the services that may be required by a U.S. citizen. The amount of cooperation provided by the host country and the quality of professional services available vary greatly from country to country.

Privacy Act Limitations

The provisions of the Privacy Act, which was designed to protect the privacy and rights of the individual, occasionally complicate the handling of cases involving citizens abroad. As a general rule, consular officers may not reveal information regarding an individual American's location, welfare, intentions, or problems to anyone, including family members and congressional representatives without the express consent of that individual. As an example, if an American citizen who has not maintained contact with family or friends is located by a consular officer abroad, neither that officer nor the officers in the Overseas Citizen Services office may report back to the family or congressional office regarding the individual's welfare or whereabouts unless the individual gives written permission to do so. Americans arrested overseas often refuse to give permission for their families or friends to be informed of their location or their plight.

Although sympathetic to the distress this can cause worried families, the Overseas Citizen Services office must comply with the provisions of the Privacy Act.

The Department's legal advisors have ruled that a congressional member is not exempt from the restrictions of the Act unless his or her request is directly connected to the functions of a committee or subcommittee and the request is supported in writing by the chairperson of such committee or subcommittee.

Arrest

The Overseas Citizen Services office monitors the cases of Americans arrested abroad and acts as liaison between the prisoners's family and Congressional representatives in the United States and consular officers overseas. When a U.S. post abroad is advised that an American has been arrested, a consular officer visits the American as soon as possible, provides information regarding the foreign legal system and a list of attorneys, and offers other assistance such as contacting family or friends on the prisoner's behalf. The consular officer's role in arrest cases is one of observation and support, regularly visiting the prisoner and checking his or her welfare, monitoring human rights and the status of the case, and advising interested parties of case developments.

The Overseas Citizen Services office may assist in transferring private funds to U.S. posts abroad for delivery to American prisoners and serves as a point of contact for concerned families and friends. When a prisoner's health or life is endangered by inadequate diet or medical care provided by the local prison, food supplements and/or medical care may be arranged. Although officers at posts overseas may be permitted to monitor the conditions of the prisoner, they cannot demand the immediate release of the prisoner, give legal advice, pay for fines or legal fees, or represent the prisoner at trial.

Financial Assistance

The Overseas Citizen Services office works with consular officers at U.S. posts abroad to assist Americans overseas who find themselves in financial trouble. If destitute American citizens turn to a consular officer for help, the officer first attempts to locate private sources of funds, usually from family, friends, or business associates. After these private funds are identified, the officer assists in transmitting the funds to the individual through Department of State facilities. If all efforts to identify private funding prove fruitless, normally the consular office abroad will request approval of a "repatriation loan" that will pay for the individual's direct return to the nearest port of entry in the United States.

As a result of a program approved by the Congress, the Department is able to provide further assistance to Americans who find themselves temporarily destitute because of loss, robbery, failure of expected funds to arrive, or similar circumstances. In these cases, the consular officer may work with the Overseas Citizen Services office to arrange for the prompt transfer of private funds from home, and may also provide the individual or family with a small Government loan until private funds arrive.

Medical Assistance

The Overseas Citizen Services office also works with and assists U.S. consular officers abroad in handling the serious problem of Americans who become physically or mentally ill while traveling or living abroad. A consular officer who becomes aware of an ill or injured American in his or her consular district advises the Overseas Citizen Services office. The office, in addition to providing guidance and support to the post abroad, locates family members, guardians, and friends in the United States and advises them of the problem; identifies and transmits private funds when necessary; and frequently collects information on the individual's prior medical history and forwards it to the post abroad. When necessary, the office assists in the return of the ill or injured individual to the United States with appropriate medical escort via special commercial air ambulance or, occasionally, by U.S. Air Force medical evacuation aircraft. The use of Air Force facilities for medical evacuation is authorized only under certain conditions when commercial evacuation is not possible, and the full expense must be borne by the citizen or the citizen's family.

Death of American Citizens

When an American dies abroad, the consular officer reports the death by telephone or telegram to the next of kin or legal representative. Often the Overseas Citizens Services office must help to locate the next of kin and provide guidance on how to make arrangements for local burial or to return the body to the United States. The disposition of remains is affected by local laws, customs, and facilities, which are often vastly different from those in the United States. The family's instructions and necessary private funds to cover the costs involved are then relayed to the Foreign Service post concerned. The Department of State has no funds to assist in the return of ashes or remains of American citizens who die abroad. The scheduled time of arrival of the remains and carrier data are provided in advance to the next of kin or funeral home. Upon completion of all formalities, the consular officer abroad prepares a death report based upon the local death certificate and forwards it to the next of kin or legal representative for use in U.S. courts to settle estate matters.

Citizen Welfare/Whereabouts

The Overseas Citizens Services office also responds to inquiries from the public and congressional offices concerning Americans traveling or residing abroad. Most cases handled by this division fall into one of two categories. The first deals with Americans who are presumed missing abroad because they have failed to return as scheduled, have not made intended connections, or have not communicated with family or friends for an undue length of time.

The second category involves Americans traveling abroad who are presumed to be safe and well but who must be located quickly because a crisis has occurred in the United States, such as the serious illness or death of a family member. In both these cases, the Overseas Citizens Services office relays the request for assistance and all pertinent data available on the individual to the U.S. Embassy or consulate responsible for the area where the individual is believed to be traveling or residing. Acting on the information provided by the inquirer, the consular officer attempts to locate these individuals, determine their welfare, pass on any urgent messages, and, consistent with the Privacy Act, report back the results of search efforts.

In case of disasters, such as earthquakes, hurricanes, and air crashes, the Overseas Citizens Services office ascertains the names of any American citizens involved and informs their families of their status.

Travel Advisories

The responsibility for informing the public and U.S. Foreign Service posts on the advisability of travel to certain countries or areas is centralized in the Overseas Citizens Services office. The source of the information disseminated is usually a Foreign Service posts. The office is responsible for issuing travel advisories when events abroad are likely to affect traveling Americans adversely. Travel advisories usually concern civil unrest, natural disasters; disease outbreaks, and long term criminal activities and potential terrorist threats directed against travelers. Many of the advisories refer to temporary conditions and are canceled when the problem no longer poses a threat. The advisories are distributed to the travel industry and the media, U.S.

passport agencies and the Department of State internet website located at:

http://www.state.gov/.

Search and Rescue

The U.S. Department of State is also responsible for monitoring search and rescue efforts outside the United States. Airplanes and/or ships search for missing American Registry planes or boats that may be carrying American passengers or crew.

AIRCRAFT OPERATIONS

INTRODUCTION

My involvement in the study and practice of aircraft operations has spanned a period of over 35 years. It began with my first class in Aviation Operations in the Marine Corps. Later as a licensed general aviation pilot I had an opportunity to fly into some of the largest airport facilities in the United States and of course on the other end of the scale some that were no more than a small strip of cleared grass and dirt. Later, as an international security consultant, I spent over 20 years traveling around the world through most of the major international airports and a few that most people have never heard of.

The following section is intended for use primarily by the professional security staff of a company that owns and operates aircraft in foreign environment however; many of the following suggestions are applicable in the U.S. as well. Based on my personal experiences, I believe several of the suggestions offered here will also be useful to owners of general aviation aircraft desiring guidelines for improving the security of their investment.

Corporate aircraft operators are not exempt from criminal activities and, should be aware of terrorists groups attempting to promote a particular cause through exploitation of the company's aviation assets. The military-defense industrial complex, international corporations with operations in countries with civil unrest, corporations whose products and operations are of a controversial nature, and corporations experiencing labor unrest, are all potential targets for acts of air piracy, sabotage, extortion, bombings and other criminal acts.

The safe operation of corporate aircraft must balance security planning with flight planning. Every pilot knows that the ultimate responsibility for the safe operation of the aircraft rest with the *pilot in command*. However; without the full support of the aircraft owner and operator, this responsibility would be a significant challenge.

Airport operators are required, in most cases, to provide for the physical security of the air operations area as an integral part of their overall responsibility for the operation of that airport. The suggestions offered here are intended to complement these efforts, where possible, and direct the user at all times to coordinate their efforts with the responsible airport operator.

The first line of defense against threats to the safety of corporate aircraft operations is the protection against unauthorized access to the aircraft and ground support facilities or areas. Aircraft owners and operators who are involved in establishing or maintaining protective measures for corporate aircraft should also consider the presence or absence of an airport security program, as required by FAA. It should be noted that since the terrorist attacks of *11 September 2001* there have been many major revisions in the rules and regulations governing both domestic and international aircraft operations. The following information should always be considered in the context of "current" local, state, federal and international rules and regulations governing aircraft operations.

GENERAL CONSIDERATIONS

A corporate security plan should be a written document detailing positive measures to protect the aircraft at its home base, in-flight, and at airports where the aircraft is parked during a transit status. Access to the plan should be limited to those who have an operational need-to-know, in order to preserve its integrity.

A security awareness program in a corporate aviation department should be established to promote initial and recurrent security training of all personnel, including clerical, maintenance personnel, flight crews, and not just the employees who are directly responsible for security. System testing should also be an integral part of the program and should include all elements of the plan.

The security plan must have the full support of the chief executive officer of the organization, and those responsible for it should be held accountable for its success to the same degree as are other corporate efforts.

BASIC AIRCRAFT PROTECTION MEASURES

The following suggestions should be considered when developing a protection plan:

- Where possible, the aircraft should be parked in a locked or guarded hangar. Dependence upon a locked hangar for protection should include strict access control measures. Placement of an aircraft within a hangar does not eliminate the necessity for securing the aircraft.

- Security of an unattended aircraft may be improved through the use of devices such as special anti-tampering tape on doors, windows, ports, inspection plates which once applied cannot be removed under normal conditions. Tape that is weatherproof, heat resistant and available with self-destroying slits will enhance the tamper detection capability.

- Due to the widespread unauthorized possession of master keys to manufacturer installed locks, and the possibility of loss of key control with the passage of time, the security of manufacturer installed locks may not always be assured. If in doubt, consideration should be given to the replacement of the locks on corporate aircraft with high quality, professionally installed locks.

- Positive key control is used to protect many valuable corporate assets; the flight department contains or transports many of them and should, therefore, be subject to the highest control standards in the corporation.

- All avionics and removable items in the aircraft should be marked for positive identification. Positive identification of each item is an absolute necessity to facilitate the investigative and recovery efforts of local, state and federal authorities in addition to providing some deterrence. A color marking, in addition to engraved aircraft registration numbers, or any other unique identifying numbers or symbols, is recommended. The engraved marking provides a means of positive identification and the color marking provides a deterrent value.

- Non-installed items of value or of unusual interest should not be stored in the aircraft if it is to be unattended for any extended period of time. If storage in the aircraft is absolutely necessary, these items should be secured.

- A thorough inventory of the contents of the aircraft should be maintained on file at its home base. The inventory should include serial numbers and other identifying data. Color photographs of the aircraft exterior and interior spaces should also be maintained with the inventory.

- Consideration should be given to the use of anti-theft devices such as alarms or removable wheel locks. While such devices are not foolproof, they are a deterrent and could result in a diversion of an attack on an unprotected aircraft. Such devices may also bring about an early detection and apprehension by authorities. This is an especially important consideration at airports where the corporate aircraft will remain unattended overnight when the aircraft is not in a hangar.

- The display of corporate logos and product or organizational identification media is not recommended. This could increase the threat of attack for several reasons.

- Aircraft parked on the ramp should always be parked in a well-illuminated area and away from perimeter gates and fencing.

- Positive identification of all passengers is a must. If a passenger is not a known corporate official or guest, identification and trip authorization should be verified before the individual is allowed access to the aircraft. Safeguards should be established assuring that all baggage to be loaded on board the aircraft matches those passengers on board, and that the baggage was not left unattended and accessible prior to its loading.
- Safeguards should be established for cargo to be transported on board the aircraft to assure that each package is received from a known source and has been authorized by the flight department.
- Procedures should be established for the search of passengers, baggage, and packages or cargo in the event of the receipt of threats, or in the event of other questionable circumstances.
- All persons working on the aircraft should be positively identified, especially at airports where other than corporate employees are called upon to perform maintenance or repair work.
- The pre-flight inspection should include efforts to detect foreign objects and evidence of tampering with the aircraft.
- Crew vigilance should be heightened while the aircraft is being re-fueled by persons representing a company which does not normally do business with the flight department.
- Once engines are started, be suspicious of any attempts to delay, stop, or otherwise impede the departure from other than air traffic control authorities.

HANGAR SECURITY

The following suggestions should be considered when developing a hangar security plan:

The Corporate Executive Survival Guide

- Aircraft should always be placed in a secure hangar whenever possible.

- Designate the hangar as a closed or restricted area and control access into it from the public side of the airport.

- Depending upon the size of the flight department, use corporate identification badges unless preceded by an airport authority operating under an approved FAA security program.

- Unless under escort, visitors should not be permitted into the hangar area where aircraft are stored, or in the immediate ramp area where the aircraft are readied for flight.

- Pedestrian doors to the hangar should deny access to unauthorized persons. Doors which open into an office area should be designated for passengers, visitors or delivery access to the flight department.

- Consider establishment of a waiting lounge for passengers to wait until boarding is announced, or pending identification and approval for boarding.

- If large, air side hangar doors are left open for ventilation, expansion type barriers should be deployed to delay unauthorized access into the hangar area.

- Where possible, visual observation of the hangar and ramp parking areas should be maintained.

- All unauthorized personnel should be challenged. Suspicious individuals should be immediately reported to the supporting law enforcement agency.

- An alarm system is recommended to protect the hangar during unoccupied periods. Guards with adequate communications equipment offer added protection of extremely valuable or threatened assets.

- Employee and non-employee parking should be separated.

- The air side should be physically separated from the public side in the vicinity of the hangar. A seven-foot chain link fence with three-strand barbed wire overhang is the minimum recommended.

- Vehicle parking or the storage of items on the ground, within 20 feet of the perimeter fence should be prohibited, as it provides an easy means to go over the fence.

- Outside illumination of the hangar and immediate fencing is highly recommended.

- Consideration should be given to lease provisions allowing control of the ramp areas where corporate aircraft are parked or are readied for flight. The controlled area should be sufficient to provide a buffer zone between the aircraft and non-controlled access areas. The marking of a controlled area as a restricted area is sometimes accomplished by lines and symbols painted on the ramp surface. Markings applied to a ramp area are very often subject to specific requirements. The airport operator should be consulted prior to applying any permanent ramp markings.

- A policy should be established and enforced requiring passengers to board through the operations office or passenger lounge, and, except for maintenance and service support, prohibiting vehicles on the ramp side.

- When cargo must be transported to the aircraft, flight department personnel should admit the vehicle to the ramp only after verification of authenticity of the shipment and the driver, and accompany the delivery van to the aircraft.

- Positive access controls should be enforced, including the positive identification and recording of all visitors.

- Assure that a comprehensive emergency or bomb threat plan is in effect and that the telephone numbers of the airport's supporting law enforcement agency and Explosive Ordnance Disposal resources are readily available.

- Ensure that the facility is periodically visited by the airport's supporting law enforcement patrols.

"REMAIN-OVER-NIGHT" AIRPORT CONSIDERATIONS

The following suggestions should be considered when an aircraft has to remain over night:

- Prior to any departure from the home base, the servicing fixed-base operator at any remain-over-night airport should be contacted in advance and advised of any unusual security requirements required to protect the aircraft while at that airport.

- The flight crew should be provided with telephone numbers of all offices and watch personnel having responsibility for protecting the area at a remain-over-night airport.

- Aircraft should be in a hangar whenever possible. If it is not, the aircraft should be parked in a well-illuminated secure area away from perimeter gates and fencing.

- In threat conditions, especially outside the U.S., arrangements for a guard on the aircraft should be considered a necessity.

- When taxiing to the parking location, a non-flying crewmember should carefully scan the area to detect any unusual conditions.

- The flight crew should visit the aircraft at least once daily at remain-over-night airports to inspect the aircraft and assure that it is properly secured and that there are no signs of tampering.

- The keys to the aircraft should never be left with the Fixed-Base Operator unless they are properly secured and controlled to the satisfaction of the *pilot in command*.

- If maintenance or repairs are required of a firm not normally providing services to the flight department, a flight crew member should be present, and the repairman should be positively identified as an employee of the servicing firm.
- A security inspection of the aircraft to detect tampering or foreign objects is critical prior to any departure from a remain-over-night airport.

IN-FLIGHT SECURITY CONSIDERATIONS

The following suggestions should be considered as part of an in-flight security plan:

- Flight crews should frequently review plans developed by the security department to handle in-flight emergencies and threats. Plans of action should include actions to take in the event of a bomb threat, attempted hijacking, or terrorist attack. These plans should be consistent, to the extent possible, with those developed to protect other corporate assets from similar threats.

- If the cockpit is separated by a door from the cabin, unauthorized personnel should not be permitted into the cockpit.

- In the event of a hijacking, the following suggestions should be considered:

A special emergency condition exists when a hostile act is threatened or committed by a person(s) aboard an aircraft which jeopardizes the safety of the aircraft or its passengers.

The pilot of an aircraft reporting a special emergency should if possible, implement standard distress or urgency radio-telephone procedures providing the details of the special emergency. If circumstances do not permit the use of prescribed distress or urgency procedures, transmit on the air/ground frequency in use at the time as many of the following elements as possible, spoken distinctly and in the following order:

>(a) Name of the station addressed including time and circumstances.
>
>(b) The identification of the aircraft and present position.
>
>(c) The nature of the special emergency condition and pilot intentions.
>
>(d) If unable to provide this information, use code words and/or transponder codes. This will alert air traffic controllers of the emergency. Transponder codes and code words should be restricted to responsible officials in the flight department. Flight crews should be thoroughly familiar with their meaning and use. Mistaken use of these codes and code words could have severe consequences.

- If it is possible to do so without jeopardizing the safety of the flight crew and passengers, the pilot of a hijacked passenger aircraft, after departing from the cleared routing over which the aircraft was operating, should consider the following:

  >(a) Maintain a true airspeed of no more than 400 knots, and preferably an altitude between 10,000 and 25,000 feet.
  >
  >(b) Fly a course toward the destination which the hijacker has announced.

- If these procedures result in radio contact or air intercept, the pilot will attempt to comply with any instructions received which may direct him/her to an appropriate landing field.

- In the event of a hijacking or any other disturbance, or upon learning an unauthorized person may be aboard the aircraft, the flight crew should:

    (a) Get the aircraft on the ground under any pretext.

    (b) Get the passengers and then the flight crew off the aircraft, if possible.

    (c) Allow law enforcement to deal with the hijackers or other disturbances.

- Only authorized officials should have access to bomb threat, search, and in-flight hijack incident management procedures.

LAW ENFORCEMENT CONSIDERATIONS

The following legal and law enforcement should be reviewed and updated as required:

- Theft, damage, or destruction of general aviation and corporate aircraft, or contents, is a criminal offense. The law enforcement agency having jurisdiction where the offense was committed typically has primary jurisdiction. All such offenses should be promptly reported to that agency for investigation and prosecution

- The interstate transportation of a stolen aircraft is a violation of Title 18 of the U.S. Code, and is a federal offense investigated by the FBI. Such offenses may be reported directly to the local FBI office or reported through the local law enforcement agency.

- Arson, malicious damaging, destruction, disablement, or wrecking of any civil aviation aircraft used, operated, or employed in interstate, overseas, or foreign air commerce; or any aircraft engine, propeller, appliance, or spare part with intent to damage, destroy, disable, or wreck any such aircraft; or, with like intent, placement of a destructive substance in, upon, or in proximity to any such aircraft or components or times used in connection with the operation of the aircraft or cargo carried; or with like intent wrecks, damages, destroys, disables, or places a destructive substance in or upon or in proximity to support facilities used in connection with the operation; or with like intent, willfully incapacitates any member of the crew of such aircraft, is a violation of Title 18, U.S. Code, and is a federal offense investigated by the FBI.

- Any forgery, counterfeiting, alteration, or false marking of a certificate issued under the authority of the Federal Aviation Act and/or the willful display of markings that are false or misleading as to the nationality or registration of the aircraft are federal criminal offenses under Title 49, U.S. Code.

- Interference with air navigation through display of a light or signal in such a manner to be mistaken for a true signal in connection with an airport or other air navigation facility, or any removal, extinguishing of, or interference with the operation of any such true light or signal is a federal criminal offense.

- Interference with flight crew members while aboard an aircraft within the special aircraft jurisdiction of the U.S. by assaults, intimidation, or threats so as to interfere with the performance by such member of his/her duties or lessen the ability of the flight crew member to perform his/her duties is a federal criminal offense under Title 49, U.S. Code, and is investigated by the FBI.

- Aircraft piracy, i.e., any seizure or exercise of control, by force or violence or threat of force or violence with wrongful intent, of an aircraft within the special aircraft jurisdiction of the U.S. is a federal criminal offense, punishable by death or imprisonment for not less than 20 years.

James R. Doyle

GUIDELINES FOR INTERNATIONAL FLIGHT OPERATIONS

The following suggestions should be considered as part of international flight operations:

- Prior to the start of any foreign trips, consult with the Department of State, Travel Advisory Service and provide a briefing for all scheduled passengers before the flight.
- When traveling to an area of economic strife, make advance arrangements to provide for a reliable security and guard service.
- Know the telephone numbers of the nearest U.S. Embassy or consulate and, if unsure of any political, economic or other local factors which might affect security, contact them directly before departure.
- Advise all crew members and passengers en-route to a foreign location to be cautious when accepting gifts or packages of which the contents are unknown. Query all aboard prior to departure of their knowledge of <u>all</u> personal or business-related goods acquired outside of the U.S.
- Physically inspect all goods for which any uncertainty exists.

CONCLUSION

Prior to the terrorist attacks of 11 September 2001 most Americans were complacent with issues of personal security. Since then, most Americans are aware that an attack can come from any source, at any time, and in any location. In addition to terrorist using civilian aircraft as tactical weapons of mass destruction, Americans are more aware of other terrorist threats including biological, chemical and nuclear.

Terrorist are not the only threat we face. Many Americans have been victimized by local crime and most of us are acquainted with victims of crime. We are constantly inundated with daily reports from the news media about a wide range of criminal activities, including burglary, robbery, rape, kidnapping and murder.

Crime is escalating throughout the world. It is a serious problem which will not be solved in the foreseeable future. Unfortunately, we cannot delegate our personal security to the police or to anyone else. Law enforcement, as we all know, is largely reactive.

As I mentioned at the beginning of this book, each of us must assume a high level of personal responsibility for our security and insure that our loved ones do the same. We must adopt an attitude of continuous awareness of our vulnerabilities and always resist the temptation of yielding to a complacent attitude of "it will not happen to me".

The Corporate Executive Survival Guide

APPENDIX

Here is what experts in the world of security have to say about Mr. Doyle and his essential manual:

"Dear Mr. Doyle,
Thank you for sending me a copy of the security manual "The corporate executive Survival Guide: Internal Operation.
Your thoughtfulness during this great transition in democracy is inspiring.
Again, thank you for your kindness...
John Ashcroft
Attorney General"

"One of my users has purchased a copy of your "Terrorist Groups – Profiles and Tactics" resource. He has requested that the library make this available on our agency intranet, which is accessible to all NSA/CSS personnel. Will you grant permission for this use?"...."CSS refers to military personnel assigned to NSA"...."I cannot give you specific numbers of users, since information about the size of the NSA workforce is not a matter of public record."

Sallie Becker, Librarian, National Security Agency.

"I have thoroughly enjoyed reading the materials you sent me; and expect that I will continue to refer to them for some time to come".

Dr. Ian Q.R. Thomas, author of "The Promise of Alliance – NATO and the Political Imagination"

"Please accept our introduction to Mr. James R. Doyle. Mr. Doyle has worked on the Peace Shield Program with the Kingdom of Saudi Arabia for many years. Mr. Doyle is known for his professionalism and integrity"

Fawaz A. Kayal, Consul General, Royal Kingdom of Saudi Arabia.
"Mr. Doyle is known for his personal and professional integrity. In addition, Mr. Doyle is known for his clear understanding of international business operations and related security considerations in Latin America."

Sergio A. Lopez, Managing Director, America Hispana Magazine.

In an interview on international terrrorism, during which Mr. Doyle stated: "We believe that Mexico is only second to Colombia in regard to risk to corporate executives" .... "During the early days of the North American Free Trade Agreement talks, we were quite often contacted by companies expressing an interest in doing business in Mexico but it was apparent that most were not aware of the risk in doing business there or any other country, Doyle said".... " "All international companies face the same challenges relative to security and most companies are aware of them" said Doyle of Emergency Data Systems. He added that: "It has been our experience that most people believe they will never be a victim. It is only after they become a victim that they put security measurers in place" "....
"Thank you very much for your comments the other day. The article regarding the kidnapping of Mr. Konno of Sanyo Video Components (USA) Corp. was carried in the Nikkei Weekly's Aug. 19 edition".

Joshua Ogawa, Nikkei Weekly, Tokyo

"On more than one occasion Mr. Doyle provided invaluable assistance to me in overcoming delays that would have seriously impaired my ability to respond to in-kingdom problems". Mr. Doyle's dedication together with his ability to "make it happen" was always reassuring".

P.J. Hillestad, Administrative Contracting Officer, Department of The Air Force.(The Administrative Contracting Officer who was responsible for all contract work done on the Peace Shield Program.)

"I read your draft and it sounds outstanding. Once again, I want to thank you for being our guest speaker and the troops have been informed this week that you're a Marines Marine".

[On presenting a gold etching to Mr. Doyle] ..."Iwo Jima Flag raising is presented with our sincere appreciation for your outstanding support. Your loyalty and dedication is living testimony that "Once a Marine, always a Marine".

M.D. Becker, Major, Commanding.

The Attorney General
Washington, D.C.

April 5, 2001

Mr. James R. Doyle
2525 Old Farm Road - 2021
Houston, TX 77063-4422

Dear Mr. Doyle:

    Thank you for sending me a copy of the security manual *The Corporate Executive Survival Guide: Internal Operation*. Your thoughtfulness during this great transition in democracy is inspiring.

    Again, thank you for your kindness.

        Sincerely,

        John Ashcroft
        Attorney General

JDA:mes

Document A

LaCelle Books
Better Bargains
Camden, NY 13316
UNITED STATES

Ship To:

**Daryl Smith
10709 CORY LAKE DR
TAMPA, FLORIDA 33647-2725**

Order No.:107-6054061-9565050

Standard

Qty	Item Name	Condition	Notes	Price Each
1	The Corporate Executive Survival Guide: International Operations - 062509-pough16	Used: Very Good	Softcover - VGC. Tight & Clean. We ship quickly.	$13.00

Customers: Please retain this packing list for your records. If you have any questions about this order, please contact the bookseller directly at info@lacellefamily.com.

Welcome to the Evening Parade

Friday, July 25, 1997

Guest of Honor:
Louis J. Freeh
Director, Federal Bureau of Investigation

Hosted by:
General Richard I. Neal, USMC
Assistant Commandant of the Marine Corps

In honor of
The Director, Federal Bureau of Investigation
The Honorable Louis J. Freeh
The Assistant Commandant of the Marine Corps and Mrs. Neal
request the pleasure of your company
at an Evening Parade
on Friday, the twenty-fifth of July
Marine Barracks, Washington, DC

A reception will precede
the parade at
The John Philip Sousa Band Hall
at seven o'clock

R.S.V.P.
(703) 614-1201

Blue White "B"
Civilian Informal

Document B